PC Magazine®
Office 2007 Solutions

PC Magazine®
Office 2007 Solutions

Joli Ballew

S. E. Slack

Jerri Ledford

Wiley Publishing, Inc.

PC Magazine® Office 2007 Solutions

Published by
Wiley Publishing, Inc.
10475 Crosspoint Boulevard
Indianapolis, IN 46256
www.wiley.com

Copyright © 2007 by Wiley Publishing, Inc., Indianapolis, Indiana

Published simultaneously in Canada

ISBN-13: 978-0-470-04683-8
ISBN-10: 0-470-04683-X

Manufactured in the United States of America

10 9 8 7 6 5 4 3 2 1

For my family and friends for their ongoing support and enthusiasm—Joli

For Alia, because you brought magic into my life—Sally

For Mom and Dad, because you said I could do anything—Jerri

About the Authors

Joli Ballew is a technology trainer and writer in the Dallas area. She holds several certifications including MCSE, A+ and MCDST, and holds a B.A. in mathematics. In addition to writing, she teaches computer classes at the local junior college, and works as a network administrator and Web designer for North Texas Graphics. Joli has almost 20 books available, including *Degunking Windows* (voted best computer book of the year by the Independent Publishers Book Awards in 2004), *Degunking Your PC*, *Degunking Your Mac*, and *Degunking Your Mac Tiger Edition* (Paraglyph Press), *Hardcore Windows XP* (McGraw-Hill), and *Windows XP: Do Amazing Things* (Microsoft Press). Joli also writes for Microsoft's Windows XP Expert Zone, is a Microsoft blogger, and has written a textbook for Microsoft's MCDST certification. In her free time, Joli enjoys golfing, yard work, and teaching her cat, Nikko, new tricks.

S. E. Slack is a writer and author with more than 16 years of experience in business writing. She specializes in technology, with an emphasis on degunking technology so the masses can both understand and use it. Slack has written numerous articles for small- and medium-sized businesses, appearing internationally in business magazines and online business sites. She has also been an executive and business transformation communications consultant to IBM, Lenovo International, and State Farm Insurance. She is currently writing *Do-It-Yourself Digital Home Office Projects* (McGraw-Hill) and *Breakthrough Microsoft Windows Vista: Your Jump-In Guide to Microsoft's Newest Operating System* (Microsoft Press). She has also written four other books. She has no free time; she has a 17-month-old daughter!

Jerri Ledford is a technology junkie who has always loved to share her passion for software and gadgets with anyone who'll listen. In 15 years as a writer and technology trainer, Jerri has written more than 800 business technology articles, and nine books, including *The Gadget Geek's Guide to Your Sony PlayStation Portable* (Course Technology), *Google Analytics* (Wiley), and *Google Powered: Productivity with Online Tools* (Wiley). Jerri also writes and teaches consumer technology courses for online audiences. When she's not working, Jerri spends time in her garden, reading, and, of course, playing with her gadgets.

Credits

EXECUTIVE EDITOR
Chris Webb

DEVELOPMENT EDITOR
Sydney Jones

TECHNICAL EDITOR
Kevin Farnham

COPY EDITOR
Maarten Reilingh

EDITORIAL MANAGER
Mary Beth Wakefield

PRODUCTION MANAGER
Tim Tate

VICE PRESIDENT AND EXECUTIVE GROUP PUBLISHER
Richard Swadley

VICE PRESIDENT AND EXECUTIVE PUBLISHER
Joseph B. Wikert

COMPOSITOR
Maureen Forys, Happenstance Type-O-Rama

PROOFREADER
Jen Larsen, Word One

INDEXER
Melanie Belkin

ANNIVERSARY LOGO DESIGN
Richard Pacifico

Contents at a Glance

Contents

Acknowledgments

Joli Ballew

I'd like to thank Chris Webb and all the folks at Wiley and PC Magazine for helping bring this book to life. And I'll send special thanks to Sydney Jones and Kevin Farnham for their diligence in the perfection department — making sure all our *i*'s were dotted and our *t*'s crossed.

I'd like to thank Jerri Ledford and Sally Slack too. They are the best coauthors I've ever had, and I've already asked them to join me on several upcoming projects (and they've both accepted). I am pleased and honored to have worked with such an amazing team. It's not often a book comes to production weeks early, but we did it, all the while never having a single miscommunication or creative disagreement. It was a great few months and I made two very good friends along the way.

In addition, kudos to my parents, family, and friends. They tiptoe when I'm writing, and don't make a sound when I'm editing. They raise the roof with me when I finish a book. They ask me about my work. They support me and seem continually awed by my transformation from public school teacher to full time author, writer, and blogger. I genuinely loved seeing the look in their eyes every time I told them I was working on a book for *PC Magazine*! My mom subscribes to it and will be thrilled when she sees mention of this book in her mailbox!

And last but not least, I'd like to thank everyone at Studio B. My agent, Neil Salkind, Ph.D., has got to be the best agent ever. He's supportive and enthusiastic, and lends an ear when I need one. Elsa Rosenberg, Amelia J-Lewis, Lisa Pere, Carolyn Mader, Dan Kinglesmith, Juliann Feuerbacher, and everyone else at the agency works hard for me every day and keeps me in blogs, corporate work, articles, and Web work, leaving me without any time to worry about my next job. Without Studio B, I would not be where I am today.

S. E. Slack

The number of people to send my heartfelt thanks to are many: Joli Ballew and Jerri Ledford, outstanding and witty coauthors who made it fun and easy to work on this book. I learn daily from both of them! Sydney Jones and Kevin Farnham — both of whom possess patience and diligence far beyond that of normal humans — thanks to both of you for keeping me honest. And of course, everyone at Wiley and *PC Magazine* for believing that both the subject matter of this book and a trio of women could be a killer combination.

My husband, Greg, and daughter, Alia, both deserve my sincere thanks — for their patience when Mom was working late, and for their quiet hours when Mom needed some silence as deadline rapidly approached. I can't do what I do without either of them in my corner and this book is for them.

Last but most definitely not least: Neil, you are an agent extraordinaire. You know which projects work for me, and you always fight for the best possible outcome. I can't thank you enough for your continued support. I will echo Joli's thanks as well to Studio B — there is no better agency for professional writers.

Jerri Ledford

Books are not the responsibility of only the authors. (Thanks, Joli and Sally. I'm looking forward to the next project.) Although we had an excellent author team, many other people are equally as responsible as we are for putting this book together.

Sydney Jones and Kevin Farnham, I echo my coauthors' sentiments. Without the two of you, this book would not be the quality resource that it is. Sydney, you're amazing. I don't know what else to say. Kevin, your eye for detail has helped to ensure that we stayed on our toes.

Of course, the team at Studio B can't go without recognition. I've worked with many people in the agency including my agent Lynn Haller and with Neil Salkind. But even there, droves of people behind the scenes make everything work the way it should. The team at *PC Magazine* is to be commended as well. The amount of work that goes into laying out and producing a book is astounding. Your efforts make us look good. Thank you.

Most important in my ability to write this book, however, have been my parents. Folks, you'll never know how much your support means to me, and Mom, thanks for dinner and a break every night. I'm forever grateful to have been so very blessed with such wonderful parents. I love you dearly.

Introduction

This book covers all aspects of Microsoft Office 2007. While there are multiple versions, this book serves as a desktop reference for Microsoft Office Professional, which includes Excel, Outlook, PowerPoint, Word, Access, Publisher, and Outlook.

Whom Is This Book For?

This book is intended for anyone who uses Microsoft Office 2007. This includes users in a corporate setting, employees and owners in a small business setting, and students and family members in a home (or dormitory) setting. It's for those who want to know how to get started with Office, how to get the most out of every aspect of Office, and how to use the newest and coolest features such as the Ribbon and the Galleries. It's also for those who want to find out how to incorporate Vista into the mix when it becomes available. This book will be an invaluable resource for years to come, as you'll find yourself picking it up again and again to learn about another new and awesome feature you've recently found hidden away in the depths of Microsoft Office 2007.

What Does This Book Cover?

Microsoft Office 2007 Professional is a multifaceted suite of applications that includes Excel, Outlook, PowerPoint, Word, Access, Publisher, and Outlook. This book aims to help you get the most out of each application by introducing new features, the new graphical user interface, and how to get immediate results with a few mouse clicks. Our goal is to teach you to use the new features to make your work easier, more fun, more intuitive, and more productive.

You can read the book straight through, but you probably won't want to do that. However, we do suggest you read Parts I, II, and III first, even if you plan to skip around later or use the book as a reference. That's because the first three sections cover how to get off to a good start, including performing a good installation, keeping Office up-to-date and secure, and understanding the basics of the new interface so you can understand where things are as you skip around or work through the remaining chapters. If you don't get off on the right foot, you'll end up missing out on some of the greatest new things since the invention of sliced bread!

The book is laid out as follows:

Part I: Getting Started

- **Chapter 1, Installing Microsoft Office 2007:** Covers what to do before installation, what Office 2007 brings to the table, and what you need to know about Product Keys, registration, and privacy.

- **Chapter 2, Protecting Against Viruses and Other Threats:** Covers virus types and how viruses can be acquired through Microsoft Office programs and popular virus software, and what to keep an eye out for to avoid getting a virus in the first place.

Chapter 3, Organizing Data Right from the Start: Covers the default options in Microsoft Office including where files are stored, file formats used, and the folder structure, and how to change the defaults to meet your specific needs. You'll also learn how to create your own folder structure to keep your data organized in the long term.

Part II: Avoiding Disasters

Chapter 4, Backing Up Your Own Data: Covers the basics of backing up to hardware and software backup options. Backup options include (but are not limited to) copying files to various media and using Office's new Search folders.

Chapter 5, Staying Up to Date: Covers how to scan for Office updates and enable automatic updates for your PC. It also covers the various kinds of updates, including security patches and service packs.

Chapter 6, Recovering from Problems: Covers how to enable and use System Restore, how to locate and recover lost files, and where and how to search the Internet for answers to problems not covered in the chapter.

Part III: Exploring the New Interface

Chapter 7, Personalizing the Interface: Covers how to change Office's skin and views, how to customize the work area, and how to change the look of the interface. Personalizing Office is an important part of exploring, because you make the applications your own while learning your way around the interface.

Chapter 8, Getting Familiar with the Ribbon: Covers the new results-oriented interface, and how to make things happen using it. Covers navigating the tabs, using the Quick Access Toolbar, and accessing and using Contextual Tabs.

Chapter 9, Obtaining Immediate Results with Styles and Galleries: Covers how to use Galleries to streamline your editing and formatting tasks, and how to employ Galleries to do your creative work for you.

Part IV: Working Together

Chapter 10, Saving and Sharing Data: Covers proper file-saving techniques, workgroup sharing concepts such as creation, permissions, caching, and testing, and working with new XML file formats.

Chapter 11, Setting Up User Access: Covers how users and groups work, including information for controlling user access and managing project data ideas.

Chapter 12, Collaborating Options: Covers collaboration options provided by Office 2007, with overviews of integrated communication options such as Web conferencing and instant messaging, extended collaborative workspaces using SharePoint Services Technology and SharePoint Server 2007, Office Groove, and shared note-taking with OneNote 2007.

Part V: Writing with Word

- **Chapter 13, Performing Common Tasks in Word:** Covers the new look and feel of Microsoft Word as well as some of the basic functions of the program including adding visual enhancements with graphics, working with lists, working collaboratively, and creating professional mailings.

- **Chapter 14, Exploring Additional New Features in Word:** Covers additional features of Microsoft Word. Learn how to use new toolbars and tool tips, take advantage of the Document Inspector, and use building blocks and styles to quickly create appealing and consistent documents on the fly.

Part VI: Presenting with PowerPoint

- **Chapter 15, Performing Common Tasks in PowerPoint:** Covers the new look and feel of Microsoft PowerPoint. Information about common formatting and creation tasks such as adding graphics and objects is also covered, in addition to collaboration.

- **Chapter 16, Exploring Additional New Features in PowerPoint:** Covers useful tips for using Microsoft PowerPoint to quickly create consistent and professional presentations. Information on creating charts and diagrams is also included.

Part VII: Managing Data with Excel

- **Chapter 17, Performing Common Tasks with Excel:** Covers the new interface and Excel Ribbon basics, new tools and features, formatting worksheets, the new Page Layout View, headers and footers, and working with functions, including the new Formula AutoComplete. Database, import/export, sorting/filtering, and charting basics are also explained here.

- **Chapter 18, Exploring Additional New Features in Excel:** Formula AutoComplete is discussed in more detail here, along with information about new things you can do with charts and chart templates. Also covered are tips for obtaining better printouts, working with larger workbooks, and obtaining and using free Excel templates.

Part VIII: Keeping in Touch with Outlook

- **Chapter 19, Performing Common Tasks in Outlook:** Covers the new interface and tools that have been added to Microsoft Outlook. Information about working with and managing e-mail as well as tips for using the calendar effectively and managing contacts are included in this chapter.

- **Chapter 20, Exploring Additional New Features in Outlook:** Covers previewing attachments without opening them and using the new To-Do Bar to get and stay organized. Additional information is also included to help you quickly become familiar with the new formats and capabilities of business cards and the RSS feed reader.

Part IX: Managing Data with Access

◼ **Chapter 21, Performing Common Tasks in Access:** Covers the new interface and tips for using the Ribbon, along with information on the Report Wizard and the new navigation pane. Also covered are queries, importing and exporting data, and the creation of tables.

◼ **Chapter 22, Exploring Additional New Features in Access:** Covers the use of Access templates and macros, as well as data collection techniques and the new XPS support feature.

Part X: Publishing with Publisher

◼ **Chapter 23, Performing Common Tasks in Publisher:** Covers the new user interface as well as information about working with text, creating attractive layouts using the Publisher tools, and adding graphics and object.

◼ **Chapter 24, Exploring Additional New Features in Publisher:** Covers design templates, and creating and using your own brand. In addition, there's information about using the content stores, design checker, and Web conversion tools with your publications.

Part XI: Doing Even More with Office

◼ **Chapter 25, Web Design with Office:** Covers using Office to create basic Web pages, understanding HTML, incorporating existing data and documents in Web pages, working with hyperlinks, and adding flair to Web pages. The chapter also covers saving and publishing your work.

◼ **Chapter 26, Using Office 2007 with Vista:** Covers what you can expect to see once you've installed Windows Vista, including the ability to use Vista's powerful new Search features. Features include searching from the Start menu, searching from inside the Office suite of applications, and using the Search results as live folders for organizing data.

◼ **Chapter 27, Exploring Office Enterprise:** Covers the various versions of Office 2007, and details the applications not included in Microsoft Office 2007 Professional. This includes such applications as InfoPath, OneNote, Groove, Communicator, and more.

PC Magazine®
Office 2007 Solutions

Part I

Getting Started

Chapter 1

Installing Microsoft Office 2007

Installing Microsoft Office 2007 is generally a simple affair. You know the drill — open the package, pop in the CD, and accept the default settings by repeatedly clicking the Next button. In less time than it takes to finish a cup of coffee, you've installed a brand new office suite. That's what we cover in this chapter: how to go about preparing for and performing the installation of Microsoft Office. Before you start flipping pages to the next chapter though, understand that there's a lot more to installing Microsoft Office than just running the installation program. You need to do some important chores before and after installation, such as backing up data and selecting an installation type. You also need to understand the differences between activation and registration once installation is complete, and how each of these affects your privacy. And once Microsoft Office 2007 is installed, you need to know just what you can expect once you're up and running with it. This chapter covers all of these things and more.

Installing Microsoft Office 2007

Microsoft offers many different Office 2007 suites, each tailored to a specific class of user, but installation is the same for all of them. Although the installation process is straightforward, you do need to make some decisions beforehand. You need to decide if you want to upgrade the Microsoft Office product you have or if you want to start fresh with a new installation. If you choose the latter option, you need to decide what you want to do with the old Office program files. You need to back up your data just in case something goes wrong, and you need to make sure your computer meets the minimum requirements to support Office. Once you've done that, you can start thinking about the actual installation.

Note

All available versions of the Microsoft Office Suite are outlined in Chapter 27, "Exploring Office Enterprise," specifically, in Table 27-1.

Before Installation

Most software you install on your system takes very little preplanning. You rarely need to do anything special to install the genealogy CD you received for your birthday or the software included with a new printer. However, installing the Office suite is a bit more complex. Although most people rarely do so, and almost every installation goes perfectly, preparing for your new Office suite is certainly a best practice.

SHOULD YOU PERFORM AN UPGRADE OR A NEW INSTALLATION?

The first thing you need to decide is whether you want to upgrade your present Office suite or if you want to perform a clean installation. An upgrade builds on the suite you already have; an upgrade preserves personal settings for things like margins, AutoComplete and AutoRecover, changes you've made to the dictionary, colors, themes, and backgrounds, page layouts, and more. While this may sound enticing, an upgrade will also preserve the gunk you've created in your existing applications and may prevent you from getting the most out of Microsoft Office 2007. If you've changed where applications save files, for instance, that will be preserved in the upgrade. If you want to see Office 2007 in its pure form, it's best to perform a clean installation.

You also have the option to install a new copy of Office while keeping your older versions of the Office suite applications intact. This means you can try out the newer application, say Word 2007, and if you find you're more comfortable with the older version of Word, you still have access to it. If you have the hard drive space, this is something you may want to consider.

This particular trick works for all of the Office applications with the exception of Outlook. If you choose to install Outlook 2007, your older version of Outlook will be upgraded. You will not have access to the older Outlook once the upgrade and installation is complete.

BACK UP DATA

It's always better to be safe than sorry. Perform a full backup of your data; include Word files, PowerPoint presentations, Excel spreadsheets, Access databases, Outlook data files and mail settings, and Publisher documents before going any further. You can burn these files to CDs or DVDs, copy them to a backup hard drive, or upload them to an online backup Web site. Don't forget to back up pictures and videos too.

MISCELLANEOUS SAFETY TIPS

Take some time now to clean up your computer and verify it's in good shape before installing Office 2007. Following the suggestions here will not only give you peace of mind, but will also help you get better performance from Office once it's installed.

- If installing from a laptop, plug it in to an electrical outlet first.

- Perform virus and spyware checks on your system. Remove any offending items.

- Get all Windows updates and any necessary driver updates.

- Check your hard drive for errors by running Check Disk. Click Start and then Run, and type **CHKDSK**. Click OK.

- Uninstall unnecessary programs, remove unnecessary data, and restart the computer.

- Log on as administrator and verify there are no errors.
- Close all programs before installation.

MINIMUM REQUIREMENTS

At the time this book was written, no final set of system requirements had been set. However, the following are excellent guidelines.

- **Operating System:** Microsoft Windows XP SP2 or later or Microsoft Windows Server 2003 or higher.

- **Computer and Processor:** 500-megahertz processor or higher, 256-megabyte RAM or higher, and DVD drive. For Microsoft Office Outlook 2007 with Business Contact Manager, you'll need 1 gigahertz and 512 megabytes of RAM.

- **Hard Disk:** 2 gigabytes for installation, although some of it will be freed after installation is complete.

- **Monitor:** 1024 × 768 resolution or higher is recommended, but 800 × 600 will work if needed.

- **Internet:** Broadband connection of 128 kilobits per second for download and activation of products is recommended. However, it's not required; if necessary, you can install from a DVD and activate the product by phone.

- **Outlook 2007 Users:** Microsoft Exchange Server 2000 or later is required for Outlook 2007 users. (This is somewhat misleading though, because Outlook can also be used with non-Microsoft mail servers. Still, for corporations that use Exchange this is important: if they are considering installing Office 2007, their Exchange version needs to be Exchange Server 2000 or later, or else Outlook 2007 won't work.)

- **Miscellaneous:** Internet Explorer 6.0 with service packs.

Installation Step-by-Step

The installation itself should go smoothly if you've performed all of the preinstallation tasks. Here's how it generally goes:

1. Insert the Microsoft Office 2007 DVD and wait for the installation program to begin. If it does not begin automatically, open My Computer, click the appropriate drive letter, and start the installation manually.

2. If prompted to proceed with the installation, click Yes.

3. In the Enter Product Key dialog box, type your 25-character key. This key is located on the packaging. Hyphens are added automatically. Click Continue.

4. Read and accept the Microsoft Software License Terms. Click Continue.

5. In the Installation Types page, select Upgrade or Custom.

6. If you choose Upgrade, the installation continues and automatically installs. If you choose Custom, you'll need to perform the rest of the steps listed here.

7. In the Upgrade dialog box, configure your preferences for installation.

    a. From the Upgrade tab, select Remove all Previous Versions, Keep all Previous Versions, or Remove Only the Following Applications. When choosing the latter, check which applications to remove.

    b. From the Installation Options tab, click the drop-down arrow beside Microsoft Office, and select Run all from My Computer to install the entire Office suite. To keep any single application from installing at all, click the arrow next to it and choose Not Available as shown in Figure 1-1.

    c. From the File Location tab, accept the default installation location or browse for a more suitable location.

    d. From the User Information tab, fill in your personal information for User Name, Initials, and Organization.

8. Click Install Now.

9. When the installation is complete, click Close or click Register for Online Services. For more about Registration, continue to the next section.

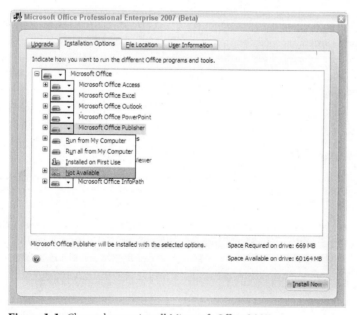

Figure 1-1: Choose how to install Microsoft Office 2007.

Installing Windows Vista

There's another new kid on the block. It's Windows Vista. Just as Office 2007 can be an upgrade to earlier versions of Office (or a clean install), Windows Vista can be an upgrade (or a clean install) to Windows operating systems such as Windows XP. The thing that's great about Windows Vista is the same thing that's great about Microsoft Office 2007; there are tons of new features and a cool new interface.

If you'd like to know more about Windows Vista visit `www.microsoft.com/windowsvista`. There you'll find all you need to know about the features, the community, and the minimum requirements. You can expect Windows Vista to be available for corporations at the end of 2006, and for home users in early 2007. You can install it as an upgrade or as a clean installation.

Understanding Product Keys, Activation, Registration, and Privacy

Before completing the installation of Office 2007, you must have a clear understanding of three key terms: product key, activation, and registration. As you already know, you have to input a valid product key to perform the installation. You may not be aware that after installation you have to activate the product too. However, you do not have to register to finalize or use Office 2007, even though you are prompted to do so at the end of the installation.

Activation and Product Keys

After installation you will, under almost all circumstances, be prompted to connect to the Internet to activate your copy of Microsoft Office 2007. Microsoft needs to verify that you have a legitimate copy of the product and activate it. (If the product is not properly activated, it will go into *reduced mode* after 50 launches.)

When you activate your copy of Office 2007, the product key is sent along with a hardware hash to Microsoft's activation system. This hash is a snapshot of your computer hardware. No personally identifiable information is sent during this time. At this point, Microsoft knows only what your machine consists of, not who you are, what your e-mail address is, or even from what city you are.

Activation is necessary because Microsoft wants to restrict you to installing Office 2007 on the appropriate number of computers, and to verify you have a legitimate copy of the product. Antipiracy technology takes care of this automatically. If you need to install Office 2007 on more machines, you'll need to purchase additional copies of the product, and they will require activation as well.

Activation limits help keep users from burning copies of the software and distributing it to others, or installing one copy of the product across an entire office. The product activation process helps enforce the software license terms that the user agreed to during the Office 2007 installation.

Note

Activation is generally completed through the Internet, but you can activate over the telephone if necessary. You'll be prompted with a phone number to call if you do not have an Internet connection. You can obtain a hardware hash number from your PC and give it to Microsoft over the phone.

Once Microsoft knows what your machine looks like, you can install and uninstall the product as many times as you want on the same machine, and Microsoft can recognize that it's the same installation from the hardware hash each time you activate it. You'll need to read the software license terms specific to your suite to see if you can install Office on an additional computer, such as a laptop. In the past, this has been acceptable with consumer versions of the product.

There are a few miscellaneous items to add regarding product activation:

- In reduced functionality mode, you cannot save, edit, or create documents, but existing documents are not deleted.

- You can activate the product or view activation status from Microsoft Office Help, a small icon available on every page. It is a small blue icon with a question mark inside.

- Activation is completely anonymous.

- Common changes to a PC's hardware, such as upgrading video cards, adding a second hard drive, adding RAM, or installing a DVD drive, will not require reactivation.

- Microsoft cannot remotely access your machine, and they cannot revoke activation approval via the Internet.

- No cookies are placed on your machine during activation.

All About Registration

We recommend selecting Register for Online Services once installation is complete. Although you will be providing Microsoft with personally identifiable information when you register, the information you give will be securely stored and protected. You will also be able to check for and immediately download and install any updates to the product. These updates are sometimes security-related and sometimes feature-related, but whatever the case, we feel strongly about registering your product to obtain them. Regarding privacy, Microsoft goes to great lengths to protect the information you give them.

When registering though, unless you specify otherwise, you will receive e-mail from Microsoft and Microsoft Partners. This can be quite a bit of mail, and may eventually become bothersome. You can specify on the first registration page whether you want to receive e-mail. After registering, you can change your preferences at any time.

Once registered there are many things you can access.

- **Outlook Calendar Sharing Service:** This service lets you publish calendars to Office Online and other servers on the Internet. You can choose with whom to share your calendar.

- **Try New Beta Software:** You can try the beta versions of Microsoft's upcoming releases, and content changes often.

- **Updates:** You can check anytime for updates to all office products.

Protecting Your Privacy

It's important to be vigilant about your privacy, not just when communicating with Microsoft but also regarding any other Web site you visit. You may be surprised just how much these companies know about you. Everything you input and every icon or link you click can be tracked and generally is. While this is a good thing when offered by legitimate sites (it personalizes your Web experience), it can become a privacy nightmare with unscrupulous ones.

As noted in Microsoft's Online Privacy Notice Highlights page (http://privacy.Microsoft.com), the personally identifiable information Microsoft acquires from you is obtained from what you give them when you create a Passport at www.passport.net, what you offer during registration, and any other information you give when accessing other Microsoft services and other companies (when logged in with a Passport). Microsoft uses cookies to keep track of your interactions with its sites and services, but of course, this is only to offer a more personalized experience. Cookies allow Microsoft to keep track of what you click when online and how you otherwise interact with Web sites. Microsoft also uses this information to send targeted e-mails if you've signed up for them. They can use the information they have to make sure you're getting information regarding services that interest you.

The amount of information Microsoft collects on people is sometimes off-putting though. For instance, if you have a Public MSN Profile (www.spaces.msn.com) you're asked to input a lot of information about yourself. This is all voluntary, but still, people do write incredibly personal information here, and make it public. MSN Profiles can include marital status, hometown, contact information, name of your significant other, personal cell phone number, home fax, personal e-mail, birthday, anniversary, and more. Be very careful what you offer. It will be kept and stored.

While some of this may sound a little scary, you can rest assured that Microsoft does not sell, rent, or lease your information to anyone. You can also stop e-mail at any time by changing your preferences at the Passport Web site.

What Office 2007 Brings to the Table

There are currently eight Microsoft Office 2007 suites ranging from Microsoft Office Basic 2007 to Microsoft Office Enterprise 2007. Each version contains a different set of office applications. This book covers the applications included in Microsoft Office Professional 2007, which are Word, Excel, Outlook, PowerPoint, Publisher, Outlook with Business Contact Manager, and Access. Each of these products has a new look and new features, and better ways to collaborate.

New Interface

The first thing you'll notice when you start using Office 2007 is the new and improved interface. There's a lot of material in this book to get you up to speed on this. The interface is completely redesigned and contrary to what Microsoft implies, is going to take some time to master. There are no longer drop-down menus; instead, you select a tab at the top of the page, and the choices change underneath the tab depending on what you've selected. Some of the old standbys are hard to find though, like settings that were easily accessed in Office XP's Word's Tools → Options. There, you could set everything from user information to formatting marks to spelling and grammar. You'll have to learn to navigate through the new interface to find those preferences now.

Look at Figures 1-2 and 1-3 and you'll understand how drastic the changes are. The figures show two tabs in Word and how the choices change when a tab is selected. You learn more about the new interface starting with Part III. Not having any drop-down lists is going to take some getting used to.

Figure 1-2: Office now has tabs instead of drop-down menus. This is Word, and Home is selected.

Figure 1-3: This shows Word with Page Layout selected. Notice how the options are different than in the previous figure.

New Features

Microsoft has certainly changed the interface, but the features you've come to rely on are still there. In Figure 1-2, you may recognize the familiar icons for Bold, Italic, and Underline, icons to add bulleted lists and numbered lists, and icons for managing other common tasks like changing a font or font size. But the changes to Word and other applications are more than just a reordering of tools and offering a new and more intuitive way to access them.

The release of Microsoft Office 2007 is a major breakthrough in office software. The building blocks in this release allow developers to create custom-made solutions for workers and home users alike. This office suite lets users from enterprise, small business, and the home take advantage of new collaboration tools, content management tools, and timesaving interfaces that together create a more productive environment.

Some of the new features are listed here:

- The new uncluttered workspace has a Web-like interface.

- Ribbon, the new sets of commands and tabs, keep all tools relevant to the task in progress at the forefront.

- Contextual Tabs offer unique sets of commands appropriate for the particular type of data being edited. For instance, in Excel, clicking a chart opens a new contextual tab with options for chart editing.

- Galleries, combined with Live Preview, provide a set of clear results for a particular project and allow you to create a professional looking presentation, document, or spreadsheet easily. With Live Preview, you can see what the final product will look like before actually applying the style or template; simply hover your mouse over the gallery style you like.

- The interface is extensible. This means that developers can add functionality to additional releases of Office so that their programs integrate with Office. That means developers can add Contextual Tabs, interface tabs, and Galleries.

Summary

Installing and activating Microsoft Office 2007 usually goes very smoothly. However, you can increase the likelihood of success by performing a few preinstallation tasks. Cleaning up your computer, backing up data, and understanding what type of installation you need are the main three. Once installed, you'll be prompted to activate and register the product. Activation is necessary, but registration is not, and there are pros and cons for the latter. We suggest you register your product immediately, and take advantage of updates, tips and tricks, and other perks.

Once installed and activated, you'll experience the new interface, complete with new tabs and no drop-down lists. You can explore Ribbon, Galleries, Live Preview, and the new uncluttered look and feel. Once you've installed and introduced yourself to the product, you can move forward to Chapter 2. If you already have even only a modest familiarity with Windows and the Office applications, you can flip around the book to locate what you need to know right now.

Chapter 2

Protecting Against Viruses and Other Threats

Computer viruses are a fact and an intrinsic part of the computing experience. It's extremely likely you have antivirus software installed on your computer, and possibly even software that protects against adware and spyware. If you don't, you should. However, installing this software, accepting the defaults during installation, and expecting the application(s) to protect you against anything and everything that comes your way is no longer a reality. These days, you need to have at least a basic understanding of viruses and other threats, including what types of viruses exist, how they work, and what you can do to help protect your computer, data, and personal information from harm.

While you can obtain a virus manually by downloading something from an unscrupulous Web site or installing a malicious freeware or shareware program, most viruses are passed from one computer to another automatically through applications like Outlook. In fact, the fastest spreading and most destructive viruses travel through e-mail in the form of attachments.

Macros you use in Excel or Access can also contain viruses. Downloading a macro or "borrowing" one from a colleague is sometimes the source of the virus, but more often than not, they arrive in e-mail attachments. Viruses can attack through Office applications if the proper security updates have not been downloaded and installed. It is therefore very important to also keep Microsoft Office protected, just as you would your computer.

Other threats exist though. You need to take personal precautions for keeping your data safe. You should sign up for security bulletins, configure high-security passwords, and do whatever else you can to thwart unauthorized access to your computer, including being vigilant about what you download and install from the Internet.

Viruses and Antivirus Programs

In general, a virus is a computer program intentionally designed to cause harm to your computer. Like their biological namesakes, viruses also replicate themselves. Viruses may rename files so they are unusable, delete files, replicate themselves through an e-mail program or other application, or simply tie up valuable computer resources such as CPU and RAM by attacking those resources.

Viruses don't generally bring down a system though. Viruses most often cause system-wide slow downs, produce annoying pop-up messages, and cause nagging error messages.

Virus Types

The most common type of virus is one that attaches to an executable file, such as Outlook, Excel, or a graphic-editing program. Most of these types of viruses, once on your computer, simply wait for you to perform the command necessary to release them, such as opening a ZIP file, running a macro, or opening an e-mail attachment. Once they're running, they replicate themselves using your computer and its resources. These types of viruses are usually called *program viruses*.

Other common virus types are those considered *malware*. These viruses may run during boot-up, when logging on to a network, or even when a specific hour and minute of the day is reached. For example, in the latter case the malware may release automatically when the system clock hits midnight of a certain year, say 2010. It may then delete all JPEG files or all documents on the computer, or create a pop-up that simply says "Happy New Year!" *Spyware* and *adware* are also considered malware, as detailed in a sidebar later in this chapter.

How a Virus Works

There are plenty of virus types, but they all generally work the same way. First, the virus gets onto your computer. This usually happens without your knowledge, although you are usually at fault for contracting it. Most of the time, the viruses are acquired through malicious software you intentionally download or open, such as trial software, screen savers, e-mail attachments, or freeware.

Once on the computer, they run. Viruses are executable files and run when you install the screen-saver, trial software, or freeware, or when you open an e-mail attachment that contains it.

Once the virus is loose, it produces symptoms and begins to replicate itself. As noted, these symptoms can range from harmless pop-up messages to the deletion of important files. Some viruses wait in the background too, in anticipation of an event such as a specific date and time.

No matter what, viruses replicate. That's why it's so important to have antivirus software configured on your computer. This software should catch a virus before it is opened, thus preventing it from doing harm and replicating to other computers on your network (or the Internet).

Caution

You can prevent the majority of viruses by being vigilant about what you download, install, and open. If you get e-mail with an attachment from someone you don't recognize, don't open the attachment. Even if you do recognize the sender, e-mail back and ask them if they meant to send you an executable file. If you're on a Web site and you are prompted to download and install a program, don't do it. Finally, don't fall for free screensavers, free emoticons, or free software of any kind on the Internet, unless you've read the reviews and license and know it's a legitimate and virus-free application.

Custom-Configure Antivirus Programs

Antivirus software, while an excellent and must-have tool, can sometimes cause your computer to perform more slowly than a mild virus would. Letting your antivirus program check for updates daily is important, but checking for updates each day at 8 A.M., just when you're logging on to the Internet, will slow down access and quickly become tedious. Configuring your antivirus software perform a system-wide virus scan at boot up is also a performance killer. Imagine the issues you'd have if you let your computer perform a two-hour scan just when you're sitting down in the morning to get some work done. The point of this section then is to learn how to use and configure your antivirus programs for the best performance possible, while at the same time protecting you and your computer from harm.

The newest antivirus programs offer more than just protection from viruses. Many also contain firewalls, privacy services, and options for permanently deleting files. You'll need to work with those accordingly.

To see what your antivirus software offers, click Start → All Programs, and select your antivirus program from the list. Figure 2-1 shows an example. In this figure, there are four options: McAfee VirusScan, McAfee Personal Firewall Plus, McAfee Privacy Service, and McAfee Shredder. Each of these offers different kinds of protection. You may have these or others.

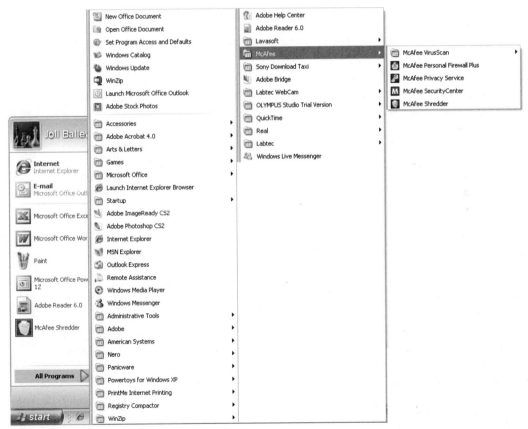

Figure 2-1: Antivirus software often contains more than virus protection.

Spend some time now and open each antivirus subprogram you have to see what's offered. Only then can you configure the program for the best possible performance. You should look for several things. If possible, set or use your antivirus program to perform the following tasks:

- Schedule a complete system scan weekly, during a time when the computer is on but is not in use.

- Check for quarantined files twice a month and either delete files you know are harmful or restore files that are not.

- Find out what viruses are currently circling the Internet by visiting your antivirus manufacturer's Web site as time allows.

- Run only one antivirus program. Running more than one can cause system instability.

- Scan incoming and outgoing e-mail automatically.

- Start when Windows starts.

- Create a rescue disk in case a virus disables your computer.

- Schedule updates to download and install at a time that is convenient for you, a time when you will not be actively using the computer or using programs that require a lot of computer resources.

- Use the firewall to warn you of potential dangers, but not automatically block them. You can then decide for yourself what is or is not a potential danger and take the appropriate action.

- Enable instant messaging protection.

- Perform a manual scan anytime you see anything suspicious, such as an odd or recurring pop-up message, changes to names of files or pictures, or a noticeable slowdown at the computer (which would indicate an attack on computer resources).

Spyware and Adware

Spyware and Adware are two more threats to be concerned with.

Spyware is malicious software that spies on you by stealing keystrokes, passwords, and other personal data. It is usually written and distributed for someone's personal monetary gain, and is generally well hidden in long licenses you agree to when downloading and installing software. Spyware can make changes to almost any part of your computer, including changes to your Internet home page or what you see when performing an Internet search. Spyware can also cause system-wide slow downs, install malicious toolbars, and collect Internet browsing history data, including passwords and personal information. It can even make changes to the Registry. At best, it's a nuisance; at worst, it's all a person needs to steal your identity or disable your computer.

Adware is similar. It's a form of spyware and it also collects information about you as you surf the Web. Adware programs use the information collected to display advertisements in the form of pop-ups, ads that are targeted directly at you based on the Web sites you've visited. Adware, like spyware, can slow down your system by hogging system resources. It can also slow down Internet browsing, by using valuable bandwidth on ads.

To avoid spyware and adware:

1. Keep your PC up to date with Windows Update.

2. Install and use antiadware and antispyware software from such reputable companies as Spybot Search and Destroy, Ad-Aware, and Windows Defender (to be released with Vista).

3. Use a personal firewall.

4. Install software only from trusted sources.

5. Do not open suspicious attachments in e-mail.

Generally, antiadware software catches tracking cookies, which collect information about your Web surfing habits.

Understanding and Avoiding Office Viruses

You can unknowingly unleash a virus from almost any Microsoft Office application. From Outlook, you can set a virus loose by opening a dangerous e-mail attachment, from Excel, by running an unsafe macro, and from any other application through a security hole (that could have been patched with a simple Office update). However you get the virus is not necessarily the point here though; once you have a virus, you have no choice but to deal with it. Here we want to talk about avoiding viruses in the first place.

Beware of Attachments

The most common virus threats come via e-mail in the form of attachments. Attachments you receive from people you know are generally harmless. They're usually forwarded e-mails, videos, pictures, Word documents, or PowerPoint presentations. If you know the person who sent the attachment, and are expecting something from them, it's usually safe to open it. It's doubly safe if you have antivirus software running that scans all attachments before they are opened.

However, viruses can and do replicate themselves without a user's knowledge. Even if the user knows they were affected, viruses replicate so quickly through e-mail programs that that person may not have time to let you know a virus is coming your way in time anyway. That being the case, the best thing you can do is to never open e-mail attachments that contain suspicious extensions such as .exe (an executable file), .bat (a batch file), and .vbs (a Visual Basic file). There is more information on this in Table 2-1.

Another way to protect yourself from viruses that come through attachments is already config-ured in Microsoft Outlook by default. Outlook automatically blocks attachments that contain file types it deems dangerous. If you try to forward one of these e-mails, you'll be prompted regarding the security threat as well.

Table 2-1 lists potentially dangerous extensions and offers a brief explanation of what each is.

Table 2-1   Suspicious E-Mail Attachment Extensions

Extension	Description
.exe	A file that contains a program (executable). Almost all executable files in e-mail attachments are viruses. Legitimate executable files are used to install software such as Microsoft Office or Adobe Photoshop.
.com	A file that contains instructions (commands) that tell your computer to do something specific. COM files are created for DOS-based systems and usually run faster than executable files, and thus can cause problems very quickly. Almost all COM files in e-mail attachments are viruses.
.vbs	A file that contains a Visual Basic script. Scripts are executed code that can access and modify data on your computer. Unless you work with Visual Basic in a work setting, consider all Visual Basic files in e-mail attachments as viruses.
.scr	A screen saver file in Microsoft Windows. Screen savers are safe as long as they come from valid sources. However, almost all screen saver files in e-mail attachments are viruses and should be deleted immediately.
.bat	A batch file that contains a sequence of commands for DOS based systems. Consider all batch files that come as e-mail attachments as viruses.
.pif	A program information file that contains information about how Microsoft Windows should run a non-Windows application. Consider all PIF files that come as e-mail attachments as viruses.
.zip	A compressed file and a common format for sending data via e-mail attachments. If you know the sender and are expecting a large amount of data, the attachment is probably safe. If you do not know the sender, do not open the attachment.

Caution

Just because a filename says it's one thing doesn't mean it is. While many ZIP files are safe and do not contain viruses, if you aren't expecting a ZIP file you shouldn't open it. Once unzipped, it could contain and run any other file type, such as an EXE or a VBS program. In other instances, attachments ending in .doc may not be a simple Word document. In reality, it may be a macro virus. Again, the warning stands: Only open attachments from people you know and trust.

Tip

Microsoft Office helps you protect against macro viruses by using the High macro security setting as the default. It is wise to leave this security setting alone, as you'll be prompted to enable macros anytime a macro is detected within a document. With this setting, you can run only those macros that are digitally signed from trusted sources, and macros you create yourself. You cannot, by default, run harmful macros. If you choose the Low setting for macros, you will not be prompted to enable or disable macros; they will run automatically.

Avoid Macros

Macros, if you aren't familiar with them, are programs created to perform often-repeated steps, and are initiated with a specified key sequence such as Ctrl+A. For instance, if you insert your name, address, city, state, phone number, and e-mail address often in the Word documents you create, you can construct a macro to do it for you. Once the macro is created, you simply click a user-defined key combination to run that macro and insert the information at any time and at any place in the document.

Sophisticated and malicious macros can also be created and sent via e-mail to unsuspecting recipients. These macros attach themselves to Microsoft Office programs and can run every time you open the program or each time you hit a specific keystroke. While these macro viruses are generally more annoying than harmful (a specific keystroke may cause something "comical" to happen), they may also replicate by using your Outlook contact list, thus continuing their destruction via the Internet.

The best way to avoid macro viruses is the same way you'd avoid any other virus. Don't open attachments from people you don't know, don't install programs from suspicious sources, and don't borrow macros from people you know or download from Web sites offering free ones. Macro viruses are the most common type of Office viruses; they are becoming increasingly prevalent with the free exchange of documents, templates, and data over the Internet.

Patch Security Holes

Some viruses are specifically written to attack a computer through known vulnerabilities in software. It is therefore extremely important to protect Microsoft Windows, Windows Vista, and Microsoft Office with security patches and updates. All updates are free and can be installed automatically with little or no intervention on your part, or manually, so you stay in control.

WINDOWS UPDATE IN MICROSOFT WINDOWS

There are two ways to install updates in Microsoft Windows operating systems and Office 2007: manually and automatically. To install an update manually, in Microsoft Windows, click Start → All Programs → Windows Update. You'll need to be connected to the Internet, and once at the Microsoft Update Web site, you'll follow the directions listed.

Installing updates manually isn't generally a good idea though; that is, unless that's the way your network administrator wants you to do it. That's because you have to remember to get the updates yourself, and most people won't remember to do that. The best way is to configure Microsoft Windows to perform the updates automatically.

To configure your computer to obtain Windows Updates automatically:

1. Click Start, right-click My Computer, and select Properties.

2. From the Properties dialog box select the Automatic Updates tab.

3. Configure the updates to occur automatically, as shown in Figure 2-2. Make sure the time configured for downloading is a time when the computer will be turned on and connected to the Internet. Note that if the computer is turned off at the specified time, the updates will occur the next time the computer is booted.

4. Click OK.

Figure 2-2: It's generally best to configure Windows Update to download and install updates automatically.

WINDOWS UPDATE IN WINDOWS VISTA

There are two ways to install updates in Windows Vista operating systems and Office 2007: manually and automatically. To install an update manually in Windows Vista, click Start → All Programs → Windows Update. In the resulting window, you are informed if updates are available, as shown in Figure 2-3. As mentioned earlier, it's best to configure the updates to occur automatically with Vista too.

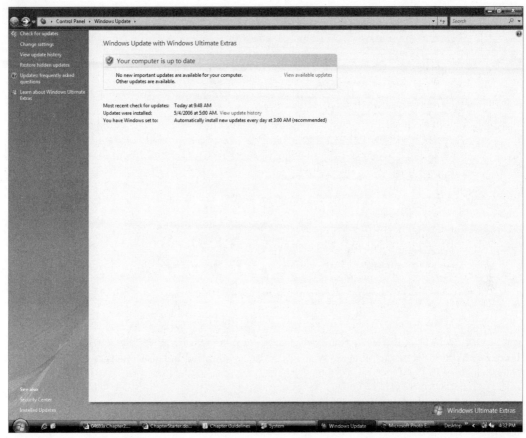

Figure 2-3: Windows Vista informs you if any updates are available, and you can download and install them manually.

To configure your computer to obtain Windows Updates automatically:

1. Click Start → All Programs → Windows Update.

2. Click Change Settings.

3. Configure the updates to occur automatically, as shown in Figure 2-4. Make sure the time configured for downloading is a time when the computer will be turned on and connected to the Internet.

4. Click OK.

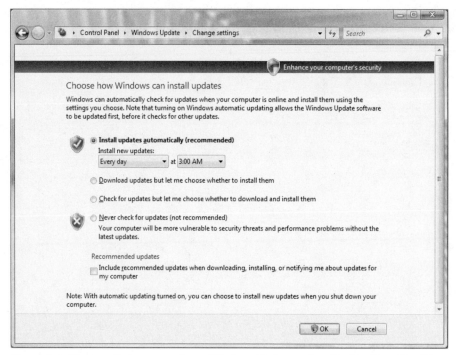

Figure 2-4: It's generally best to configure Windows Update to download and install updates automatically.

OFFICE UPDATE IN MICROSOFT OFFICE 2007

You can use Automatic Updates to get updates for Microsoft Office 2007. If you've already done that, you don't need to gather the updates manually. However, the only way to update the suite is to do so manually. To update Microsoft Office manually:

1. Click the File button in the top-left corner of any application and choose the application's Options button.

2. Click Resources.

3. Click Check for Updates, shown in Figure 2-5.

Tip

After getting all necessary updates, sign up for Microsoft Security Bulletins at www.microsoft.com. Perform a search for Security Bulletins and select the alerts for your operating system and Office product. You'll receive alerts via e-mail.

Figure 2-5: All Office programs have an Options dialog box where updates can be manually obtained.

Taking Additional Security Precautions

As you would probably expect, protecting yourself from viruses and security holes isn't all there is to managing your security issues. There are threats beyond the Internet bad guys, threats that come from right inside your home or office.

Physical Safety

You'll want to start with a few physical precautions. These include placing your computer tower away from kids and pets, avoiding spills, and making sure you lock your office door when you go to lunch or leave for the day. You'll also want to avoid smoking around your computer, as this can cause damage to the inside of the tower.

Continued

Taking Additional Security Precautions *(Continued)*

Here are a few other things to consider:

- Keep your backups in another room or building. If there's a fire or similar threat, at least your backups will be safe.

- Keep installation CDs, product keys, and passwords secure and together. You might consider a fireproof safe.

- If you do keep coffee or sodas near your computer, create a no-spill area for them, such as a half-open drawer.

- Use surge protectors for all hardware.

- Avoid permanently sharing folders on your computer, especially on your desktop, unless necessary. There are inherent risks to allowing data to be so easily accessible by too many people.

Passwords

You'll also need to take some generic computer precautions like configuring high-security passwords and creating a screen saver that's password protected.

High-security passwords are those that contain upper and lower case letters, numbers, and special characters like exclamation points or asterisks. Use a high-security password on your login screen for both computer and network access. The same password will automatically be configured when you enable a screen saver that requires a password once it is active. (You can do that from Display Properties → Screen Saver; just right-click in an empty area of your Desktop and select Display Properties.)

Summary

You must take precautions to protect your data and your computer from viruses, adware, and spyware. This includes installing, configuring, and keeping on top of related antithreat software programs, and, being careful about what you download and install from the Internet. Many viruses attack through Microsoft Office programs, mostly in the form of e-mail attachments and macros. It's important to be vigilant there too.

Other threats exist. You can protect yourself even more by signing up for security bulletins, configuring high-security passwords, and doing whatever else you can to thwart unauthorized access to your computer, including being vigilant about creating and using passwords and keeping your computer physically safe.

Chapter 3

Organizing Data Right from the Start

The best way to improve efficiency in any work environment is to create an effective, extensible organizational system. In this chapter, we address the organizational system you have in place for the files and folders already on your computer. If you're like most people, you have some regrets about how you initially set up your filing system, including where you save files by default, and you may have even outgrown the system you initially created. You might also feel frustration when trying to back up data quickly or locate a file you worked on a month ago. All of this is normal, and the problems you have now can be fixed.

This chapter covers organizing data, saving files, and Office 2007's new file formats. We show you how to reorganize your folders and files now, and how to keep them organized and accessible in the future. With the proper plan in place, you'll enjoy the added benefit of being able to quickly and easily perform a backup of everything, everyday. You'll never again have to worry about lost data.

Configuring Default Saving Options

If you chose to upgrade instead of installing a clean version of Microsoft Office 2007, you likely will not experience that fresh out-of-the-box sensation that you get with a brand new software program. That's because when you upgrade, you keep all of your old settings, like where you save files (among many other things). While upgrading is often a convenience, there's a lot to be said for installing clean, and we prefer it when given a choice. The only way you're going to see Microsoft Office 2007 in its default form is to install a clean installation of it.

The default settings shown in this chapter are those of a clean version of Microsoft Office 2007. It doesn't matter if you've upgraded to follow along, but the screen shots and written examples here refer to the default settings with a clean installation only. Your settings may be different if you upgraded. Let's look first at some of the default settings on Word 2007.

Basic Default Options

You can access any of the Office applications' options by clicking the File button in the top-left corner. In the resulting dialog box, click that application's Options button. Figure 3-1 shows an example from Word 2007.

Figure 3-1: Click the application's File menu in the top left corner of the screen and then select the Options button to view default settings.

After you click the Word Options button in Microsoft Word 2007, you see the Word Options window as shown in Figure 3-2.

Figure 3-2: The Options window offers a place to change just about any setting imaginable.

If you're ever not sure what one of these items does, just hover your mouse over it for a brief explanation. Figure 3-3 shows an example.

Top options for working with Word

- ☑ Show Mini Toolbar on selection ⓘ
- ☑ Enable Live Preview ⓘ
- ☐ Show Developer tab in the Ribbon ⓘ
- ☑ Open e-mail attachments in Full Screen Reading view ⓘ

Color scheme: Blue ▾

ScreenTip style: Don't show feature

Show Developer tab in the Ribbon

The Developer tab includes macro and template authoring tools, as well as XML-related features.

Figure 3-3: Get information about any item by hovering your mouse over it.

Go ahead and work though the categories on the left to see what options are available to change. You may want to make a few minor modifications now, like what color the interface is or how AutoCorrect works, but for the moment, don't make any changes to where files are saved, what will be shown in the Quick Access Toolbar, and other things that will veer off too far from the defaults. If you make changes now, your screen may not look like ours when working through the examples provided in this chapter and others.

Tip

Before going any further, click Resources in the Word Options window. Make sure you're connected to the Internet and then click Check for Updates. You want to start out on the right foot, with all the latest features and security updates.

Changing Where Files Are Stored by Default

If you look in Word's Options, in the Save section, you see the defaults for saving files in Word. They are to save files with .docx filename extension in the user's My Documents folder. (.docx is the new filename extension for Word 2007 document files. Previous versions used a .doc filename extension.) Often, this is just fine. Many people save everything to the My Documents folder and subfolders they create inside of it, and they save files using the default file type.

SHOULD YOU CHANGE THE DEFAULT OPTIONS FOR SAVING FILES?

There are many instances when changing the default location for saving files is appropriate. In a business setting, the most common modification is setting the files to be saved to a network drive or network share. If your files are not kept on your desktop computer but on a network server, it makes sense to change the default setting from My Documents to the appropriate folder on the network. Once you do, you'll no longer have to use the Save As window to browse to My Network Places, and then on to the folder you need. (When data is stored on a network server, network administrators can easily perform backups for everyone's data each night after everyone's gone home — that's the point of that.)

If you have a PC with a partitioned hard drive — perhaps one partition for applications and operating system files and another for saving data — you'll want to change the default location for saving files to the partition that holds your data. When there are two partitions, this is generally done by changing the default from the My Documents folder on the C: drive to some other folder on the D: drive. If you want to do this, read the section Creating New Organizational folders first, before continuing here.

You might also change the location of the data you save if you have a complicated organizational structure or multiple projects. For instance, maybe the work you do in Word has to be saved to a network project folder for the publishing department, while the work you do in Excel needs to be saved to a network folder for the accounting department. You may also have private folders on your own hard drive that contain presentations you've created in PowerPoint for a small business you have at home. Each of these instances would require a change in the appropriate options.

Finally, you can use Word to create one specific type of file, such as HTML files for Web pages, or older Works files that end in .wps. In the same vein, you might create only templates in Excel, or only Web pages in PowerPoint. You can make these changes to simplify your work as well.

In all of these circumstances, you can and should change where files are saved and/or what types of files are created by default.

HOW TO CHANGE THE DEFAULTS

If you've already decided that you want to change where default files are saved or in what format they are saved as, go ahead and work though this section to make the changes. If you aren't sure yet, or if you're not happy with your current organizational structure, skip this part, finish the chapter, and come back to it once you're better organized.

To change the default location to save files:

1. Open any Microsoft Office 2007 application. In this example, we'll use Word.

2. Click the File menu in the top-left corner, and select Word Options. (You'd do the same in any other Office application.)

3. In the Word Options window, in the right pane, select Save.

4. Locate the Default File Location window and click Browse.

5. In the Modify Location window shown in Figure 3-4, browse to the location of the folder you want to save to. In Figure 3-4, it's a shared network folder on the computer Cosmo. This is how the Modify Location window looks on Windows XP. Figure 3-5 shows how the Modify Location window looks on Windows Vista.

6. Click OK, and OK again to close the window.

7. Repeat this procedure for all of the Office applications you use. You can select a different folder for each application.

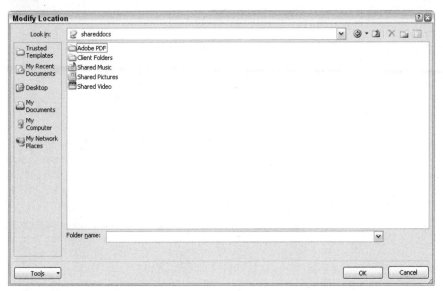

Figure 3-4: Browse to the location of the folder to save files to by default. This is on Windows XP.

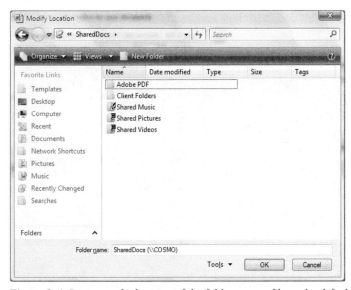

Figure 3-5: Browse to the location of the folder to save files to by default. This is what you'll likely see on Windows Vista.

To change the default file type for any application:

1. Open any Microsoft Office 2007 application. In this example, we'll use Excel.

2. Click the File menu in the top-left corner, and select Excel Options. (You'd do the same in any other Office application.)

3. In the Excel Options window, select Save.

4. Locate the Save Files in This Format window, click the down arrow, and make a selection from the resulting drop-down list. The choices are shown in Figure 3-6.

5. Click OK to close the window.

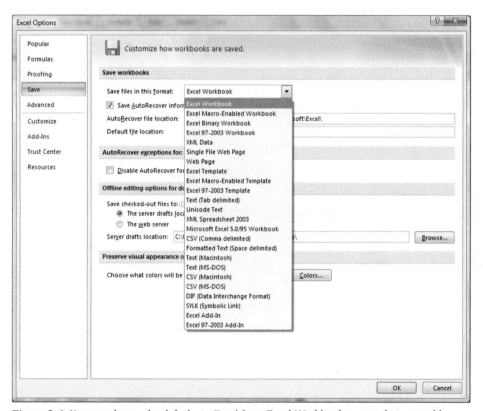

Figure 3-6: You can change the defaults in Excel from Excel Workbook to any choice you like.

Go ahead and look at what's available in the other sections of both Word and Excel's Options window. Don't make any changes though; you don't want to stray too far from the defaults until you have a good idea of what's available.

Note

You never have to accept the default settings when saving a file. If you ever want to override what you've configured in this section, just click the File menu, and select Save As instead of Save. You'll see the window shown in Figure 3-5, and you can save anywhere you want to. Saving in this manner will not change the defaults you've previously set.

About Office's New File Formats

You may have noticed a new file format in Word 2007 that uses a new filename extension: .docx. This was not a file format in earlier versions of Word. Things have changed a lot though, and the new file formats are a big part of that change.

This new file format is based on XML, or Extensible Markup Language. The World Wide Web Consortium (www.w3.org) has demonstrated that XML is truly a standard that has been embraced by the entire computer/software/Internet community. In using XML as the basis for Office's new file formats, Microsoft is moving away from proprietary file formats, and allowing more compatibility with other applications.

Office XML files offer the following features for the end user:

- Automatic compression of files, reducing file size by an average of 75%. This feature works by zipping the files when they are stored, and unzipping them when they are opened. This is all done automatically, with no special help from the user or the installation or purchase of special software.

- Better damaged-file recovery, which allows a file to be opened even if part of it is corrupt, such as a chart or table.

- Improved privacy and better control over personal information with Document Inspector.

- Better integration with documents, worksheets, presentations, and forms, all with XML data interoperability framework.

You'll see two new file type extensions, those that end in *x* and those that end in *m*. An *x* means the file is saved in XML format and does not contain macros; an *m* means the file is saved in XML format and contains macros. That's pretty much all you need to know about the new file formats!

Creating New Organizational Folders

If you work in an office, store your data on a network server, and/or do not have the power to change your current folder structure, you might think there would be no need to read this section. However, the tips detailed here don't pertain just to a work setting. You can apply what you learn here to properly organize the folders you have on your home, tablet, mobile, or small business PC.

Getting Organized

Whatever organizational system you have in place now isn't going to improve itself without interaction from you. Sure, there are a handful of people who can keep everything in the My Documents folder and in subfolders they create on an as-needed basis. If that works for you, fine. However, most people don't do that. Most people haphazardly save all kinds of files straight to their desktops, create folders anywhere, or work directly from their C: drive. Even if people do use the My Documents folder, it usually looks like what's shown in Figure 3-7, and contains a mishmash of data.

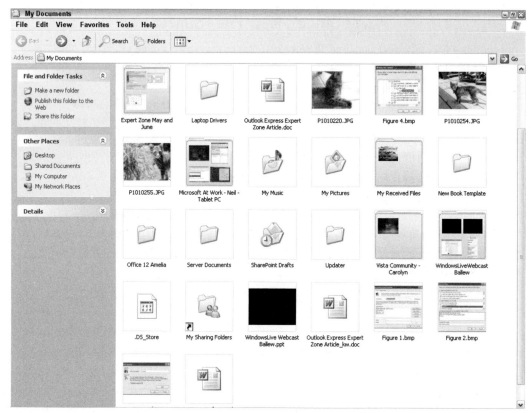

Figure 3-7: Even if you use the My Documents folder, it could probably stand some cleaning up.

There's no point in having a brand-new Office suite if you're not going to be any more productive with it (file and folder-wise) than you were before you upgraded! It's going to take the same amount of time to find the files you need and wade through the junk on your PC as it did before, even with all of Office's new features. So, taking some time to clean up the data you have and create a working organizational structure for the future will make you much more productive and efficient.

The My Documents folder in Figure 3-7 contains quite a bit more than organized subfolders. It contains images (which should be in the My Pictures folder), music (which should be in the My Music folder), documents (which should be in the appropriate project subfolder), and a PowerPoint presentation (which should also be in a project folder). If you have something like this going on, you need to clean that up.

To do that, first drag the stray files into their appropriate subfolders. Right-click when dragging and choose Move, otherwise you'll just create a copy — adding to the mismanagement of your PC! Repeat this with any other folders and subfolders you have. Make sure you have music only in the My Music folder for instance, and that you have photos only in the My Photos folder. Drag anything to its appropriate folder as you come across it.

Finally, before moving on, clean up your desktop, the Unzipped folder if you use the program WinZip, and the root drive too. The object is to move everything that's misplaced to an existing folder, so that there are no stray files laying about the place.

Caution

If you have an Office file that links to a folder on your hard drive to provide up-to-date information each time you open the file, don't move that particular item. Otherwise, when you open the file that uses it, the file won't be able to find the information it needs.

Creating Your New Folder Structure

Once you've cleaned up your files and folders, you can think about how you really want to organize your data. For some, a simple desktop folder system will suffice. Figure 3-8 shows one of ours. There's a shortcut to an external backup device, shared folders for My Documents (that has lots of subfolders inside it, including Finished Projects), a shared folder for this book, a shared folder for another book, and a shared folder for Keystone Learning. With this system, no matter what we're working on, this book, another book, learning videos, or an odd project in the My Documents folder, we can easily drag the folder to the external hard drive for back up at the end of each day. This is a workable and easily extensible system.

Figure 3-8: Even a simple desktop system can work effectively.

Some people would rather have a clean desktop; they have additional partitions or they need a larger system of folders. Perhaps you work on 25 different projects at work, have 10 hobbies at home, and create Web sites for people on the side; perhaps you have a computer with three partitions or you own your own home-based business. Any one of these situations may call for a more sophisticated organizational system.

To begin, if you're going to do this, go through the folders and subfolders currently on your computer and make a list of each category. Think about what you need folders for. In a business situation you may need to create a structure that includes level-1 folders like Publishing Projects, Accounting Projects, Presentations, Marketing Projects, Spreadsheets and Databases, and the like. You'd create subfolders inside of them that would be considered level-2 folders, perhaps subfolders for particular departments, clients, or file types.

For a computer with multiple partitions, consider a folder structure on each to manage different kinds of data, with folders and subfolders that meet your particular needs. You can use any of the techniques here to do that.

For a home-based business (for instance, an advertising company) create a system with level-1 folders for Artwork, Clients, Clip Art, Web Graphics, EPS files, Scanned Art, E-Mailed Artwork, and Backup. You can create level-2 subfolders that are appropriate for each. For instance, level-2 subfolders under Clients could contain a separate folder for each client you have. You could even include level-3 folders to hold the graphics, invoices, fonts, and other items you have on file for them.

Finally, if you have a home-based business, you'll probably also need folders for Hobbies, Pictures, Music, Video, and Kids, with subfolders to match.

Look at Figure 3-9. This is the folder we're using for this book. Look at all of the subfolders. It is extremely organized; it is a shared folder and contains subfolders for each chapter, for chapter guidelines, and for templates and instructions. Because everything is in a single folder, backing up each day is a piece of cake. Additionally, in Figure 3-10, you can see the subfolder for this chapter, Chapter 3.

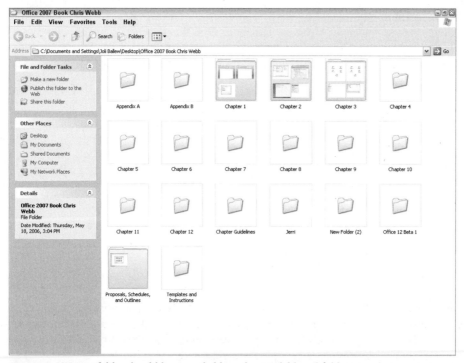

Figure 3-9: Every folder should have workable and extendable subfolders.

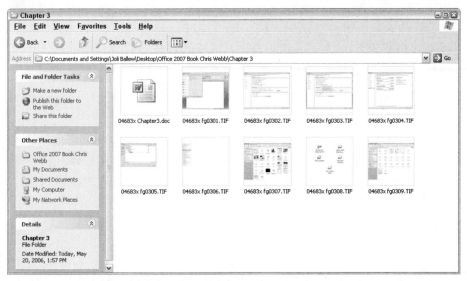

Figure 3-10: Subfolders should also be organized and contain items related to it only.

You'll need to take some time to write everything down, and draw out a system of folders and subfolders just as we did. Once you know what you want to do, creating folders and moving the data into them is easy:

1. Decide where you want to keep the level-1 folders you'll create. This would be akin to a My Documents folder or one of our book folders. You'll have several level-1 folders. You may choose to create these on a partition or a root drive, inside My Documents, or right on the desktop. (We prefer the desktop because it makes backing up much faster.) Whatever you choose, browse there.

2. Right-click, point to New, and choose Folder.

3. Name the folder.

4. Locate any existing folder that you want to put in that folder (as a subfolder), right-click it, and drag it to the new level-1 folder. When prompted, select Move or Move Here.

5. Repeat this until you've created all your-level 1 folders and moved all existing data into the proper folders.

6. Open each level-1 folder and consider the subfolders. You can either right-click again to create additional subfolders, again dragging to move data there, or you can rename any subfolders you've dragged there.

7. Continue in this manner until your new folder structure is created.

8. If you want to, now is the time to return to the previous sections and change where files are saved. You may want to open PowerPoint, and change the default location for saving files to a folder you've created just for presentations. You can open Excel and change the location for all saved files to your Taxes folder or your Accounting folder.

Now it may take a little time to achieve perfection in this matter. You may find that you need to rename folders once you work with this scheme for a while, or that some subfolders can be combined. You may occasionally move subfolders from one folder to another once that particular project is finished. We have a folder for Current Projects. As projects are completed, the related subfolders are moved to the My Documents → Finished folder. The Current Projects folder usually only contains five or so subfolders.

Caution

When a shared folder is moved, it is no longer accessible to those who used it prior to the move. After you've completed the new organizational folder structure, configure sharing again, and inform your network users of the new name and location.

Staying Organized over the Long Run

Staying organized over the long run is about as hard as keeping a house clean after a good scrubbing. Just like a house, your computer will collect trash, unwanted items, and well, junk. You will need to continually monitor what folders contain finished projects, items you no longer need, and clients you no longer have. It's not as difficult as it sounds though. Here are a few tips to stay neat and clean:

- Move, don't copy data. If you copy data, you'll find yourself not only with a hard drive full of duplicate data, but you may have problems determining what document or image to use.

- Always browse to the correct location to save a file. You won't always need to save a file to the default location. For instance, if you've configured Word to save to My Documents, remember to always select the proper subfolder before saving.

- Make sure you back up the folders you've created. This can be done using a simple drag-and-drop technique to a flash drive, external hard drive, or network drive.

- Keep only the data you need. Delete the rest.

- Don't be afraid to create more subfolders. Generally, it's easier to navigate among many descriptively named subfolders than having to wade through a few nondescript ones. For instance, instead of a single folder named Pets, create subfolders for every pet you own.

- Move finished projects to a folder just for those types of documents and presentations.

- At the end of every workweek, get rid of any stray items on your desktop or in folders or subfolders by deleting them or moving them to the appropriate folder.

Summary

With new features, a new, sleeker interface, redesigned tabs and contextual tabs, and more templates and ready-to-use features, Microsoft Office 2007 will help you be more productive and make your job much easier than before. However, if you had to wade through a complicated folder structure before the upgrade to find or save the data you use and keep, you're still going to have that problem after.

In this chapter, you learned how to create a new folder structure and why you should take the time to create it. With appropriately named folders and subfolders, you can always find what you want quickly. You can even change the defaults for saving files to save to a particular folder automatically, so that one click does it all. You can even save automatically to a network drive, without having to browse the network to find it. Not only does all of this make working with data easier, it makes backing up more efficient too. It's well worth the time it takes to get organized; with organization, you'll find yourself being much more industrious.

Part II

Avoiding Disasters

Chapter 4

Backing Up Your Data

If you've ever had a hard drive crash, you know how important it is to back up your data. If you've yet to have a hard drive crash, consider yourself lucky. Your computer or hard drive will give out sometime, probably when you can least afford it. Knowing this, the time to create your first backup is not when your hard drive starts whirring and making painful noises. You need to have a backup plan in place at all times, have the items on hand you need to make the plan work, and take the time to implement the plan on a regular basis.

Backing up doesn't have to be an agonizing task though. This isn't the olden days when you had to have a sophisticated tape drive or a stack of floppy disks. You can back up your data to CDs, DVDs, external drives, flash drives, and even to online servers. You can drag files to a writeable CD folder or drive, or upload to a network or online server.

Backing up e-mail is another story, though. Most people never take the time to do it, most likely because it isn't very intuitive and because they don't really trust the backups anyway. (This is likely because they don't understand how to recover using them!) You can't really just drag files, and copy and burn, when backing up e-mail. There's a little more to it than that. You have to back up your e-mail, address book, and contacts if you really want to be safe. To do that, you have to know a little about how Outlook works.

If you have Vista, you can use Search Folders to create a backup of your recent documents or a specific type of data. Search Folders in Office is detailed in Chapters 10, 11, and 12, but in this chapter we'll introduce a kind of generic Vista Search Folders technique for backing up data. Backing up is an important task, and we want to get you started doing it on a regular basis!

Understanding Backup Media

Losing data through a hard drive crash is kind of like being robbed. One minute, life is going along normally, and the next, you're suddenly missing some very valuable stuff. And, you aren't sure how to go about replacing it, or even if you can. While a thief might take jewelry, money, and personal identification, a failed hard drive can claim family pictures and movies, music, personal files, and more. In an office setting, data loss can wreak havoc as well. If you haven't backed up that project you've been working on for a month, a publication you're putting together for Friday's printing deadline, tax or client information, or something equally important, losing it could mean losing an account, your job, or worse. Bearing that in mind, let's first look at the types of backup media that exist, so that you can choose the one that's right for you.

CDs and DVDs

Forget floppy disks — those days are gone. Zip drives are on their way out too. What's in are CDs and DVDs, external hard drives and flash drives, and intranet (network) and Internet drives. CDs and DVDs are the easiest, so let's start there.

CDs offer a universal way to back up files and folders. Almost all PCs these days come with writeable CD drives, but you can add one for under $100 if you don't have one. Disks are inexpensive too, and they're getting cheaper by the day. Backing up to CDs offers several advantages over other backup options because you can store the backups off-site, reuse them (if they are rewriteable CDs and you have a rewriteable drive), and restore your data from the CD to any computer, even a new one.

The only problem with using CDs as your sole backup option is that you'll probably have much more data than will fit on a couple (or dozens) of CDs. A CD holds only 650MB of data; that's not a lot when you have a 200GB monster hard drive. If you used CDs only, you'd likely need 50 or more to do a good backup, and data would be scattered across them. CDs deteriorate over time too. So we suggest you reserve this option for short-term and weekly backups, or to back up projects once they're finished.

DVDs are another story. DVDs hold 4.7GB of data, and the newer dual-layer DVDs hold almost twice that. We suggest you use DVDs to burn copies of large folders of media, such as pictures, videos, and music, and to create backups of programs you've downloaded from the Internet or that you've purchased from a computer store.

The problem with DVDs is that the setup is more expensive than CDs, and the disks cost more. A dual-layer DVD burner starts at around $100 and disks are about $5 apiece at the time this book was written. However, backing up 8.5GB of data in a single shot is a great option for those with lots of data.

External Hard Drives

External hard drives come in lots of shapes and sizes. One of our favorite backup devices is an 80GB Western Digital. It's old, but it works like a charm. External hard drives are simple to use, and you can back up literally gigabytes of data with a single click. They connect easily to your PC via USB or FireWire, and you don't need to purchase additional media. With an external drive, even the most paranoid users can feel safe. If you wanted to, you could perform a complete backup of your system every night of the week.

We can't think of too many disadvantages to this method. You can remove the external drive and take it off site, it's fairly inexpensive (considering it's a total backup system), and there's no additional media to purchase, like CDs or DVDs, and, it's completely reusable!

Tip

A second internal hard drive can be used in place of an external one. However, you can't take an internal hard drive off site, and if you spill a cup of coffee on your computer, you might ruin both your root drive as well as your backup internal drive.

Flash Drives

Flash drives, thumb drives, pen drives, portable MP3 players, or whatever you want to call them make great backups too. Pocket PCs and smart phones that have a memory card can also be used. Some drives are small enough to take off-site every day, and you can attach them to your key ring or put them in your pocket. Newer drives hold more information than ever too; the latest (and probably most expensive) ones hold several gigabytes of data. They're Plug and Play, so installation is a breeze, and you can use them to restore data to any computer that has a USB drive.

The only disadvantage that we can see, and it's a big one, is that they're easily lost. You may find your missing flash drive in the clothes dryer, on the floor of your car, or you may never find it at all. If it has personal information on it and someone finds it, you could be in for far more than some lost data. We'll say this about flash drives: They make for a great short-term backup, like when you're on a business trip (or vacation) and don't want to haul around blank CDs or DVDs, an external drive, or a Zip disk, but for the long term, you should have another backup strategy.

On the plus side, flash drives are excellent for carrying files you may want to give to someone else; for files you may receive from someone else, for example at a conference or a meeting with customers; or for carrying files between your work and home computer (when your work computer is not accessible from your home computer). In that sense, flash drives are today's version of floppy disks — they can be used for backup, but are best used just for short-term backups or for temporary transport of files.

Network Drives

In a corporate setting, your working drive (where the documents you work on every day are stored) is usually a network drive on a corporate server, not a disk drive on your own PC. Typically, an administrator will back up the network drive every day, so you don't have to do anything at all regarding your own backups. However, some companies do configure a setup where data is stored on your own PC, and you have special disks and network drives designated for backup. It is then your responsibility to perform a quick backup before leaving each day. Whatever the case, network drives are generally backed up by someone else, to insure data is safe in case of a disaster. This type of setup makes network drives the optimal way to back up data.

Network drives are used like external drives, meaning you can drag files nightly to back up the day's data. In a corporate setting, you'll usually save directly to the network drive while you are working, and not to your PC. So, in this case, you don't have to do backups at all! If you're confused about whether you have a network drive where you work, ask. In a small business or home environment, you're probably better off with other backup options.

Internet Options

There are several places you can save your data online. If you go with a reputable company, you can rest assured that your data will be safe. There are several good companies; Xdrive (`www.xdrive.com`) and IBackup (`www.ibackup.com`) seem to be popular. With these companies, you pay a monthly fee and upload your daily backups to a safe and secure server, far from where your office is. This is a good thing because if your office is destroyed by a fire or flood, you'll know your data is safe. You can also access your data from anywhere, so if you're on a business trip and need to get or save data, you can do so just by logging on. These sites also let you share data with people you give access to. Xdrive offers 5GB of space for $10 a month.

For home or small business users, an inexpensive option is Yahoo! Business Email. For around $20 a year, you get 2GBs of e-mail space. You can then create a "backup" folder, and configure an e-mail filter that automatically directs all e-mails with the word "backup" in the message subject into it. At the end of the day, or any time you want to save a copy of your current work, just attach the file to an e-mail and send it to your Yahoo! account with a subject like "current work backup." It's a cheap and simple way to back up e-mail and work any time you like.

Copying Files Manually

If you've decided that you'll use a CD, DVD, or external hard drive to back up your data, dragging files is your best bet. You can drag (or copy and paste) to any of these mediums. Figure 4-1 shows an example of a computer with several backup options. Notice it has two hard drives, and one is named PCBackup. It's an external hard drive. There are also three drives under removable storage, a floppy drive, a DVD drive, and a rewriteable CD drive. In this case, the two best options are to back up to the rewriteable CD drive or the external hard drive. (The DVD drive is only a player, not a recorder.)

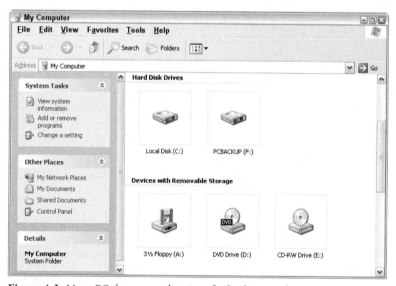

Figure 4-1: Many PCs have several options for backing up data.

Drag Files to Any Drive

With an external hard drive such as shown in Figure 4-1, all you have to do to perform a daily backup is to drag the folders that contain the data to back up to the appropriate folder on the external drive. You generally do this by opening the folder on your PC that you want to back up in one window, opening the folder on the external drive you want to back up to in a second window, and dragging the data from one to the other. Figure 4-2 shows an example.

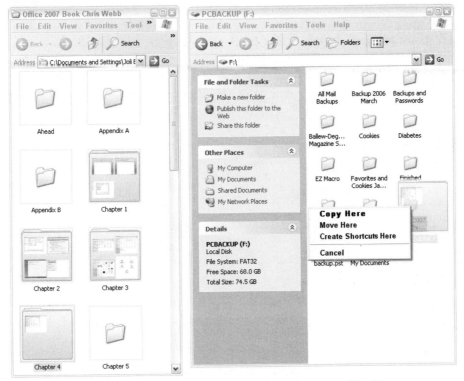

Figure 4-2: Drag from your PC to your external drive to perform a quick backup.

Caution

Always verify you're backing up from your PC's hard drive to the external drive. If you back up the other way around, you can bet you'll lose important data.

If you right-click while dragging, you'll get the option to copy or move the data. If you left-click and drag, the data will automatically be copied and you won't be given the options shown in Figure 4-2. This happens only when you're dragging data from one drive to another. Dragging a folder from one area of a drive to another area on that drive will, by default, copy the data. That's why we always suggest right-clicking; you'll always have the option to copy or to move, and you can know you're making the right choice.

Burning CDs and DVDs

Just as dragging to an external drive works to back up data, dragging to a rewriteable CD drive also works. Once you've dragged the data to the drive though, you'll need to tell Windows XP you want to copy the files to the CD, or choose something similar if you're using a third-party program or another operating system.

To copy data to a DVD, your best bet is to put the DVD in the drive and wait for the prompt from Windows. If you're using Windows Vista (Microsoft's latest operating system), you'll see a prompt like the one that's shown in Figure 4-3. The dialog box for Windows XP is similar. Choose Burn a DVD data disc. You'll be prompted to name the disc and then you'll be able to select items to add to the disc once it's prepared. With the Vista build that we're using, once you drag the items to the DVD writeable folder, Windows immediately prepares to copy and then copies. There's no need to do anything else. Figure 4-4 shows a copy in progress with Vista.

Figure 4-3: When you input a DVD into a DVD drive, you are prompted to choose appropriate tasks.

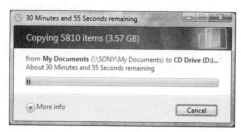

Figure 4-4: Vista copies data to a DVD almost automatically.

If you need to burn a specific type of DVD like a DVD image or a DVD that can be used to boot a PC, you'll need to use the DVD's software to make that happen. Windows XP (and Vista) create data and media discs only. When using a third-party program, insert a writeable DVD in a writeable DVD drive, and choose an option from the prompt or start the program manually.

Backing Up E-mail

Most people never back up their e-mail, not because they don't feel it's important, but because they don't know how. Backing up e-mail is just as important as backing up any other data on your computer, and in a business setting, perhaps even more so. Think about it: even if you lose a receipt, software code, or verification from a client that the project you've been working on is a go, you likely have the same data in an e-mail folder somewhere. If you collaborate on projects, you probably have the latest project file in your Sent Items folder. Last but not least, an okay from your boss to take the day off or miss an important meeting might be something you'll need later when it comes up during your yearly review. That being said, it's important to know how to back up your e-mail. In the following section, we do that in Office Outlook.

Back Up Outlook 2007

Unless you are using a Microsoft Exchange Server e-mail account or an HTTP account such as Hotmail, all of your Outlook data is saved in a Personal Folders file (with a .pst extension). Each Personal Folders file contains your Inbox, Calendar, and Contacts, as well as other folders including Sent Items, Deleted Items, and others. You can back up your e-mail using the Import and Export tool in Outlook 2007.

To back up your Outlook 2007 data:

1. Open Outlook 2007.

2. From the File menu, click Import and Export, and select Export to a File. Click Next.

3. In the next dialog box, select Personal Folder File (.pst). Click Next.

4. Select Personal Folders to back up everything in Outlook 2007, and select Include sub-folders as shown in Figure 4-5. Click Next.

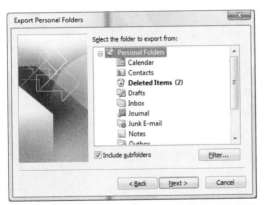

Figure 4-5: To back up all e-mail, including subfolders, configure the dialog box like this.

5. Browse to the location where you want to save the file. Replace any duplicates with items you export by choosing the default setting Replace Duplicates with Items Exported. Click Finish.

6. When prompted, if you desire, configure a password and a new name for the backup folder. Click OK.

The process may take moments or minutes to complete depending upon how much material you are backing up.

Restore Outlook 2007

The only way to be positive that your backup worked is to restore from it. The first time you perform a backup, you may want to do just that. Once you know you've backed up properly, you won't have to test again, but for starters, and just to be safe, it's best to make sure your backup worked.

To restore Outlook 2007 from backup:

1. Open Outlook 2007.

2. From the File menu, click Import and Export, and select Import from another Program or File. Click Next.

3. In the next dialog box, select Personal Folder File (.pst). Click Next.

4. Browse to the location where you saved the original backup file.

5. Replace any duplicates with items you export by choosing the default setting Replace Duplicates with Items Exported. Click Next.

6. Select the folders to restore. You may want to select Personal Folders to import the entire backup.

7. Import the items back into the original folders. The configuration is shown in Figure 4-6. Click Finish.

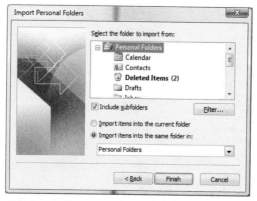

Figure 4-6: To restore all e-mail, including subfolders, configure the dialog box like this.

The process may take moments or minutes to complete depending upon how much material you are restoring.

Using Search Folders

There's one more way to back up data that's worth mentioning: incorporating Vista's new Search Folders. With Vista, you can create folders that contain search results, using the exact technology you'll find in the new Microsoft Office applications. Although there is plenty more about Search Folders throughout this book, Vista's Search Folders are worth a brief look here.

Vista's new Start menu has a Search box, as shown in Figure 4-7. When you type something into the Search box and select Search this Computer, a new window opens up with the results. Once you get to know Vista, you'll learn that it keeps certain data indexed by default.

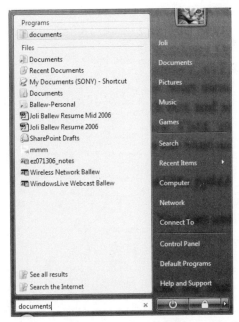

Figure 4-7: You can use the Search box on the Start menu to perform searches quickly.

You can then click any selection to open the resulting file or folder. In this instance, clicking Recent Documents opens a Search Window with your most recent additions.

It's easy now to click Save Search in the Search window, name the new Search Folder, and then burn that folder to a CD or DVD. This makes for a quick end-of-the-month backup option, one you can reuse each month, applying names that represent the month that the data is from. You can perform similar searches for media. You can even search e-mail, e-mail attachments, music, and pictures; you can then save and even share those saved folders.

You'll learn a lot more about Search Folders later in this book, and as you move up to Vista. For now know this: Backing up data is changing. In the near future, you won't be backing up by the folder; rather, you'll be able to quickly specify exactly which data you want to back up.

Summary

Backing up data is extremely important. It's best to create, perform, and verify backups regularly. Remember, your data is only as good as your latest backup. Without a backup, you could lose everything — business proposals, family pictures and videos, client receipts, project files, and more.

Chapter 5

Staying Up to Date

You know it's important to keep the set security features in your office up to date, including changing your computer passwords often, maintaining and testing backups, and configuring and managing firewalls. And everyone knows how important it is to have antivirus and antiadware software installed and up to date too. But there's one other thing to remember to keep up to date, and that's your software.

The easiest way to keep your software up to date, and thus secure and in good working order, is to obtain and install the recommended updates regularly. You can do this by configuring Automatic Updates for your operating system and for Microsoft Office. In this chapter, we discuss how to get these updates and why they're important.

Setting Up Automatic Updates

In order to keep your operating system in good working order, you need to configure Automatic Updates to retrieve the most important updates for your computer automatically. Updates come in many categories, including critical updates, security updates, service packs, software updates, and upgrades. Each of these types plays their own role in keeping your computer safe and up to date, and each has a certain level of importance. As you might guess, critical updates are just that, critical. These updates generally address known bugs in software or security holes in applications. And upgrades, as you may guess, are optional updates that add features to the products you already have installed.

Office Update and Windows Automatic Update are tightly integrated. If you turn on Automatic Updates in your Windows operating system, you'll get all of the necessary Office updates too. It's very important then, to follow our advice here, and double-check that Automatic Updates is enabled.

To configure Windows XP to automatically get critical and high-priority updates:

1. Click Start, right-click My Computer, and select Properties.

2. Open System.

3. In System Properties, select the Automatic Updates tab.

4. Select Automatic (Recommended).

5. Configure a time to download and install the updates. Make sure to choose a time when the computer will be on. If you leave your computer on all the time, select a time in the

middle of the night. If you have your computer on from 9 A.M. to 5 P.M. only, configure it to check during your lunch break. (If your computer is not on when updates are to be retrieved, they will be at the next boot up.)

6. If you do not want the most important updates to install automatically, you can select from one of the remaining three options:

- **Download updates for me, but let me choose when to install them.** Select this option if you use your computer with high-resource software or for resource-hogging tasks like photo rendering. You wouldn't want any resources to be used while you're trying to work (or play a video game). You should also choose this option if you want to review what updates are being downloaded and installed.

- **Notify me but don't automatically download or install them.** Select this option if you want to see what updates are being installed, and to select what you do and don't want. Select this option if you have limited hard drive space.

- **Turn off Automatic Updates.** Select this option if you do not want any updates automatically installed. You'll have to remember to visit the update Web site once a week though, if you want your computer to be secure.

7. Click OK.

Some of this information was covered in Chapter 2; in this chapter though, we go into a bit more depth. For instance, with Automatic Updates, optional updates won't be installed by default. Because of this, you should know that you'd still need to visit the Microsoft Update site occasionally, just to see if there are any driver updates or updates for additional software you own that you'd like to have. You learn how to get updates manually in the next section.

Note

You should also look into setting up automatic updates for your other software. Antivirus and antiadware software always have automatic update options, including options to scan your computer for viruses and other ills daily or weekly. Refer to Chapter 2 for more information on this.

Getting Updates Manually

One way to check for, select, and install updates is to do so manually. There are two ways to do this; from inside any Office application or by going to the Office update Web site. Either way, you'll end up with the same choices, so it really doesn't matter which one you choose. The first thing that will happen when you check for updates is that your computer will be scanned for the information it needs, such as the version of Office you have and its product ID.

The first way you can get updates manually is to connect to the Internet and go to http:// update.microsoft.com/microsoftupdate. Watch the title bar in Internet Explorer to see if you need to install ActiveX controls. If you're prompted to do so, click the title bar to perform this installation.

You can also get updates from inside any Office application. To do this, click the File menu, and choose the application's Options button. Click Resources, and select Check for Updates. Figure 5-1 shows what happens after doing either of these.

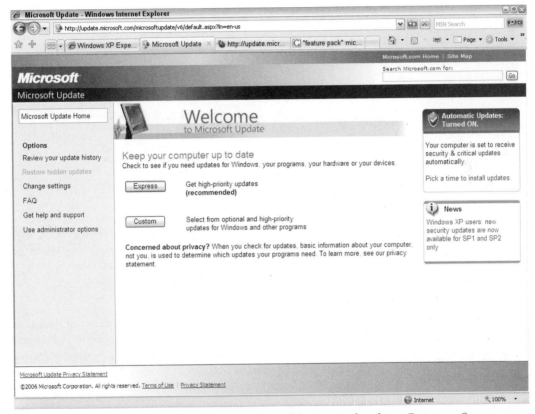

Figure 5-1: Before Microsoft Update performs a scan, you'll be prompted to choose Express or Custom. Choose Custom.

When prompted, select Custom. Selecting Express is recommended by Microsoft, but you won't see all of the available updates by default. With Custom, you'll see everything that is available, and you can make decisions regarding what to install.

Once the scan has finished you'll see how many updates are available, and what kind there are. You may see High Priority; Software, Optional; Hardware, Optional; or other types as shown in Figure 5-2.

Figure 5-2: Choose Custom so that you can see all of the available updates, not just select ones.

Click each of these to see what's available. You should install everything that does not have the word *Optional* beside it, especially any High Priority or Critical updates. To install any High Priority or Critical update, click it and select Install. The process changes occasionally, but it's usually a simple affair, as the installation happens with little interaction from you.

Installing an Optional update is somewhat less automatic. To install an optional update:

1. Select the update category on the left side of the page.

2. Click any optional update in the Select Optional Updates page.

3. Read the description of the update.

4. If the update pertains to you, place a check by it to select it for download. If it does not pertain to you, do not check it. Figure 5-3 shows an example of an optional software update that does not pertain to any of us.

5. Once you've selected the updates to install, click Review and install updates. You'll be prompted again to verify you want to perform the installation. Click Install Updates.

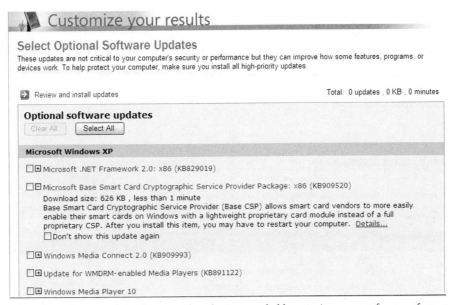

Figure 5-3: The optional software update that's expanded here isn't necessary for any of us, so we will not install it. You need to make similar decisions.

6. Wait while the installation completes as shown in Figure 5-4.

7. If prompted, restart your computer. If you do not get all of the updates you want, repeat the steps here until you do.

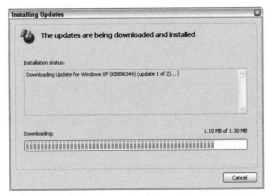

Figure 5-4: Wait while the updates are being installed.

Tip

After updates have finished installing, you see a Results screen. You'll see what was installed correctly and what failed, if anything. You'll also be able to view your update history. It is a good idea to look over this information, just to make sure everything went the way it was supposed to. Here you can see that one of the updates failed. Look at Figure 5-5.

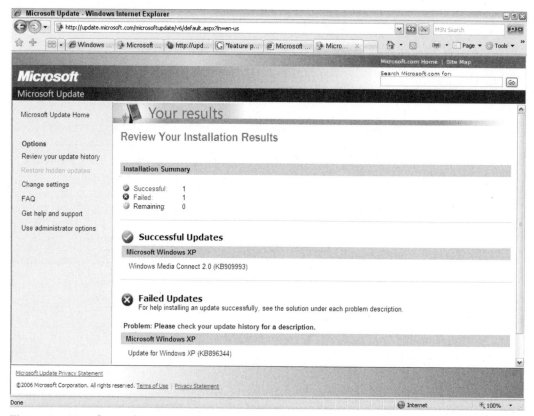

Figure 5-5: View the Results screen to see if any updates failed to install correctly. Take the necessary action to remedy the problem, as prompted by Microsoft.

Understanding Update Types

As you've seen, there are many kinds of updates. There are Critical updates and Security updates, both of which are extremely important. But there are others you may see from time to time as well. In the next few sections, you'll learn a little about each of them.

Critical Updates

Critical updates are broadly released fixes for a specific problem that address a critical issue, but one that is not related to security. Critical updates may be released to fix an error in the software; for instance, perhaps there is a bug that causes a program to shut down unexpectedly. You should install all of these updates.

Security Updates

A security update is also a broadly released fix for a specific problem, but in this instance the problem is security related and applies to a specific product such as Microsoft Office Word or Outlook Express. Microsoft rates these updates by their severity: low, moderate, important, and critical. You should get all security updates, even if their severity rating is low.

Service Packs

A service pack is a collection of all hotfixes (fixes for specific problems, sometimes only customer or organization-related), security updates, critical updates, and updates. These service packs may also contain design changes to the software itself, including new and improved features. Service Pack 2 for Windows XP for instance, added new features to the Control Panel. You should install all service packs. It may be wiser, however, to install the service pack on a test machine first, or wait for a month or so after its release, to make sure it will not cause more problems than it's worth.

Software Updates

A software update is any update, service pack, feature pack, critical update, security update, or hot-fix that will improve Microsoft Office. It may also solve problems related to the software, such as a bug or a known issue. You may or may not need to install these updates. Read about the update if installing manually, and make a decision based on the description.

Upgrades

An upgrade is an entire software package that replaces an installed version of the software you currently have. The replacement is a newer version of the same product. An upgrade won't install clean, you'll still have your current settings. Upgrades for a product generally change the interface by adding new features, make existing features more secure, and leave your application's configuration intact.

Feature Packs

A feature pack is a fun and optional item that you do not have to install. Feature packs provide new functionality for a product, functionality that is usually included in the next release of the product.

Exploring Privacy Issues

Microsoft does collect some information when you visit its site for updates. Microsoft does this so that you can receive the updates that are best for your computer configuration and software. Microsoft does not collect your name, address, phone number, or e-mail address, and does not know where you are specifically located.

Some information is collected, however, including the following:

- Computer make and model
- Version numbers of operating systems, browsers, and software
- Plug and Play ID numbers for hardware devices
- Region and language settings
- Globally unique identifier
- Product ID and product key
- BIOS name, revision number, and date

This information is used only to help Microsoft decide what software you have, what you need updates for, and whether you have a valid copy of Windows and Microsoft Office. The globally unique identifier is used to identify your specific computer and does not contain any information that could identify you. If you'd like to see a sample of what is collected, visit any Microsoft Update page, scroll to the bottom of the page, and select Microsoft Update Privacy Statement. Scroll down that page to View Sample Data.

Summary

It's important to keep your computer up to date with the latest antivirus software, to keep doors locked, and passwords secure. There are other things you can do though, and one of those is to get operating system and Microsoft Office updates regularly. The best way to do this is to configure Automatic Updates in Windows XP. In this chapter you learned how to do that, as well as how to get updates manually.

Chapter 6

Recovering from Problems

Most of the time, things go along just as they're supposed to. You create, save, and back up data; you shut the computer down and boot it back up without incident. You always find the data you need, and it's always in the folder you saved it to. Notice we started that first sentence with the phrase *most of the time,* though.

Occasionally, something will happen to break the cycle of certainty. If you've ever been in the middle of a project when the power went out, you know what we mean. A power outage can wreak havoc on an open file. Problems can also arise when you open a file from an e-mail attachment or network drive, work on it, click the Save button (vs. Save As), and then close the file. If you've ever done this, you know how difficult it is to locate the file when you're ready to work on it again. Problems can also occur when you install faulty software, get a virus, or work on a read-only or shared file with a colleague.

When any of these things happen, you need to know how to recover. An operating system problem (a problem that affects the entire computer) may mean using System Restore to revert the computer to a previous state. If it's a problem that affects Office only, you may need to use Office Diagnostics, a new feature in Office 2007. If it's a lost file, perhaps searching the computer is the answer. If you've lost a file during a power outage or computer crash, you may need to incorporate complicated search techniques, such as browsing through recovered files in Office. In this chapter, we address the most common problems you'll run across and detail their solutions.

Using System Restore

System Restore is a feature of Windows XP and beyond; it lets you reverse harmful changes you've made to your computer. Harmful changes cause the computer to perform poorly, hang up, or barely boot. Most of the time, an installation of third-party software or a "new and improved" device driver causes these changes. With Office applications, it could also be a third-party Office add-in, a rogue macro, or perhaps even a virus.

You use System Restore to return your computer to its state on a *restore point* from an earlier date that you choose, a date when the computer was working properly. You can think of a system restore point as a snapshot of your computer, and if you ever need it, you can return to that snapshot without losing any data you've recently created. You'll use System Restore to return to a stable computer state if your PC ever becomes unstable.

System Restore won't solve all your problems though. If you have a virus or if a macro has done irreparable harm, you may have to take another route. However, it never hurts to try System Restore, although for viruses, antivirus options are a better choice.

Although System Restore returns your system to a previous state, it does not change the files you are working with. You can be sure that the application will not destroy (or lose) any of the following files:

- Personal files, such as work documents, spreadsheets, or presentations

- Media, including music, pictures, and videos

- Cookies and Internet history

- E-mail, attachments, contacts (even those created after the restore point)

Restore points, the snapshots of your system we talked about earlier, are created automatically and for different reasons. Restore points are created at the following times:

- When you install a new application that is System Restore API compliant, which almost all programs are

- When you install a Microsoft update

- Before a Backup Recovery operation

- Before installing an unsigned driver

- At 24 hour intervals

- When you create one manually or turn off and then turn back on System Restore

A restore point includes registry settings and the entire registry, Windows File Protection files, COM+ database, Windows Management Instrumentation database, IIS metabase, local profiles, and more. System restore points do not include Windows XP passwords, Content Advisor passwords, contents of redirected folders, files not monitored by System Restore (third-party application files with unknown origin), and similar items.

Tip

If you can boot the computer, you should give System Restore a shot at correcting whatever problem you have. If you can't boot normally, try booting in safe mode (press F8 during boot up).

If you want to use System Restore to recover from a virus, hijacked home page, or malware, it's always best to let your antivirus software have a go at it first. If that doesn't work, then try System Restore. After any successful removal of a virus, turn System Restore off and back on to remove any lingering viruses that may be hanging around in your restore points.

Enabling System Restore

System Restore is enabled by default, so you probably don't need to do anything here but check to make sure it's turned on. The only reasons it would not be on are if you have less than 200MB of free disk space, you've manually turned it off, or a network administrator has disabled it.

To check to see if System Restore is enabled, and to configure the available options for System Restore:

1. Right-click My Computer and select Properties.

2. In the System Properties dialog box, shown in Figure 6-1, select the System Restore tab.

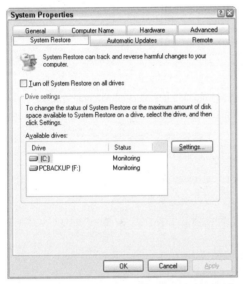

Figure 6-1: To view System Restore settings, select the System Restore tab in System Properties.

3. Verify that Turn off System Restore on all drives is not checked. If it is checked, deselect it.

4. Select the drive that's being monitored; if more than one is available, select each one separately to configure and perform the rest of the steps on each.

5. Click Settings.

6. In the Drive Settings dialog box, shown in Figure 6-2, note how much hard drive space is allotted to System Restore data. By default, this setting is 12%. For this computer, that's almost 10,000MB. You can move the slider to the left to allot less. However, we prefer to leave the defaults as they are, unless we're low on hard drive space.

7. Click OK to close the Drive Settings dialog box, and OK again to close System Properties.

Figure 6-2: You can move the System Restore slider to allot
less space to System Restore, but we advise against that.

Creating a Restore Point

Although System Restore creates restore points by default, you may want to manually create one if
you suspect you're about to do something risky, such as install software or a screensaver you've
downloaded from the Internet.

To create a restore point manually:

1. Click Start, point to All Programs, point to Accessories, point to System Tools, and select
   System Restore.

2. From the System Restore Welcome Page, shown in Figure 6-3, select Create a restore point.
   Click Next.

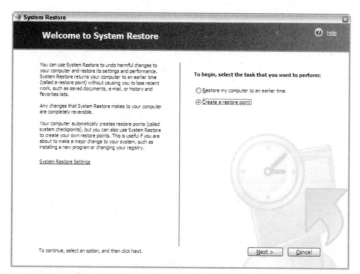

Figure 6-3: To create a restore point manually, select Create a restore point
from the Welcome to System Restore page.

3. Name the restore point with a descriptive name, such as the reason you're creating it. Click Create.

Restoring to an Earlier Time

To use System Restore to restore your computer to an earlier date and time:

1. Click Start, point to All Programs, point to Accessories, point to System Tools, and select System Restore.

2. From the System Restore Welcome Page, select Restore my computer to an earlier time. Click Next.

3. From the Select a Restore Point page, use the arrows to move through the calendar, and select a point to restore to. Figure 6-4 shows an example. Click Next.

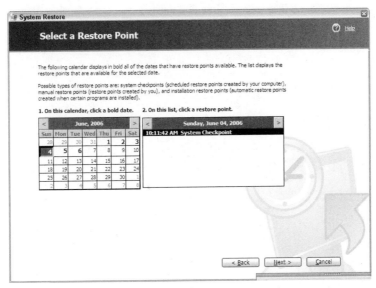

Figure 6-4: Select a restore point.

4. Verify that you want to make this change by selecting Next.

5. Wait while the process completes; your computer will reboot.

System Restore is a good choice when you've installed harmful software on your computer. Sometimes, System Restore works to repair problems with rogue macros and viruses too. However, for viruses, it's best to let your antivirus program have a go at it first. System Restore will not recover open files that are lost when there's a power outage though, and it won't cause missing files to magically reappear. For those tasks, you need to take a different approach. However, System Restore is an effective tool when you need to get your system back to a state prior to when a third-party application caused a specific conflict or problem.

Using Office Diagnostics

Office Diagnostics is a new feature of Office 2007 and can be found in any Office application's Options page. If something is wrong with an Office application but nothing seems to be wrong with the computer itself, run this diagnostic to repair it before reverting to System Restore. If this does not solve the problem, use System Restore next.

To perform an Office Diagnostic:

1. Open any Office application and connect to the Internet. The Office Diagnostic tool often goes to the Microsoft Web site to get the latest updates.

2. Click the File menu in the top-left corner and open the application's Options page.

3. Select Resources.

4. Click Diagnose (to the right of run Microsoft Office Diagnostics).

5. Click Continue to run Office Diagnostics. Note that this process can take up to 15 minutes. In the figure below, you can see the interface.

6. Click Start Diagnostics.

Several tests will run, including a search for known problems and solutions, testing memory, updates, compatibility, disk, and setup. You can watch the progress as shown in the following figure.

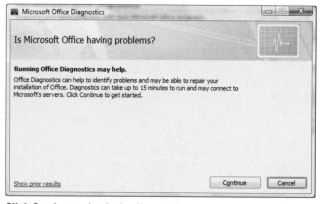

Click Continue to begin the diagnostic.

After the diagnostic is finished, you'll see a summary screen.

Locating Lost Files

Everyone's done it; we've all lost files. Either you can't remember where you saved it, or you can't remember if you saved it. Perhaps you can't remember what you've named it. With the new features in Office 2007, you stand a better chance of finding the file now than you did in the past. If you can remember anything about the file, anything at all, you can probably locate it with a little time and effort.

Using the Office Interface

Remember the olden days when you'd open an attachment in Outlook (or Outlook Express), save the file, and it would default to some obscure folder in some temporary holding area on your hard drive? Heaven help you if you saved your work there, you'd never see it again. Well, those days are gone. Now when you open an attachment in Outlook and save it, My Documents opens by default and you're prompted to save there. Small changes like this make using Office 2007 easier than ever. You'll notice that, unless you specifically configure it otherwise, the Office applications will save to an intuitive folder, or the last folder you saved to.

All of the new Office applications provide access to the File menu with a button in the top-left corner, and clicking that button shows the last files you've worked on. You can easily find forgotten files there. Figure 6-5 shows an example. Not only are the latest files listed, if you hover the mouse over them, you can see in what folder they're stored.

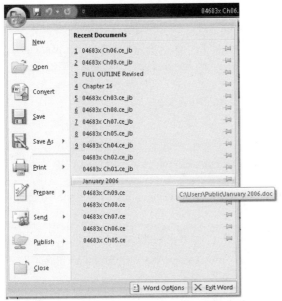

Figure 6-5: Information is available in all Office applications from the File menu button, including recent files.

If you're missing a file, try the tips in the following list to locate it; often, you'll find what you're looking for with these techniques. Later you'll learn about additional options. First, try these:

- Look in the My Documents folder and subfolders.

- Look in your Network drive(s).

- Look in your external hard drive. Open files if you aren't sure what they are. You can always close them.

- Click Start, then Search, and type a word you think may be in the document's title. (There is more on using Search in the next section.)

- Click the File menu button of the application you think you created the file in, and look at the list of recent documents.

- Click Start, and select Recent Documents. If the file is recent, it may be there.

- Look through your recent backups.

Using the Operating System's Search Tool

Search features in Windows and the upcoming Windows Vista are highly effective when searching for missing files. In Windows XP, you'll use the Search option in the Start menu; in Vista you'll use the new Search box in the Start menu.

Note

Microsoft plans to release Windows Desktop Search for Windows XP (now currently in beta) for users of Windows XP. With that product, you'll have access to the new search features you'll also find in Vista, the features mentioned in this section.

SEARCHING IN WINDOWS XP

In Windows XP, Search is found in the Start menu. To perform a search using Windows XP:

1. Click Start, and then Search. This opens the Search Results dialog box. This is shown in Figure 6-6.

2. Under What do you want to search for?, select All files and folders.

3. In the All or part of the file name: window, type ***.doc** to search for all files with a file name that ends with the .doc extension. These are Word document files.

4. In the Look in: window, select the disk drive you'd like to search. By selecting an entire drive, you'll see all of the .doc files on it. Note that you can also search a folder, although this is not nearly as comprehensive as searching the entire drive.

5. Click Search. Figure 6-7 shows the results.

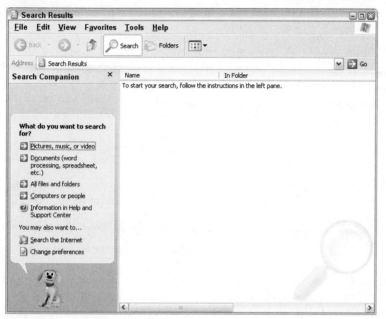

Figure 6-6: The Windows XP Search Results window offers many ways to search for the data you want.

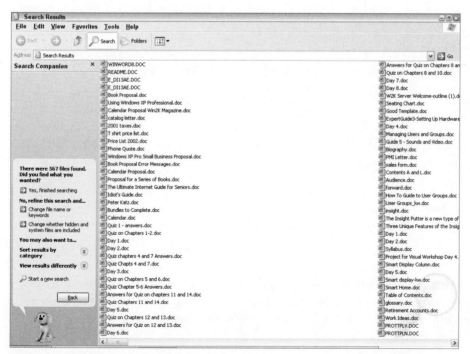

Figure 6-7: You'll probably find many Word documents.

Note
Clicking Start and then Search opens the Search Results window. As shown in Figure 6-6, our Search Window settings are the standard settings that are the default for Windows XP. If your screen doesn't look like the one in the figure, click Change preferences, Change files and folders search behavior; then select Standard. Your Search Results window will now reflect the settings we're using.

Refining Search Results
With the search complete, you can now right-click in an empty area of the Search Results window, point to View, and then select from Thumbnails, Tiles, Icons, List, or Details. You can further cull the results from the View tab, by pointing to Arrange Icons By, and selecting from Name, Folder, Size, Type, or Modified. As you'll find out quickly, you probably have hundreds if not thousands of Word documents on your computer, and understanding how to organize the results becomes quite important.

Searching for Specific Words or Phrases
In addition to searching for entire documents, you can choose to type a word or phrase that you know is inside a specific file. For instance, if you know you created a document that had to do with "the third-generation widget," typing in that phrase will produce a list of documents that contain it. Here's an example of searching for a specific keyword:

1. If you've already performed a search, click the Back button to return to the previous search screen.

2. If you're starting a new search:

    a. Click Start, and then Search. This opens the Search Results dialog box.

    b. Under What do you want to search for?, select All files and folders.

3. Under A word or phrase in the file, type the word you're looking for.

4. Under Look in, select the drive or folder to search.

5. Optionally, type ***.doc** to search document files, ***.ppt** to search PowerPoint files, and so on.

6. Click Search.

Tip
You can search for a specific file type by putting an * (asterisk) in front of the file's suffix. Common file type searches include *.doc (documents), *.jpg (images, generally photos), *.xls (Excel files), *.ppt (PowerPoint files), and *.accdb (Access database files). You can see a list of file types by going to www.google.com and searching for file name extensions.

Using Advanced Search Options

You can change the Search function's behavior by changing the default preferences for a search from Standard to Advanced. Once you make the change, you'll have quicker access to advanced search features. To change the preferences to Advanced:

1. Click Start, and Search.

2. Under What do you want to search for?, click Change preferences.

3. Click Change files and folders behavior.

4. Click Advanced. (Note that you can repeat these steps to return to Standard mode if desired.)

5. Click OK.

Once you've changed your Search preferences to include Advanced search features, you can incorporate even more detail into your searches. Here are a few examples of how you can use these options to successfully find a missing file:

▪ Click the arrow next to When was it modified? to narrow your search to the last week, month, year, or specific dates you choose. This is optimal if you know you created the file last week or last month, but can't remember anything else about it.

▪ Click the arrow next to What size is it? to narrow your search to a specific size file. This is a good choice if you know the file is extremely large or small, so much so that it would stand out from other files on your computer.

▪ Click the arrow next to More advanced options to configure where to search, including system folders, hidden files and folders, tape backup, and more.

▪ Experiment with the other two options: Other search options and Change preferences.

SEARCHING IN VISTA

At the time this book was written, Vista RC2 was available to beta testers. Vista offers a new and improved search technology that will revolutionize searching forever. As with Windows XP, you can search from the Start menu. With Vista though, the Search box is integrated into the Start menu. Figure 6-8 shows an example of this new Search box. Here, we've searched for Office. Notice the categories and the search results. This search offers three: Programs, Favorites and History, and Files. You can open any of these by clicking it.

When you type something into the Search box as shown in Figure 6-8, you'll have two additional options: Search the Internet or Search the computer. Selecting Search the computer opens a window where you can further define your search. In Figure 6-9, we've searched for the word "Office" on a network computer named SONY. Notice you can search just about anywhere. The options for searching are endless.

Figure 6-8: Vista offers a new and improved search technology.

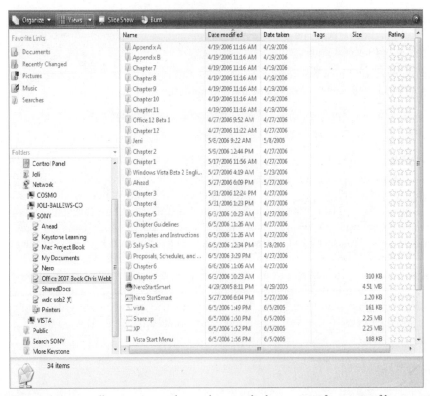

Figure 6-9: Vista allows you to easily search networked computers for missing files, among other things.

The last thing we'd like to say about Vista and its new search features is that Microsoft Office and Vista go hand in hand. Just click the File menu button of any application, click Open, and the Open window will have a search box you can use to locate the file you want. Figure 6-10 shows an example. This Open window looks nothing like the old Open window you're used to dealing with.

Figure 6-10: Office 2007 and Vista work seamlessly to offer exciting new search features.

There will be much more information on this technology in Chapters 10, 11, and 12. For now, consider this a sneak peek!

Working with Recovered Files

Microsoft Office applications automatically try to recover files when something, such as a power outage, goes wrong with your computer. The recovered file may not have all of the data that was originally included in it, but it will usually have what was there prior to the last save. This makes it even more important to let the applications automatically save the document every few minutes. In rare cases though, no information is retained even if AutoRecover is running. In our experience, a partially recovered file is better than no file at all.

Making Sure AutoRecover Is Turned On

You can see where recovered files are stored from an application's Options page, and change or configure AutoRecover options:

1. Open Word 2007.
2. Click the File menu button, and select Word Options.
3. Click Save in the left pane. This is shown in Figure 6-11.

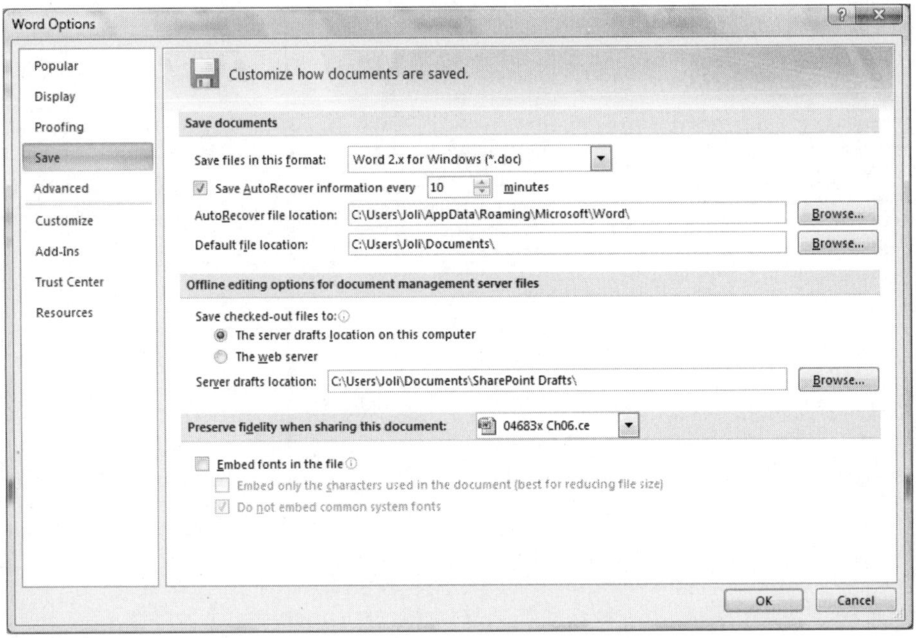

Figure 6-11: The Save tab is where you'll configure AutoRecover.

4. Make sure Save AutoRecover information every 10 minutes is checked. You can change this to any number of minutes you'd like. This is also shown in Figure 6-11.
5. Note the AutoRecover file location; in our computer it's C:\Documents and Settings\Joli Ballew\Application Data\Microsoft\Word.
6. Click Browse to change this location. We will advise against this for now though, at least until you have the approval of your network administrator or have more experience with Office 2007.

Locating Recovered Files

Generally, when a file is lost, you don't have to go looking for it. The next time you open the application, you'll be given options for selecting from the recovered files Microsoft Office has collected.

These recovered files are shown in the Document Recovery task pane, which you'll see on the left side of the application's interface.

The Document Recovery task pane allows you to open files and view what was repaired, and compare recovered versions. Generally, you'll want to select the version that was the last one saved; it will usually contain the most data. You can then save or delete the other versions, and begin work again on the recovered file.

Tip

If you still can't find the files you're missing, use Office 2007's Search features, detailed in Chapters 10, 11, and 12.

Surfing the Web for Answers

Sometimes you'll run across a problem that isn't addressed here or when searching with the Microsoft Office Assistant. These problems take many forms and can include but are not limited to the following:

- Errors in Office after installing updates

- Errors when you try to print or save, or quit a program

- Runtime errors that cause a program to close unexpectedly

- Errors related to missing dynamic link library (DLL) files

- An inability to open files created in Office 2007 in other versions of Office

- Windows installer starting each time you open an Office application

- Inability to open files or folders with long names

These problems are all known issues and listed in Microsoft Knowledge Base articles at http://support.microsoft.com. If you run across a problem that you can't solve using this chapter or Microsoft Help and Support inside the application, you'll need to take additional steps by browsing through these articles.

Using the Microsoft Office Assistance Home Page

The Microsoft Office Home page is currently located at www.microsoft.com/office and offers help and support for Office products. You can browse by program, suite, or technologies, just to name a few. You can view free training videos, or search Microsoft for the help you need.

To find the Microsoft Assistance Home Page, go to www.microsoft.com and type the title in the Search window. Once at the Microsoft Office Assistance home page, just type in information about the problem you're having, and click Go. You'll usually find the information you're looking for in the results.

Accessing Newsgroups and Online Communities

Newsgroups and online communities let you post a question to a large group of people (just like you), and receive answers. A newsgroup is an online community where people exchange questions, answers, and ideas on a specific topic. It's a public place where posts are created for public viewing. Anyone who has completed the required registration (there's generally no cost to do this) can post and reply.

Specifically, you'll want to post your difficult questions to a newsgroup created by and for Microsoft Office 2007 users. To find one, go to www.microsoft.com/office, scroll down until you see Office Community, and click it. You can then search the Microsoft discussion groups for answers, or, post a question yourself. You'll notice there are discussion groups on almost anything you can think of regarding Office. Figure 6-12 shows an example.

Figure 6-12: A Microsoft Office discussion group is a good way to get started with newsgroups.

Once you've found a newsgroup you like, create a user name and password as prompted by the group (for Microsoft you'll use your Passport), and follow the directions to create a post. You can select to be notified of any replies, or, you can refresh the site often to see if you post has been answered.

Summary

Microsoft Office 2007, Windows XP, and Vista are designed to minimize the likelihood of system operation and data loss problems. However, sometimes things do happen, and problems occur. These problems can be due to a power outage, faulty software, a virus, or poorly planned data management.

When any of these things happen, you need to know how to recover, so you can get back to work as quickly as possible. You may have to use System Restore to repair your operating system, use Office Diagnostics to repair Office, or incorporate various search techniques to recover lost files.

Part III

Exploring the New Interface

Chapter 7

Personalizing the Interface

The main thing you'll notice when you open an Office 2007 application is that the interface is completely different from any other version of Office. If you have difficulty dealing with change, this is going to be a shock to your system. However, once you spend a few minutes with the applications and start to see where everything is, you'll begin to feel a little more comfortable with it. To make the transition easier, let's spend a few minutes personalizing Office. While doing so, you'll get to know the interface, what's available, and build a little bit of a comfort zone around your new applications.

Personalizing Office with Your Language, Name, and Initials

If you didn't do so during installation, you'll need to tell Microsoft Office what language you prefer, and what your name and initials are. Chances are pretty good the language is right, but your name and initials may not be. By default, initials are configured as user.

Whatever the case, take a look at what's configured for these three options and make changes as needed:

1. Open any Office application. In this example, we'll use Word 2007.

2. Click the File menu button and click Word Options.

3. Click Popular in the left pane.

4. Under Personalize your copy of Microsoft Office, verify your username and initials are correct. Make changes by typing in the correct information.

5. Click Language Settings.

6. Verify that the settings are correct. There are over a dozen entries for English, so if that's your language, you need to verify that the correct version of English is selected.

7. Click OK to apply the language changes, and click OK again to close the Options window.

Changing the Skin

At the time this book was written, there were three options for Office 2007's skin: Blue, Silver, and Black. A *skin* is an element of an interface that you can change to alter the look of the application without affecting its functionality. The Office 2007 interface skins change only the color of the application's interface, whereas many skins for other applications generally make additional changes.

To further explain what a skin is, Figure 7-1 shows the Windows XP Media Player 10 in its default form, and Figure 7-2 shows Windows XP Media Player 10 with the Headspace skin applied. Look closely at the latter and you can see the rewind, pause, stop, fast forward, and play buttons. This is an extreme skin, and completely changes the look of the media player. Not all skins are so intense. Notice there is still lots of functionality after applying a skin, but tools are accessed in a different way.

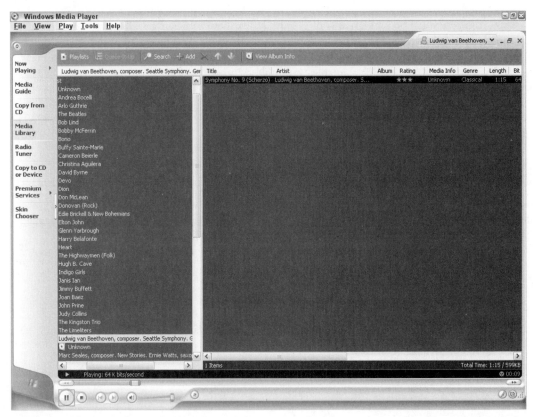

Figure 7-1: This is Windows XP Media Player 10 (11 is currently in beta at this time) without a skin applied.

Figure 7-2: This is Windows XP's Media Player 10 with the Headspace skin applied.

To change Office's skin from the default, Blue:

1. Open any Office application. In this example, we'll use PowerPoint 2007.
2. Click the File menu button and click PowerPoint Options.
3. Click Popular in the left pane.
4. Change the Color Scheme to Black.
5. Click OK. Figure 7-3 shows the result.

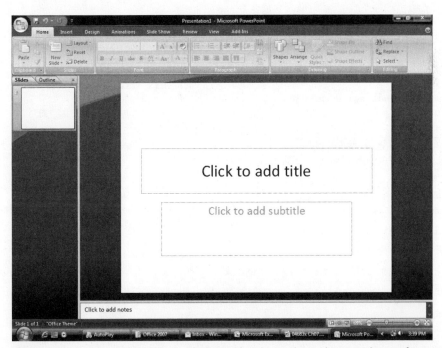

Figure 7-3: The change from Blue to Black isn't that drastic, but it does give the interface a new look.

Note that even though you change the skin using the options page for a particular program, in the previous example PowerPoint, the change affects all programs in your Office 2007 suite. In other words, you can't have different skins for different programs in the Office 2007 suite. Whichever skin you select, and no matter which program's options page you use to make the change, your selection affects all the Office programs.

You can be sure that by the time you get Office 2007 and this book in your hands, there will be many more skins to choose from. In fact, you'll most likely be able to go to Microsoft's Office Web site to download just about any color skin you'd like, even skins with themes. Themes will likely include such things as customized mouse pointers to match the skin you've selected. For now, knowing the option is available is enough to get you started with personalizing Office.

To View or Not to View

When you hover your mouse over an icon, selection box, or other feature in Microsoft Office 2007, a ScreenTip usually appears. By default, ScreenTips are set to show Enhanced ScreenTips. Figure 7-4 shows an example of an Enhanced ScreenTip. It offers a pretty detailed description of what the File menu button does. Figure 7-5 shows an example of a regular ScreenTip.

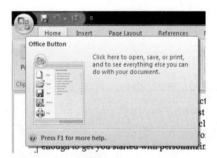

Figure 7-4: This is an Enhanced ScreenTip.

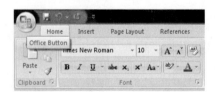

Figure 7-5: This ScreenTip is not enhanced.

You can configure what kind of ScreenTip you'd like to see, or, if you'd rather not see any at all. To do this:

1. Open any Office application. In this example, we'll use Word 2007.

2. Click the File menu button and click Word Options.

3. Click Popular in the left pane.

4. Under Top options for working with Word, next to ScreenTip style, make the feature descriptions in ScreenTips

   ▪ Don't show feature descriptions in ScreenTips

   ▪ Don't show ScreenTips

5. Click OK.

We prefer to leave Show feature descriptions in ScreenTips enabled initially. Having ScreenTips available makes it easy to see what something is without having to open Help to find out. Sometimes, the ScreenTip is all you need to continue working without interruption. As with skins, the ScreenTips setting that is selected in one Office program automatically becomes the ScreenTips setting for all programs in the suite.

Saving in Compatible Formats

The default format for saving files in Office 2007 are far different from the default formats for saving files in earlier versions of Office. In fact, if you save a file in Word 2007 using the default document format (.docx) and e-mail it to a colleague who is still using Microsoft Word 2003, they will not be able to open it. That's because this new file format is not backwards-compatible. So if you're the only one at work using the newer version of Office and everyone else is using something else, you'll need to change the default format to something your colleagues can open and work with. Under these circumstances, you'd choose the Word 97–2003 format. A file saved in this format will be fully compatible with previous versions of Word.

The same is true of other Office applications. In Excel for instance, the new default file format for saving a workbook has an .xlsx suffix. Again, this format is not compatible with earlier versions of Excel. This could cause quite a few problems and could frustrate the recipients of the documents you create, so it's in your best interest to change it now.

To change the default choice for saving files in any application:

1. Open any Office application. In this example, we'll use Excel 2007.

2. Click the File button and click Excel Options.

3. Click Save in the left pane.

4. For Save files in this format, select Excel 97–2003 Excel Workbook, as shown in Figure 7-6.

5. Click OK.

Note that unlike the previous settings for a Skin and for ScreenTips, you need to change your default file format for each program individually. That is, selecting the "Excel 97–2003" setting won't make Word also save its files in the Word 97–2003 format.

Figure 7-6: You can change the defaults for saving files so they'll be compatible with earlier versions of the related Office application.

Personalizing AutoCorrect

AutoCorrect is still around, and it's still one of our favorite features. You can use AutoCorrect for more than just correcting misspellings though, you can use it to shorten the amount of typing you have to do to get a job done by personalizing the AutoCorrect options. And there's a new feature of AutoCorrect just for mathematical symbols when you're typing in Word. If you're an engineer or statistician, you'll love this feature.

Using AutoCorrect to Save Key Strokes

You can create your own AutoCorrect terms to replace longer words, and have AutoCorrect do the typing for you. For instance, you can create an AutoCorrect term from your initials, and then each time you type your initials, your entire name and anything else you've added after it will be typed automatically. Here's an example:

1. Open any Office application. In this example, we'll use Word 2007.

2. Click the File menu button and click Word Options.

3. Click Proofing in the left pane.

4. Under AutoCorrect options, click the AutoCorrect Options button.

5. From the AutoCorrect tab, under Replace:, type in your initials.

6. Under With, type your full name followed by your position or credentials.

7. Click OK to close the AutoCorrect dialog box, and OK again to close Word Options.

8. Open a new Word Document, and type your initials followed by a space or any punctuation mark. Your initials will be replaced with your full name. From now on, each time you need to write your full name, simply type your initials!

Knowing What Symbols are Available

You'll still use AutoCorrect to add words that you commonly misspell, but there's more to it than that. Open AutoCorrect again and take a closer look at some of the entries. Look at the first dozen or so.

Notice the first few entries that represent symbols. When you type in a less than sign (<), followed by two equal signs (==), you'll automatically get this symbol: ←. When you type in a less than sign (<), followed by an equal sign (=), followed by a greater than sign (>), you get this symbol: ⇔. That sure beats inserting the symbol manually! Experiment with some of the entries here. Open a new Word document and type them. Watch what happens!

Tip

If you use AutoCorrect a lot, consider adding it to the Quick Access toolbar. There is more on this in the next section.

Using AutoCorrect to Add Mathematical Symbols

Finally, there are some Mathematical AutoCorrect options you should be aware of. They're in the AutoCorrect dialog box, under the Math AutoCorrect tab. This is shown in Figure 7-7. Not all Office 2007 applications offer this particular feature; this screenshot is from Word. Microsoft Excel 2007 does not offer this option, probably because you don't do very much typing there; it's more numbers and mathematical functions and calculations.

Figure 7-7: Math AutoCorrect is also quite useful.

Don't be confused. Math AutoCorrect entries aren't for performing mathematical operations; they're for writing mathematical symbols. It's a form of AutoCorrect. Type the proper wording and the desired mathematical symbol will appear. By default, Math AutoCorrect rules do not apply outside of math regions, but you can change that behavior if you need to.

A few examples of Math AutoCorrect are shown in Table 7-1.

Table 7-1   Examples of Math AutoCorrect Symbols

Type This in Word 2007	*To Get This*
\div	÷
\sigma or \sum	Σ
<=	≤
\subset	⊆
\sqrt	√
\Omega	Ω
\ne	≠
\infty	∞

It's important to know things like this are available when personalizing Office 2007. You can add your own flair to AutoCorrect to make the tool work for you a little better than it would otherwise. Knowing that you can type your initials and have an entire line of text appear automatically could literally save you thousands of keystrokes a year. If you really work at it, you could probably reduce the amount of keystrokes you actually have to type by a third or more.

Customizing the Quick Access Toolbar

The Quick Access Toolbar is the area of the interface that's to the right of the File menu button, above the tabs for Home, Insert, and so on. By default, there are four menu icons:

- Save
- Undo
- Repeat Typing
- Customize Quick Access Toolbar

As you would expect though, you can remove these icons or add others. Let's say you e-mail most of the files you create to your boss for approval before you do anything else with them. It would benefit you to have an icon for e-mailing on the Quick Access Toolbar. Perhaps you add a digital signature to everything you create; you should put the icon for Add a digital signature on there too. And, if you prefer, you can place the Quick Access Toolbar below the Ribbon instead of above it.

To make changes to the icons on the Quick Access Toolbar:

1. Open any Office application. In this example, we'll choose PowerPoint.

2. There are several ways to change the Quick Access Toolbar, and one way is to click the File menu button, select PowerPoint Options, and select the Customize tab.

3. In the Customize page click the arrow under Choose commands from and select All Commands. This way, you'll be able to see every command you can add to the toolbar. This is shown in Figure 7-8.

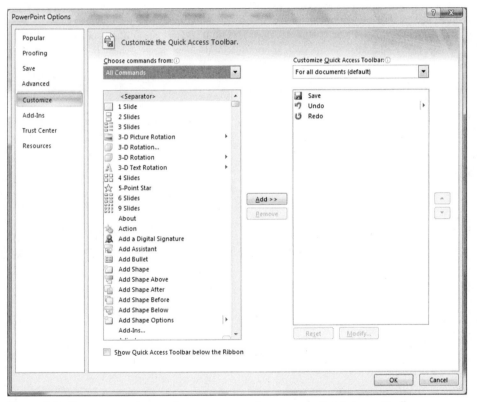

Figure 7-8: Here you can choose what you want to show on your Quick Access Toolbar.

4. Scroll through all of the commands. This will help you become familiar with the available commands, and will give you an opportunity to get to know this application. If you see a command you often use, select it and click Add.

5. When you're finished, click OK.

How you set up the Quick Access Toolbar is up to you. We prefer to add only those items we use a lot every day. If you have a crowded Quick Access Toolbar, you can actually hamper your progress by having too much on there, and thus, too much to sift through to find what you need.

Sign Up for Microsoft Office Newsletters

In order to keep up with what's new, like new skins, themes, add-ons, templates, and other items to more fully personalize your copy of Office 2007, consider subscribing to any of the Office 2007 newsletters. They'll come to you via e-mail, and you can read them at your leisure. There are two you may be interested in, and you can sign up from Microsoft's Office Web site at `www.microsoft.com/office/using/newsletter.mspx`:

- **Inside Office:** This newsletter is a monthly e-mail with the latest news and tips.

- **Inside Office — Product Update Alert:** This special alert lets Office users know when a new product update has been released. Product updates include security patches, performance enhancements, and more.

Summary

Spending time personalizing the Office applications is one of the best ways to get to know the product and its applications. By making small changes to the interface, AutoCorrect, file-format defaults, and the like, you can make Office suit your needs more effectively. Personalizing Office is a good first step for getting to know the program too. With introductions out of the way, we can now move on to specific parts of the interface. Next up, the Ribbon.

Chapter 8

Getting Familiar with the Ribbon

As Microsoft said in its initial introduction of the Ribbon, "Say goodbye to traditional toolbars and menus." The new Office system uses the Ribbon instead of the traditional tabs across the menu bar, which results in an entirely new interface, an interface like nothing you've ever seen before. The Ribbon runs across the top of your screen and is included in every Office application.

The Ribbon has its own tabs. These tabs allow you to more easily access what you need. With the Ribbon, you can find tools more quickly and more simply than ever before. At least, that's what Microsoft wants you to believe. If you're left-brained and prefer everything to be in a nice, neat pull-down menu, you'll likely find the transition a little more difficult than you'd expect. Where the heck is everything? If you're right-brained and prefer to use contextual groupings of tools, graphical icons and interfaces, and point-and-click access to items you need, you'll probably find it a welcome change.

That said, the Ribbon is an awesome graphical, results-oriented interface. The idea behind the Ribbon that you can select a tab, and when you do, the options in Ribbon change to offer tasks directly related to that tab. For instance, Microsoft Word has tabs for writing, inserting, changing the page layout, reviewing your work, and more, while PowerPoint's Ribbon has tabs for inserting data, adding animations, reviewing your work, and changing the design of a presentation's content. Just click any tab to access the tools related to the task you want to perform.

Once you're inside any tab, you can access additional (contextual) menus by clicking an element in the document. For instance, if you click a chart you've created in Excel, the chart tools appear under their own contextual tab. After you've edited your chart and click away from it, the chart tools go away. In Word or PowerPoint, click any picture you've inserted and picture editing tools appear. After you've edited the picture and clicked away from it, the tools disappear. These things and more make the interface and application more intuitive and easier to use.

Introducing a Results-Oriented Interface

The Ribbon was created to allow users to get results quickly and easily, not to simply add more commands for the user to sift through. The Ribbon contains icons and graphics for features that are organized by scenario, like writing, editing, or formulating data. This helps bring power-user functionality to even the most inexperienced user.

The results-oriented interface, the brainchild of Microsoft developers, allows you to see any changes you make to a document in real time too. There is no more applying changes, waiting for the results, clicking Undo, and trying again. With a results-oriented interface, results are fast and accurate, and you can preview and apply them immediately.

To give you an idea of how the Ribbon differs from application to application, and to get a feel for what the Ribbon offers, we've added a few figures. Figure 8-1 shows the Ribbon in Word 2007.

Figure 8-1: The Word 2007 Ribbon.

In Word, notice the Home, Insert, Page Layout, References, Mailings, Review, and View tabs. Clicking any tab changes the options underneath it. This makes it quite simple to understand where to go to insert a picture or table, and where to go to change the page layout. You can also see that it's quite intuitive to change the style of the document by simply clicking an example of what you'd like from the Home tab. Figure 8-2 shows the Ribbon in PowerPoint.

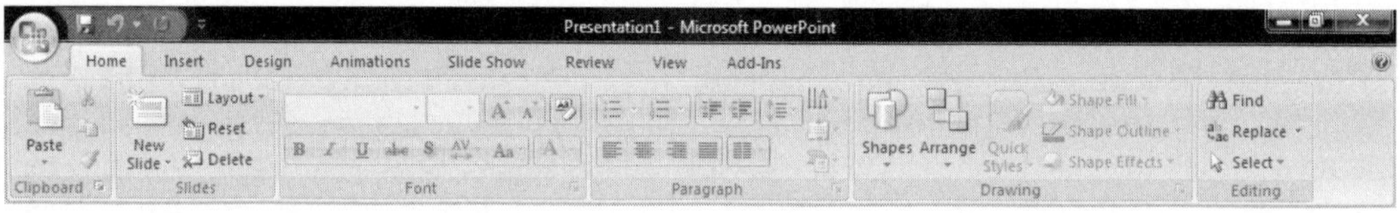

Figure 8-2: The PowerPoint 2007 Ribbon.

In PowerPoint, notice the tabs are a little different from what you see in Word. In PowerPoint, you don't need a Page Layout tab, what you really need is a Design tab. And it's there, as are tabs for inserting items, viewing a slide show, and formatting the presentation. Figure 8-3 shows the Ribbon in Excel.

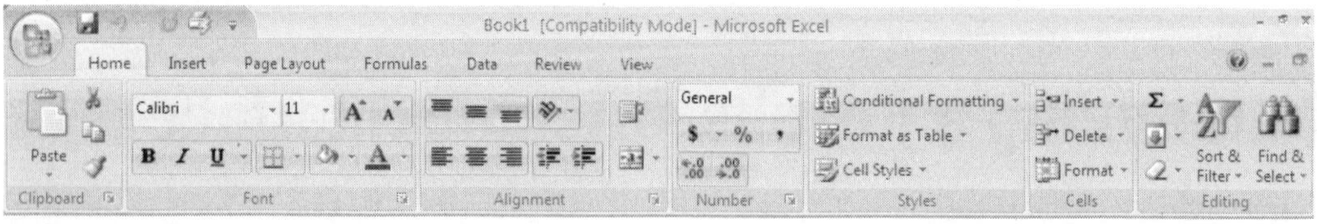

Figure 8-3: The Excel 2007 Ribbon.

In Excel, notice the all-important Formulas tab. There's also a Data tab. Apart from the Home tab, that's likely where you'll spend most of your time when working in Excel.

The Ribbon and its results-oriented interface are all about getting results using visual cues and icons, and getting those results in an intuitive manner. Once you're used to the new technology, you'll find it is indeed quite an improvement.

Exploring the Home Tab

You'll probably spend most of your time under the Home tab. Figures 8-1, 8-2, and 8-3 show the Home tab for three of the Office applications. The Home tab is where you'll create your documents, spreadsheets, and presentations. You'll edit and enhance them from the other tabs.

Take a look at the Word 2007 Home tab in Figure 8-1. All you have to do is start typing, and from the Home tab you can perform many tasks:

- Cut and paste

- Copy formats within a document

- Apply bold, italic, and underline styles

- Add highlighting and color to text

- Configure alignment

- Work with Clipboard

- Add bullets or numbered lists

- Indent

- Sort

- Apply styles

- Perform simple editing

The Home tab in other applications is similar. The Home tab is where you perform your most frequently repeated tasks and create a basic document or presentation.

Exploring the Other Tabs

Once you've created a basic document, you can use the other tabs to add flair to it. Each tab contains a logical grouping of tools for performing a specific task or tasks. Back at the Word 2007 interface, look at the options under the Insert tab, as shown in Figure 8-4.

Figure 8-4: The Word Insert tab on the Ribbon.

All you have to know to get started here is that you want to insert something. Perhaps it's a picture, clip art, chart, or a hyperlink, or maybe it's WordArt, an equation, or a symbol. Whatever you want to insert, you can insert it intuitively here.

The same is true of the other tabs. In Figure 8-5 you can see Word's References tab. Note the options to add endnotes and footnotes, bibliographies, a table of figures, and more.

Figure 8-5: The Word References tab on the Ribbon.

As you can see, the idea behind the Ribbon is to group tools by task or scenario. Since you're new to Office 2007, the best thing you can do right now is to click each tab in each Office application you use regularly to see what options are available and where they're located.

Using the Command Tabs

The best way to get comfortable with the Ribbon and the new command tabs is to open Word, Excel, and PowerPoint and click the tabs that are available in each application. Not all applications have a Ribbon; Publisher doesn't, for example. And Outlook has a completely different feel from Word, Excel, and PowerPoint. In the following sections then, we'll look at Word, Excel, and PowerPoint.

What you'll probably appreciate most from this exercise is the ability to preview changes before you actually make them. This is one of our favorite features of the new Office program!

Tip

Click the Save icon in the Quick Access Toolbar to save the documents you create in this section. You can use them later for more experimentation. Especially, you'll want to save the Excel spreadsheet. You'll use it later in this chapter.

Word: Changing Font Types, Font Size, and Styles

We will assume that Word is probably the most-used program in the Office suite. With that in mind, let's start there.

To add text, and then change the font, heading, and font size, among other things:

1. Click Start, point to All Programs, point to Microsoft Office, and click Microsoft Office Word 2007.

2. Click the Home tab if it isn't already selected.

3. Type a sentence or two in the new Word document.

4. Drag the mouse over the text to highlight it.

5. Click the arrow next to the font size. This is shown in Figure 8-6.

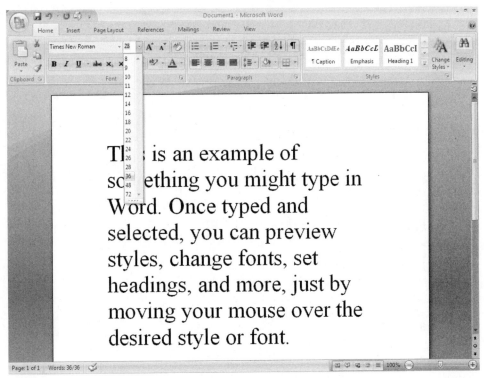

Figure 8-6: You can preview changes to any text by moving your mouse to the desired font size or style.

6. Drag your mouse down through the font size list. Notice that the font changes automatically as you drag. You no longer need to apply a change to view it. Select a font size by clicking it.

7. Select the text again. This time, click the arrow next to the font name.

8. Drag the mouse through the font list. Watch the font change automatically on the page.

9. Select a font type by clicking it.

10. Select the text again.

11. Hover your mouse over the available styles in the Styles boxes. Notice the arrow to the right. Click it to see more styles. Figure 8-7 shows an example. Notice how the style of the selected text changes automatically so you can preview it.

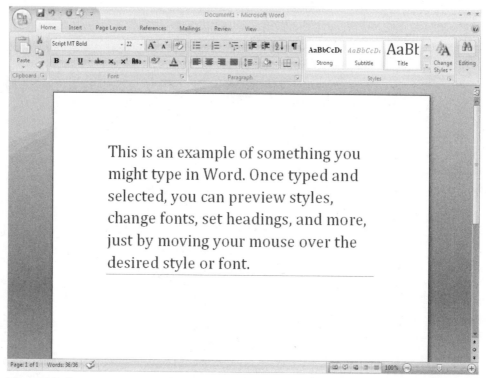

Figure 8-7: You can even preview styles from the Styles box.

12. Select the text again. Right-click the text. Notice the floating formatting toolbar that appears. Note that right-clicking highlighted text brings up the floating formatting toolbar and a floating edit toolbar (with Cut, Copy, Paste, Font, and so on). You'll learn more about that later.

PowerPoint: Inserting Objects

Let's experiment a little with PowerPoint now. To insert and work with an object in PowerPoint:

1. Click Start, point to All Programs, point to Microsoft Office, and click Microsoft Office PowerPoint 2007.

2. Click the Home tab if it isn't already selected.

3. On the new slide, add a title. (Click the Click to add title option and type something.) Click to add a subtitle too.

4. Highlight the entire title with your mouse. Click the arrow next to the font name in the Home tab ribbon. It's in the Font section. Run your mouse down the font list and watch the selected font in the title change automatically.

5. Click the Insert tab.

6. Click Clip Art.

7. In the Search for: box, type Animal. (Click Yes if you're prompted to look for clip art online, or choose No if you don't want to.)

8. Browse through the animals to select one to add. Figure 8-8 shows Steps 5, 6, and 7 in action. Take a good look at the Ribbon, and what's showing on the Insert tab. Click the image to add it.

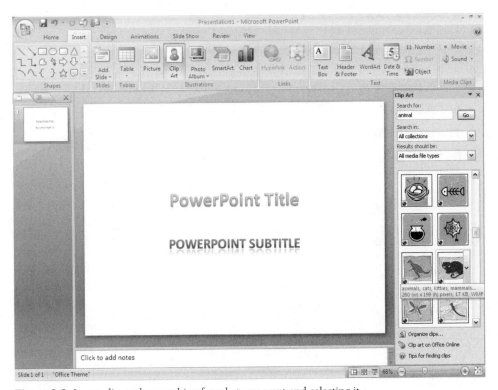

Figure 8-8: Insert clip art by searching for what you want and selecting it.

9. The Ribbon changes when the picture is selected. (We discuss *contextual tabs* later in this chapter.) Drag the image anywhere on the slide. Drop it there.

10. Drag from the corners or sides of the image to resize it.

11. Click away from the image to deselect it.

You've now added clip art, and moved it around the document.

Excel: Working With Formulas

Now let's look at Excel's Ribbon and interface. As with other Office applications you can preview font selection, font sizes, and themes by running your mouse through a list; however, what we'd like to introduce here is the new and powerful way to apply formulas to cells.

To apply a simple formula to a cell without the hassle of creating your own equation:

1. Click Start, point to All Programs, point to Microsoft Office, and click Microsoft Office Excel 2007.

2. Click the Home tab if it isn't already selected.

3. In cell A1, type today's date. Do not press Enter, otherwise cell A2 will become the active cell.

4. Move your mouse to the bottom right corner of cell A1 until the mouse pointer changes to a plus sign (+). It should be a thin black plus sign, different from the cell selector plus sign, which is white and wide, outlined in black. Drag downward to cell A15. You'll notice that dates fill in the cells from A1 to A15.

5. In cell B1, type **10**, in cell B2, type **20**, in cell B3, **30**, and so on. Fill all the cells between B1 and B15 with multiples of 10. Cell B15 should have a value of 150.

6. Click the Formulas tab.

7. Click cell B16.

8. In the Function Library, shown in Figure 8-9, click the arrow by Math & Trig. Scroll down and select Sum.

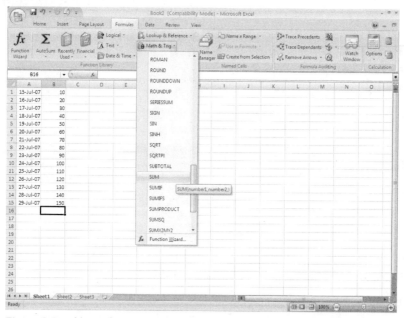

Figure 8-9: Adding a function is easier than ever before with the new Formula tab.

9. In the Function Arguments box, click OK. By default, Excel knows to add cells B1 to B15.

10. The value of 1200 appears in cell B16.

11. Click cell B16 and hit the Delete key.

12. Select More Functions from the Function Library. Point to Statistical and select Average. Click OK in the Function Arguments box, by default, Excel assumes you want to average all of the numbers in that list.

13. The average of the numbers, 80, now appears in cell B15.

14. Save this file.

Again, there are many other uses for this tab. This exercise is included here only to get you familiar with the Ribbon and to help you see how useful it can be. The more you experiment with the interface and its new features, the more impressed you'll be. You learn more about the interface throughout this book.

Using Contextual Tabs

Contextual tabs show the tools you need in the Ribbon only when you need them, and they go away when you're finished and don't need them anymore. For instance, if you insert a picture in PowerPoint and click it, a new part of the Ribbon, a contextual tab, appears, that allows you to edit that picture using the Live Preview features you saw earlier. Add a chart in Excel, select it, and the chart tools appear. Once you've edited the chart and clicked away from it, the tools go away. It's an awesome feature that you have to see for yourself to appreciate.

Introducing Contextual Tabs in PowerPoint

Follow this short example to see exactly what contextual tabs are and what they have to offer. If you can't sit at your computer and follow along, take a close look at the images included here. You'll get the idea.

To use contextual tabs in PowerPoint, we'll first add a shape, and then edit that shape using the resulting contextual tabs:

1. Click Start, point to All Programs, point to Microsoft Office, and click Microsoft Office PowerPoint 2007.

2. Click the Home tab if it isn't already selected.

3. If you still have PowerPoint open from the last exercise, click the File menu button, click New, and double-click Blank Presentation.

4. Click the Insert tab.

5. Click the arrow next to Shapes, and click once on the oval (under Basic Shapes).

6. Move the mouse to the slide, click at the top of the slide, and drag to draw the oval.

7. Let go of the mouse to create the oval.

8. Double-click the shape. The result is shown in Figure 8-10. (You can remove the text boxes behind the picture by selecting a different slide type. More about this in later chapters.)

Figure 8-10: The resulting oval has editing options, and the Ribbon changes to reflect these options.

Notice how the options on the Ribbon changed when the shape was added. When the shape is selected, you can use the new contextual tabs, specifically the drawing tools and options, to edit it. Here's how:

1. With the oval selected, move your mouse over the Shape Styles in the contextual tab menu options. You can make the shape any color. Be patient, the change might not appear as quickly as you'd assume.

2. Click the down arrow to the right of the Shape Styles to preview all of the available styles.

3. Browse through the other options to preview them and get a feel for what's available. Try these:

   ▪ **Shape Fill:** Includes Theme Colors, Standard Colors, No Fill, Picture, Gradient, and more. In Figure 8-11, we've chosen a picture.

   ▪ **Shape Outline:** Includes Theme Colors, Standard Colors, No Outline, Weight, Dashes, and more.

   ▪ **Shape Effects:** Includes Shadow, Reflection, Glow, Soft Edges, Bevel, and more.

Figure 8-11 shows what can be applied to a simple oval.

Figure 8-11: Making a shape take its own personal form is now easier than ever.

Introducing Contextual Tabs in Word

Let's look at Word for a minute. Word, like all other Office applications that include the Ribbon as a graphical tool, also includes contextual tabs.

To use Word's contextual tabs to add SmartArt:

1. Click Start, point to All Programs, point to Microsoft Office, and click Microsoft Office Word 2007.

2. Click the Home tab if it isn't already selected.

3. If Word was already open, and you have a document there, click the File menu button, click New, and select Blank Document.

4. Click the Insert tab on the Ribbon.

5. Click the SmartArt button in the Illustrations box.

6. Click Cycle, as shown in Figure 8-12.

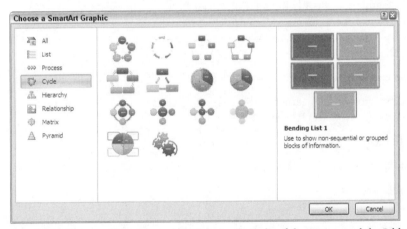

Figure 8-12: Create an illustration with a few simple clicks of the mouse, and the Ribbon.

7. Select the upper-left cycle graphic, which is titled Cycle 2, the first choice in Figure 8-12. Click OK.

8. For the first bullet, type **Start**. Press Enter. A new bullet appears and a new cycle item in the diagram. For the second bullet, type **Process 2**; press Enter. For the third bullet, type **Process 3**; press Enter. For the fourth bullet, type **Process 4**; press Enter. For the fifth bullet, type **Process 5**; and for the last bullet, type **End**.

9. You can now delete any bullets you do not need by selecting them in the left pane and clicking Delete on your keyboard.

Note

The extra cycle items can also be deleted within the graphic section of the window. If you use arrow keys to move up and down the bullet edit list, no extra bullets and cycle items are created. You might find the different responses to the Enter and arrow keys a bit frustrating at first, but it's actually a sensible user interface once you get used to it. This is also how normal bullets work within Word documents when pressing Enter or the arrow keys.

10. Close the text box, select the illustration, and use your mouse to preview different styles in the Ribbon, change colors, or perform other changes.

Introducing Contextual Tabs in Excel

For this example, you'll want to use the spreadsheet you created earlier. We'll use the data you input to create various tables and charts with the Ribbon, and edit them with contextual tabs.

To create a table from data already in an Excel spreadsheet:

1. Click Start, point to All Programs, point to Microsoft Office, and click Microsoft Office Excel 2007.

2. Click the Home tab if it isn't already selected.

3. Open the file you created earlier in this chapter by clicking the File menu button and choosing the file from the Recent Documents list.

4. Highlight the data you input in cells A1 to B16.

5. Click the Insert tab.

6. Click Table.

7. Look at the Ribbon, then click OK to verify the cells you've selected. Look at the resulting table and the new contextual tabs. Design is now selected.

8. Hover your mouse over the Design options to preview them.

9. Click Undo on the Quick Access Toolbar (located in the upper-left corner of the Excel window) until the data returns to its original state.

To create a chart from the original data, follow these steps:

1. Click the Insert tab.

2. Select the data in cells A1 to B15. Do *not* select cell B16.

3. Click Column. Select any 3-D column. Click the chart.

4. Hover your mouse over the other options in the Design Tools menu to change the color or type of chart.

Summary

In this chapter, you learned all about the Ribbon. The Ribbon lets you access tools only when you need them. Because they're available only when you need them, they're never in your way when you don't. The Ribbon also includes contextual tabs. These tabs appear only when a specific item in a document, spreadsheet, or presentation is selected like a picture, chart, or table. Getting to know the Ribbon and understanding how it works will make your life easier and your work more productive.

Chapter 9

Obtaining Immediate Results with Styles and Galleries

I n our opinion, Galleries and Quick Styles in Microsoft Office 2007 are two of the most important and innovative additions to the Microsoft suite of Office applications ever created. Galleries and Quick Styles are what we've all been waiting for: a clear set of choices to format documents, spreadsheets, presentations, and databases, all applied using only a single click of the mouse. By viewing and choosing from a single set of predefined results, you can effortlessly give any piece of work a professional look. In this chapter, you'll learn how to use Galleries and Quick Styles to spice up your work, both at the office and at home.

Galleries and Quick Styles Explained

You surely remember the olden days of Microsoft Office; to format a document or text, say in Word, you had to choose a font and font size from a list, choose the font color, choose the layout, apply color and sizes to headings, and apply other formatting options manually. You also had to apply those changes to the document to see if you liked them, and if not, you had to undo what you'd done and start again. That's all gone with Quick Styles and Galleries. With Galleries and Quick Styles, you can view and select from a collection of predefined results, somewhat similar to what has always been available in PowerPoint.

Figures 9-1, 9-2, and 9-3 show three examples. In these examples, we're using an article written about Vista, and we're applying three of the many styles available from the Ribbon interface.

In Figure 9-1, you can see the Formal style applied to the document. In our opinion, this is worthy of submittal without any extra formatting!

Figure 9-2 shows the Fancy style. This is less formal, as you can tell by the name, and a little more elegant. This particular style would be well suited for a wedding invitation or an informal office-meeting announcement, like a birthday.

Figure 9-3 shows the Simple style. This is your basic, get-'er-done font and style. You can use this style for cover letters, office-meeting reminders, and for posting notes on a bulletin board.

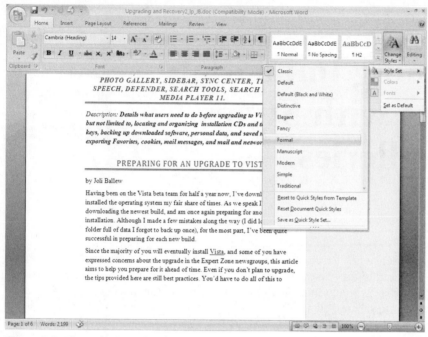

Figure 9-1: This is the Formal style.

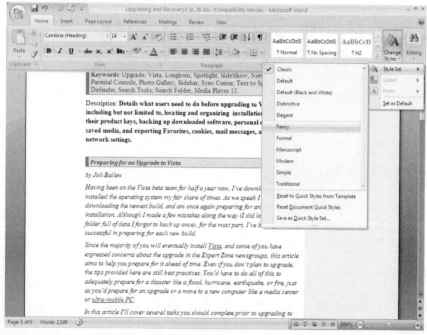

Figure 9-2: This is the Fancy style.

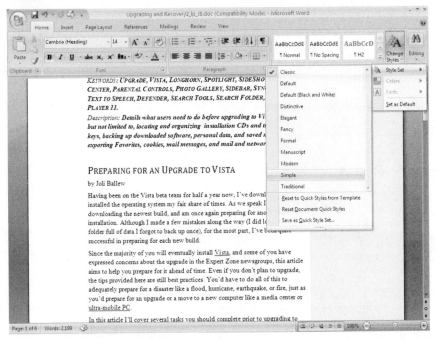

Figure 9-3: This is the Simple style.

These are called Quick Styles. Beyond applying styles to an entire document using the Quick Styles though, you can instead just change the fonts without adding any special formatting such as those shown in the previous examples. By highlighting any part of the document, perhaps the title or a paragraph, you can change only the style for that particular part of the document.

All of these formatting options are on Word's Home tab. As you work with the formatting choices on the Home tab, you'll find even more styles. There's so much to talk about we could write almost an entire book on this feature alone! Think about it, in all of the figures so far, we've shown only a smidgeon of what can be done in Microsoft Word — from the Home tab. Galleries and Quick Styles are available from other tabs in Word, in PowerPoint, Excel, Access, and all of the other Office applications.

Exploring Basic Features

To get started, let's explore a few basic style features. Highlight some text in a Word document. Next, click the arrow next to the Font list, and hover your mouse the font names. You can actually watch the font for the text change without even applying it. This was detailed in Chapter 8, but bears repeating here.

Tip

If the font list covers the text you've highlighted, you can shrink the length of the font list by clicking and holding the bottom of the list with your left mouse button, then raising the edge of the list. After doing this far enough, you can see the text you highlighted that previously was hidden.

Now for something a little more exciting, click the arrows next to the other formatting options on some of the other tabs and see what happens. Figure 9-4 shows one option on the Page Layout tab. Here, we've clicked the arrow next to Page Color, and we can watch the page color change when we hover the mouse over any color in the list.

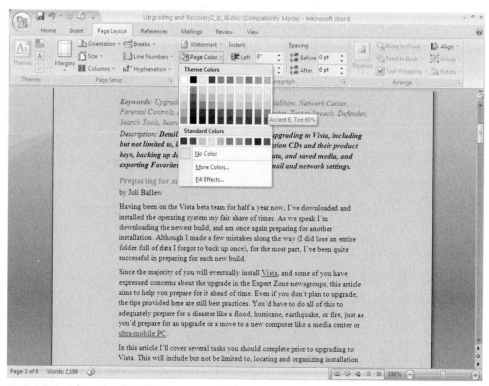

Figure 9-4: Other tabs also offer automatic styles.

Finally, in some instances, selecting a style will result in an actual Gallery of choices. Experiment with the Insert tab, choosing to insert page numbers at the bottom of the page. When you do, you can see the Gallery of choices on the left. By browsing through them, you can find the perfect style for your document.

Now that you have some idea of what Galleries and Quick Styles have to offer, let's spend some time applying them, step by step.

Using Quick Styles and Galleries

You know a little about Word's Quick Styles and Galleries from the previous section, and you can probably figure out how to apply them just by looking at the figures in this chapter. For the most part, in Word, you simply click the down arrow by any formatting option and browse through the results offered. So, let's focus on PowerPoint.

Open a PowerPoint presentation that you previously created. If you can't find it and have Vista installed, use the new Search tools to locate it. If you don't have a PowerPoint presentation to work with, see if you can get one from a coworker. (If you can't find one that's already been created, you'll need to create a simple presentation that consists of two to four slides so that you can see how Styles and Galleries work with PowerPoint.)

To apply Quick Styles and work with Galleries in PowerPoint, follow along with these steps:

1. Open Microsoft PowerPoint 2007.

2. Open any presentation you've previously created. You can see recent documents by clicking the File menu button in the top-left corner of the PowerPoint interface.

3. From any slide, use the mouse to select some text.

4. On the Home tab, click the arrow next to Quick Styles, and use your mouse to move your pointer over the available styles. Notice how the selected text and text box change to represent the highlighted styles. Look at Figure 9-5.

5. Select the Design tab.

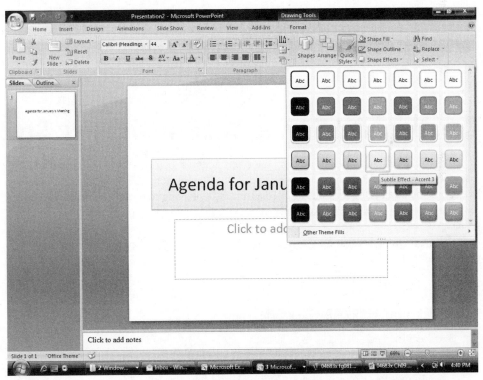

Figure 9-5: As with Word, many styles are available for immediate viewing and application in PowerPoint.

6. Under Fonts, move your pointer over the available fonts.

7. In Themes, move your pointer over any theme in the Ribbon, and then click the arrow to view and try new themes.

8. Select the Animations tab.

9. Move your pointer over the Transition to this Slide options. You can transition from slide to slide in many ways. Check out the checkerboard option.

10. While still under the Animations tab, click Animate. Move the mouse over the options.

As you can see, we've barely touched on the available Styles and Galleries available in PowerPoint, just as we touched only the surface of what's in Word. It's up to you to explore galleries and styles as you open every application. For the most part, it's all the same though. You can apply Styles and Galleries to tables, charts, shapes, and more. It'll all become clearer the more you work with Galleries and as you progress through this book.

Tip

As you work through this book and each of the chapters on the different applications, you'll learn more and more about the available Styles and Galleries. In order to avoid repeating what will be covered later, we leave this chapter short and sweet, offering only a taste of what's to come.

Creating and Saving Your Own Quick Style

The style you want and need to apply most often may not be one of the choices in the Gallery. For instance, your company may require you use a specific font, font size, and font color for all headings in documents or all category titles in Access. Instead of having to configure that manually each time, or cut and paste from the Clipboard, why not just create the style you need and save it to the Gallery? It's easy!

To create a Quick Style and then save it to the Gallery, we'll work in Word (but keep in mind this works in all applications):

1. Open Word 2007.

2. Type some text in a new document. For this example, we'll use Meeting Agenda.

3. Select the text.

4. Format the text to meet the company's standards; in this example we'll choose Bold, Italic, centered, font color blue, font Cambria, and font size 22.

5. Right-click the selected and formatted text, select Style from the drop-down list, and click Save Selection as a New Quick Style.

6. In the Create New Style from Formatting dialog box, name the style and click OK. See Figure 9-6.

Meeting Agenda

Create New Style from Formatting	
N̲ame:	
Meeting Agenda	
Paragraph style preview:	
Style1	
OK M̲odify... Cancel	

Figure 9-6: Save the new Quick Style and name it appropriately.

7. To see the new style in the Styles Gallery, click the down arrow next to the styles on the Ribbon, and locate the style in the Gallery. You can see the new style Meeting Agenda.

To remove a style from the Styles Gallery, right-click the arrow next to Styles in the Home tab and select Remove from Styles Gallery. This does not delete the style from your computer; the Change Styles pull-down menu will still list all of the styles in the document.

Working with Shapes, Tables, and Charts

In this chapter, so far, we've mainly been focused on applying Quick Styles and Galleries to text. There are many more uses, which you'll learn about throughout this book. However, to give you a sampling of what else can be achieved using these features, we'll look at some other types of data.

Working with PowerPoint Shapes

Let's look again at PowerPoint. In PowerPoint, you can add text, apply themes, change slide orientation, add animations, and even record narration to your slide show. You can also insert things. You can insert a picture, a table, Clip Art, SmartArt, charts, and more. One of the things you can input is a shape.

When the shape is added and selected, the Format tab opens up and Shape Styles are available. Clicking the arrow next to the Shape Styles offers up a Gallery of options, as do Arrange options.

You can also choose from Shape Outline, Shape Fill, and Shape Effects. Each of these offers a Gallery of choices too. You can add Quick Styles for the fonts too, and Theme Colors, Text Outline, and Text Effects; and that's just the start.

Working with Excel Charts

You can use Quick Styles and Galleries to format any chart you can create in Microsoft Excel. (You learn how to create charts in Chapters 17 and 18.) Once a chart is created, click on the chart with your mouse, and then from the Design tab, click the arrow next to Chart Styles, and make a selection from the Gallery. The choice you make is applied to your chart. Figure 9-7 shows an example of what you may see when looking at the Chart Styles Gallery. Note that what you see might differ, as the results depend on what type of chart you've created and are currently working with.

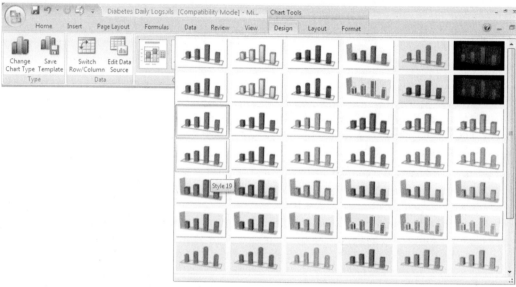

Figure 9-7: Even charts have their own Gallery in Excel.

As with other applications, you can also apply Quick Styles and choose from Galleries for text, SmartArt, WordArt, and more. Spend some time experimenting here to see what else you can do.

Working with Publisher Data

Publisher may seem to you to be mostly a collection of Galleries and Quick Styles. From the moment you open it you are offered choices from a list of options. On the Welcome to Microsoft Publisher page, you must choose a document type. There are several including:

- Brochures
- Business Cards
- Calendars
- Flyers
- Greeting Cards
- Labels
- Newsletters
- Postcards

And that's just to name a few! Clicking any of these specialty publication types opens a Publisher document that's ready for editing. Talk about your predefined styles!

Publisher helps with both the appearance and the content of your documents. For example, clicking any one of the business card templates not only brings up a predefined business card that prompts you to input your business's information, but also allows you to change and edit the styles available as desired. As you can see, there are literally thousands of options among the available applications.

Summary

Each application in the Office 2007 suite offers a variety of Quick Styles and Galleries. Depending on what you select to format, you'll see varying Gallery options. In this chapter, we focused on Word and PowerPoint, to keep things simple initially. In chapters following this one, chapters related to a specific task or application, you'll learn even more. For now, try to focus on opening each application, adding some text, a shape, or a table or chart, and see what formatting options are available to you. It's the best way to get familiar with Galleries and Quick Styles.

Part IV

Working Together

Chapter 10

Saving and Sharing Data

Creating great content is important but it's not much good if no one else ever sees it. That's why saving your data is just as critical as sharing it — anyone who has ever worked on a document only to discover it was lost forever (for some inane reason known only to computer gods) knows this is true. It just takes the loss of one file or document because you didn't save it to ingrain in your brain the importance of saving — often!

The ability to share data and other information is typically why content is created in the first place. While you may create personal documents to help you manage your daily life, the chances are good that you create many more documents for business reasons. Those documents need to be readily available and easy to access when needed, in addition to being properly protected. If others can't read or access the data you have developed, then you've wasted a lot of precious time.

In this chapter, we cover the basics of file-saving and protection techniques and discuss several key ways you can share the information you have saved. The Office 2007 suite offers a new XML-based file format for three programs — Word, Excel, and PowerPoint — so you will learn how to save in this format as well. Some of this chapter, however, is directed toward Windows system administrators or people who assume that role for their project team. If you do not have one of those roles, you do not need to read the sections between "Applying File Protection in PowerPoint" and "Saving in XML File Formats."

Applying Proper File-Saving Techniques

Have you ever saved a file on your hard drive — really *known* that you saved it — and you just couldn't find it? In the end, you probably wound up recreating the document from start to finish, muttering unmentionables every step of the way. We've all done it, so don't feel bad. But what happened to your document? Well, the reality will vary depending on the person but chances are that you didn't pay close attention when you initially saved the document. Then, when you went to look for it in the spot where you thought you saved it, it simply wasn't there.

In Office 2007, just as in earlier versions of Office, there are defaults that automatically choose a document's saved location for you. Knowing these defaults can save you time and frustration, plus it gives you a good place to start getting organized. Let's take a look at how you can organize your files, where the defaults are, and what to watch for when you initially save a document.

Note

Some of these techniques were introduced briefly in Chapter 3, "Organizing Data Right from the Start," but this chapter goes into much more detail.

Organizing Your Files

Before you save anything, think logically about where it should be stored for easy access later. Maybe it's a private location on your hard drive, maybe it's as a shared folder for others to use. (See "Using a Workgroup Share" later in this chapter.) Most people find organization easiest when they have established a hierarchy of folders under the My Documents folder.

Think of this hierarchy as having a nicely defined file drawer. When you open the My Documents drawer, you can quickly skim through the folders to find what you need because each folder is smartly named and in alphabetical order. Simply open the folder to find the document you need. One key thing to consider is whether your folders are accurately named. Too often, a folder gets named something like "Personal" and then becomes a dumping ground for anything remotely personal. Consider naming things clearly when you create a general file like that. Try placing individual subfolders inside it — like "2006 Taxes_Supporting Documents" — instead of just dumping all your tax documents as separate items into the Personal folder with no rhyme or reason. You'll thank us later when you can quickly find those documents during an audit, instead of digging frantically for dozens of documents randomly placed in the Personal folder.

If you find yourself searching too often for files that should be at your fingertips, that's your first clue that your current organizational method may be too complex or haphazard. However, it might be that you have difficulty because of the view you use to locate your files. People have different ways of seeing things, and Office 2007 views are the same as before. But maybe now is the time to change your view.

Once saved, Office 2007 programs display your documents in the Thumbnail view shown in Figure 10-1 on your computer, unless you specify another view. The Thumbnail option is available for anyone who likes a larger, more picturesque view of folders and their contents. Less visually oriented people might find it easier to change the view to List or Details.

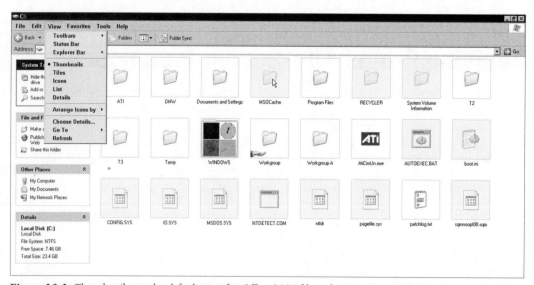

Figure 10-1: Thumbnails are the default view for Office 2007 files when viewing them on your computer.

Organizational Tips

Is your current filing system too complex or disorganized? Using the standard Explorer view, try these steps to help get things under control:

1. Create new folders on your hard drive by going to the location you desire, right-clicking, and selecting New → Folder.

2. Rename your files and documents to give them very descriptive titles. Sometimes, it's hard to find files because the names don't accurately describe the contents. You can rename a file or folder by going to File and Folder Tasks, selecting Rename this file (or folder), and typing in a new name. Don't forget to maintain the proper document extension!

3. Move documents to more appropriate folders by opening two folders: the one containing the document you want to move, and the one where the document will be moved to. Left-click on the document you want to move, go to File and Folder Tasks, select Move this file and then select the new location in the Move Items window that appears, as shown in the following figure.

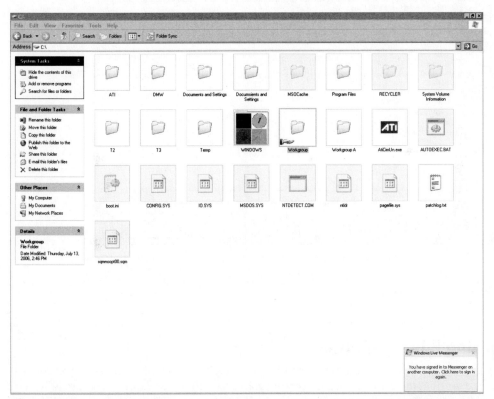

File or Folder Tasks gives you the option of renaming or moving files. The Rename and Move options are located in the left-hand task pane.

Using Office 2007 Save As Default

The first time you save any Office 2007 document, the Save As window pops up. That's not unusual — it's always done that. If you're not paying attention, you won't realize that Office 2007 programs automatically save your files to the general My Documents folder, as shown in Figure 10-2 unless you direct otherwise. This isn't unusual either. And it may be perfectly fine with you — maybe you store everything in one place under My Documents. Saving too many documents in that place, however, will cause you to eventually become overwhelmed. Apply your organizational techniques and develop a good system for filing your documents, despite the defaults established.

The real change in Save As defaults is discussed in the "Saving in XML File Formats" section of this chapter. If you don't read that section, you'll miss learning how a key Office 2007 Save As default has been changed.

Shows where file is saved

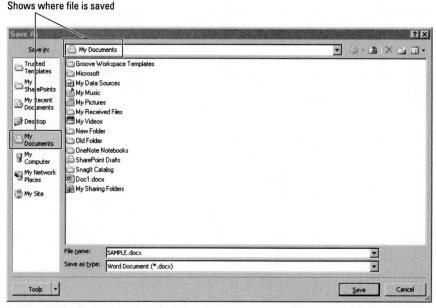

Figure 10-2: Office 2007 programs automatically save your documents to the My Documents folder. Notice in this example there are two locations that indicate where your document is being saved.

Applying File Protection

When you save a file, it's easy to forget that it might need individual protections. But as you'll see in the next section, there are options for sharing your files with others. Unless you carefully determine which files others can see or edit, someone might just see or edit something you don't want them to.

APPLYING FILE PROTECTION IN WORD

With Word 2007, you can easily protect a file by selecting the Review tab and choosing Protect Document. You have three things to decide when you protect a Word 2007 document: formatting restrictions, editing restrictions, and when to start enforcement. Formatting restrictions are helpful when you have a document that has special or multiple formats — sometimes, people will try to change a table or other item that you have created and that seemingly simple change can wreak havoc in your document. Editing restrictions can be used to limit others to simply reading the document, adding comments only or making changes only with the Track Changes feature.

APPLYING FILE PROTECTION IN EXCEL

In Excel 2007, things work slightly differently. You can prevent people from editing items in locked cells, for example, or prevent changes to the actual structure of a workbook, such as the addition or deletion of worksheets. You can also apply password protections to ensure privacy.

1. Select the Review tab, shown in Figure 10-3.

2. On the Ribbon, you'll see two options: Protect Sheet and Protect Workbook. Each one gives you a separate dialog box with selections. Take a minute to view each window so you can see the differences. Notice that you have the option to provide a password to protect worksheets.

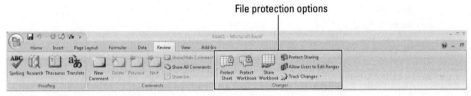

Figure 10-3: In Word and Excel 2007, you use the Review tab to apply file protections. (Shown is the Review tab in Excel 2007.)

APPLYING FILE PROTECTION IN POWERPOINT

PowerPoint 2007 works very differently — you don't use the Review tab at all.

1. Instead, you select the Save As option.

2. Click Tools → General Options. (See Figure 10-4.) Here you will find two protection options: Password to Open and Password to Modify. You can assign one or both passwords; if you use both at the same time be sure to give each one a different password.

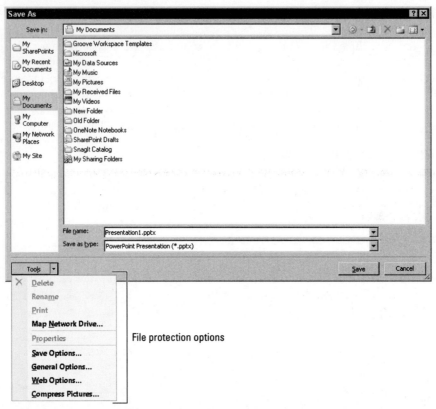

File protection options

Figure 10-4: PowerPoint 2007 applies file protections during the Save As process through the use of the Tools button.

Using a Workgroup Share

Workgroups are a great way to share files on a network or server. There are a couple of good reasons to use workgroups, starting with the simple fact that confusion over document versions when you have a team of people working on or reviewing the same document is pretty much eliminated. That's because only one person at a time can work in a document and make edits or other changes. When that person is finished, the document is reposted and the new version can now be edited or changed by others with proper permissions. If you're a control freak (not a bad thing!), you will also like the power workgroups give you in determining who can do what with a given document. Note: Workgroups cannot be created on local XP systems. If you are not on a network or server, this section will not apply to you.

Creating a Workgroup

To create a workgroup, you first need to establish a new folder on your hard drive in any location you desire.

1. Once that folder has been set up, right-click it.

2. A menu appears with the option Sharing and Security, as shown in Figure 10-5.

3. Select this option to open the Properties window for your folder.

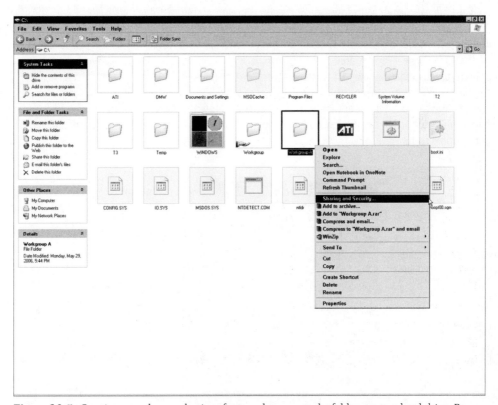

Figure 10-5: Creating a workgroup begins after you have created a folder on your hard drive. By using the Sharing and Security option as shown here, you can make the folder and related documents accessible to designated people on your network or server.

Sharing Folders

There are two tabs in this window that are important to saving and sharing workgroup files: Sharing and Security. (Note: Some systems may show these tabs together.) Let's review the Sharing tab first. When you select it, the Windows default is Do not share this folder. This ensures you the privacy you want when working on a network or server.

To make this folder accessible to others:

1. Select Share This Folder.

2. Windows defaults the Share Name to the same name you gave the folder on your hard drive; if you want team members to see a different name then make the change in the Share Name box. Be certain the share name is something easy to find and remember — don't give it an obscure name, give it something obvious for participants who might quickly forget and need to find it in a hurry.

Careful! Although Windows allows you to create a shared folder with spaces in the name, this may cause problems when others try to find your shared folder. For example, if you name a shared folder "May Calendar," some operating systems will show an error because it stops the name search at the first space it encounters. This means it will attempt to find the shared folder named "May," which doesn't exist.

The Sharing tab, shown in Figure 10-6, also allows you to limit the number of users; the default goes to the number of users that Windows allows. Note: Servers allow an unlimited number unless the administrator has set a fixed number, but Windows desktop operating systems allow 10 concurrent connections.

Share this folder must be selected to properly enable the workgroup

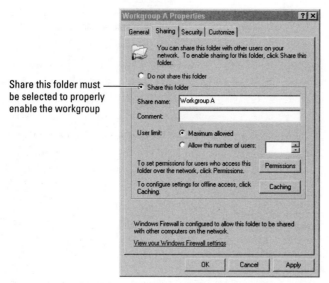

Figure 10-6: The Sharing tab allows you to share a folder with others, set user limits and permissions, and configure settings for offline access.

Caution

Last save wins! If you and another user open the same file offline at the same time, whoever saves it to the workgroup folder *last* overwrites earlier versions.

Working with Permissions

Notice that on the Sharing tab shown in Figure 10-6 there are two buttons: Permissions and Caching. Selecting the Permissions button takes you to a new window (see Figure 10-7) where you can determine how much control to give others. There are three different permissions you can apply: Full Control, Read, and Change.

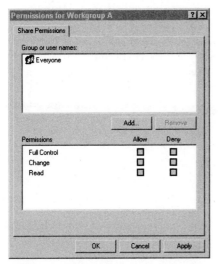

Figure 10-7: Three types of access permissions are available with shared folders in Office 2007: Full Control, Change, and Read.

Full Control is the default permission given to all new workgroup shares. This permission applies to the Everyone group, so tread carefully — do you really want everyone in your group to have full control? If you leave the default as it, everyone will have all the Read and Change permissions as well as be able to change permissions and take ownership. (Note: The last two permissions apply to NTFS files and folders only.)

Read permission allows the user to perform the following tasks:

- View file and subfolder names, even those folders where they have no permissions at all

- View data within files

- Run program files

The key here is that reading is the only thing Read users can really do — they can't make changes to your documents and they can't edit it or make comments.

Change permission gives the user all the Read permissions, plus the ability to do the following:

- Add files and subfolders

- Change data within files

- Delete subfolders and files

The Security tab, shown in Figure 10-8, displays the names of everyone with access to your workgroup share. You can add or remove names as desired. The bottom portion of the window displays the Permissions for Administrators. Note that the Allow boxes may be checked and faded; these are permissions that have been inherited from the parent folder. They can't be changed from the current settings; however, permission can be denied to override the Allow setting that is present. Use caution when denying administrator permissions on folders that are on servers. Most software that backs files up to tape require administrator permissions to access the files and folders. Denying these could prevent data from being backed up, resulting in loss of data.

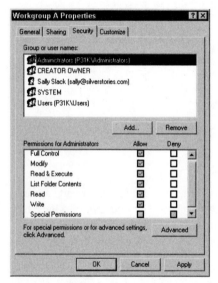

Figure 10-8: The Security tab allows you to set permissions for administrators and view the names and titles of all users with access.

Caching

Windows Server administrators are often in charge of configuring workgroup shares and must establish caching settings as a result. If you are not an administrator you probably don't need to read this section, but if you can't contain your curiosity, be our guest. Caching ensures your documents are available to you while you are not connected to the network, or offline. There are three settings you can choose from (shown in Figure 10-9).

- **Manual caching of documents** is the default option in Windows. It allows offline access only to specific files. This is a good option when

  - Private files must be kept in a shared folder along with public files.

  - Multiple people will create, access, and/or modify documents in a single shared folder.

- **Automatic caching of documents** allows users offline access to every file in a shared folder. In addition, this selection automatically deletes older copies of files as newer ones are saved. This is a good option to

  - Eliminate version confusion.

  - Ensure multiple people can access all files in a single shared folder.

- **Automatic caching of programs and documents** allows users off-line access to shared folders that contain files that cannot be changed. This is a good option when:

  - Users are limited to read-only access.

  - Network traffic is heavy. (Off-line files are opened directly without accessing the network versions.)

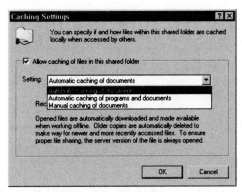

Figure 10-9: The drop-down menu shows three choices when it comes to caching your shared files and folders.

To set caching settings, follow these steps:

1. Open up the Properties window for the folder you are working with.

2. On the Sharing tab, click the Caching button. Note: This button will be available only if you have selected Share this folder.

3. Select the setting you want as shown in Figure 10-9.

4. Click OK.

Caution

Offline Files must also be enabled in order for Caching to work properly. Go to My Computer → Tools → Folder Options and be sure Enable offline files is checked in the Offline Files tab. Click the View button to verify that the folder you have cached is available offline.

Testing Access for Your Workgroup

Now that you've set up your workgroup, it's time to make sure everyone you've designated can actually access the folder and files they need to. It's not hard, but it's worth taking the time before someone says, "Oh, that file? I couldn't get to it so I just created my own."

First, take a look at your computer to see whether the folder you designated for sharing is showing on your system with the shared icon. If the hand is shown holding the file (see Figure 10-10), you're all set. If not, go back and confirm that Share this folder is checked under Properties, Sharing. (See "Creating a Workgroup" in this chapter.)

Figure 10-10: The workgroup icon (a hand holding a file folder) will appear if you have properly shared the folder. In this example, Workgroup is a shared folder and Workgroup A is not.

Assuming the folder is showing up properly as a workgroup icon, now you just need to send participants an e-mail with the information so they can find it. Usually, if it is a network share, it will look something like \\computername\sharename and a server share will be \\servername\sharename. Remember, users will need to open files within the folder to verify they have the proper permissions.

You can call people via phone, of course, but let's face it: If you've taken the time to set up a workgroup, you and the people you work with should be at least a bit technically savvy. Get that e-mail sent and get to work!

Saving in XML File Formats

Data comes from so many places these days — databases, Web pages, spreadsheet files, e-mail, and many more sources. Not all of these sources are in Microsoft format because larger companies often create their own software to perform the same activities that Microsoft applications do. As a result, the competing applications don't always integrate well and the sheer number of sources and formats involved can make it difficult to assemble documents, mine data, and reuse content. That's where XML data comes in handy: It can literally be adapted for use within any environment where information is moved from one place to another.

XML Defined

The acronym XML comes from the term Extensible Markup Language, which is a technology that allows data to be structured, validated, reorganized with each new use, and repurposed as needed. XML is now a widely accepted standard among power computer users and systems, although it is still little known to the general public. Essentially, XML allows someone to produce a document in say, Excel 2007, give it to someone with no Microsoft programs at all, and the recipient will still be able to read it, make changes and resave it if they have an XML reader.

While Microsoft has been a major player in XML since its inception with the use of XML in products such as SQL Server, BizTalk, and more, the company previously provided very limited use of XML in Office products. It first offered it as part of the HTML file format in Office 2000, then as an optional file formats in Excel 2002 and Word 2003. Some custom-defined XML schemas were also supported in Word 2003 and Excel 2003, and Microsoft even introduced an XML-based forms application, InfoPath 2003.

But overall, XML is not something that was really well-known or used by most Office users, no matter which version of Office they used. With Office 2007, however, that's likely to change.

How XML Affects You

In Office 2007, Word, Excel, and PowerPoint will all use the new Office XML format, along with formats currently available. Truthfully, you really won't notice much difference unless you are a power user, although everyone will need to get used to the new document extensions. (An example is shown in the XML Save As Defaults section of this chapter.)

The real benefits, such as the automatic ZIP compression used by XML or the improvement in the recovery of corrupted documents, won't really be noticeable to most people. The ZIP compression (which does not require any action on your part) will make it easier for you to store more files on your hard drive and send or receive files by e-mail, on the Web, or even across a network because it can reduce document sizes by as much as 75 percent over Office 2003. If you do happen to notice an improvement there, you can thank XML.

XML Default Document Extensions

Earlier in this chapter, we discussed the Office 2007 Save As default. You may have noticed in Figure 10-2 that there was a new default document extension in the File name and Save as type boxes. In the Word 2007 example shown, the extension is .docx. (See Figure 10-11.) The x at the end of the old .doc extension clues you in to the fact that the document is automatically being saved as an XML file. But not everything in XML will be saved with just an x tacked on to the extension. Read Tables 10-1, 10-2, and 10-3 to understand how different versions of the same file can have different extensions depending on whether it's a document, template, or macro-enabled.

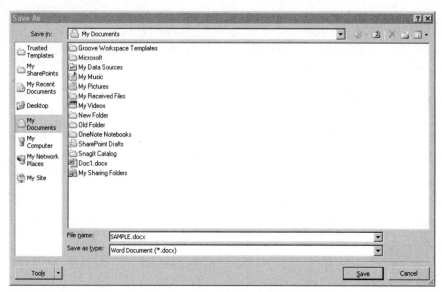

Figure 10-11: In Microsoft Office Excel, PowerPoint, and Word 2007, the Save As defaults are now in XML format, as shown here. The Save as type drop-down list still offers the option of using other formats.

Table 10-1   XML File Types and Correlating Extensions: Word 2007

File extension	XML file type
.docx	Document
.docm	Macro-enabled document
.dotx	Template
.dotm	Macro-enabled template

Table 10-2   XML File Types and Correlating Extensions: Excel 2007

File extension	XML file type
.xlsx	Workbook
.xlsm	Macro-enabled workbook
.xltx	Template
.xltm	Macro-enabled template
.xlsb	Non-XML binary workbook
.xlam	Macro-enabled add-in

Table 10-3   XML File Types and Correlating Extensions: PowerPoint 2007

File extension	XML file type
.pptx	Presentation
.pptm	Macro-enabled presentation
.potx	Template
.potm	Macro-enabled template
.ppam	Macro-enabled add-in
.ppsx	Show
.ppsm	Macro-enabled show
.sldx	An autonomous slide file
.sldm	Macro-enabled slide
.thmx	Office theme

Because the new defaults are based on XML, you don't have to perform a special save action to open and automatically edit Word 2007, Excel 2007, and PowerPoint 2007 files with an XML processing program. This change makes it easier to access data from Word, Excel, and PowerPoint files and integrate that information with back-end systems and processes.

Compatibility checkers and file converters are included in Office 2007. The compatibility checker helps when you open and work on a file created in an earlier version of Office and then try to save it in the new format. It checks to be sure you have not introduced a feature that the earlier version doesn't support.

If you don't want to save your document in XML format or if you have people who need to read it who aren't yet on Office 2007, you still have the ability to select a different document format. Just use the drop-down menu and choose the format you prefer.

Anyone receiving Office 2007 documents but not yet using the suite can download a compatibility converter pack from Microsoft to make Office 2007 documents readable in earlier versions of Word, Excel, or PowerPoint.

Caution

The converters in the File Format Compatibility Pack will not work unless the user's version of Microsoft Office has been updated to one of the following service packs: Microsoft Office 2000 Service Pack 3, Microsoft Office XP Service Pack 3, or Microsoft Office 2003 Service Pack 1.

Now that you've been reminded of the basics of file-saving techniques and how to share the information you develop, take some time to play around with Office 2007 on your own. The changes are subtle, but significant in some cases. As Office 2007 finds its way into the mainstream over time, you'll be leaps ahead of the pack in producing files that are protected but still easy to access.

Summary

This chapter covered a lot of ground, from the basics of file-saving and protection techniques to several key ways you can share the information you have saved. Some of the information applied to systems administrators, although anyone working on a network or server could take advantage of the details provided concerning security, sharing, workgroups, and caching. The XML-based file format, with its ability to compress files automatically and the use of new file extensions, is an important new aspect of the Office 2007 suite. Remember, saving your data is just as critical as sharing it. Do both wisely.

Chapter 11

Setting Up User Access

Chapter 10 explained the concept of using a workgroup share, along with an outline of permissions available for that kind of group collaboration. If you work in an administrative role, then you know that setting up user access can be far more detailed when working with users and groups in other capacities.

In any network or server arrangement, every object has an owner. Controlling permissions for each object — how the permissions are established and which users are entitled to which permissions — are key to ensuring the environment is safe and secure for the organization but not oppressive for users. In this chapter, we'll explore how users and groups work and then go into some detail about controlling user access and managing project data ideas. If you don't work in an administrative role, this chapter is not the most important one in the book for you. Read it more as an overview so you understand the kinds of things administrators must consider when setting up user access for you and so that you understand your role in a network, but don't worry too much about the actual steps involved.

Users and Groups Overview

Access control — the process of authorizing users, groups, and computers to access objects on the network — is a key consideration in network design. As in earlier versions of Office, access control in Office 2007 is still comprised of ownership of objects, permissions, inheritance of permissions, and object auditing.

Don't let the technical term *object* scare you. It's really just an item that is described by a distinct, named set of attributes. Typically, an object is a file, folder, shared folder, printer, or Active Directory object. The description of one of these objects might include a name, location, and size. If you're dealing with Object Linking and Embedding (OLE) or ActiveX, objects can get a little fuzzier. They can be literally any piece of information that can be linked to or embedded into another object. For purposes of this chapter, we will not be referring to OLE or ActiveX objects.

Consider each of these aspects when you set up your network; the more detailed you are in your thought process up front, the easier the administrative tasks will be down the road.

Assigning Owners

Owners are assigned to objects at the moment of creation. That's by default; if you create something, you should own it, right? Regardless of whether you're in an NTFS volume or Active Directory, the owner will always be able to control how permissions are set on the object in question.

Network administrators are typically the ones who create and own most of the objects in Active Directory and on network servers because they are the ones who typically install programs on the server involved. The average user, however, can also create and own objects. This usually occurs when a user creates something on a home directory or is allowed permission to access certain data files on the network.

This concept works fairly well most of the time, except in cases where an owner is no longer allowed access to the network. For example, what if an employee leaves your company? In that and similar situations, a safety net has been built in to ensure you can always access everything on the server: *ownership transfer.* Essentially, an administrator can take ownership of an object at any time (if, for instance, the departing employee is a disgruntled one) or the object owner can designate Take Ownership permission to another user.

Determining Folder Permissions

Figure 11-1 shows how group or user names are listed for a folder. To check owner or user permissions on one of your own folders:

1. Right-click on the folder.

2. Click Properties.

3. Click Security.

4. Review Permissions.

The Group or user names pane will list those with access to that folder.

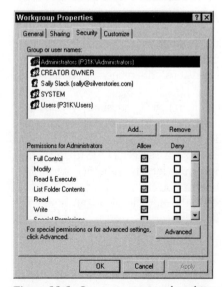

Figure 11-1: Owners are assigned to objects at the moment of creation, and indicated by the CREATOR OWNER option under Group or user names.

Caution

Even though a current owner can grant the Take ownership permission to another user, the second user must actually take ownership to complete the transfer. If the second user does not, then the object can remain in limbo if the original owner leaves. At that point, an administrator must step in and take ownership. Administrators cannot transfer ownership to others, but they can give a new user the ability to take ownership of an object. The new designated user is then responsible for taking ownership.

Granting Permissions

Once an object is created and an owner established, permissions are used to define the type of access granted to users, individually or in groups. Later in this chapter, we go into more detail about permissions but for now, you should understand that permissions are applied to any secured objects; these include files, Active Directory objects, and registry objects.

While you can certainly assign individual permissions to users, save yourself some headaches and assign permissions to groups whenever possible. For example, human resources employees might be assigned Full Control permission as a group for the file retirees.dat. There are times, of course, when assigning blanket permissions to a group just won't work. In those cases, the most commonly assigned permissions are Read, Modify, Change Owner, and Delete. Figure 11-2 shows how permissions are listed in the Properties dialog box for a folder.

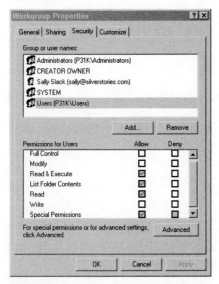

Figure 11-2: Permissions can be granted to individual users or in groups and can be applied to any secured object. In this example, Read & Execute, List Folder Contents, and Read are allowed permissions for general users.

Understanding Inheritance of Permissions

When you view the permissions of an object, you'll sometimes notice that there are inherited permissions attached. (See Figure 11-3.) This happens when permissions are set on a parent folder — new files and subfolders created in that folder automatically inherit the same permissions as the parent folder unless designated otherwise. If you design your folder structure and top-level permissions carefully, inherited permissions aren't a problem. But often, these structures and permissions are established by a variety of people and aren't well-planned. You can avoid pesky inheritances by selecting This folder only in Apply onto when you set up special permissions in the parent folder.

There may be times, however, when you want most of the files and subfolders to inherit the permissions while preventing others from those permissions. In those cases, you can set advanced permissions on files and folders by using Permission Entry for *<File or folder name>*.

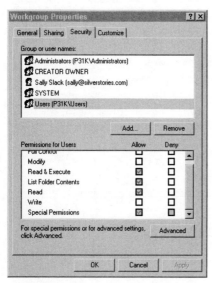

Figure 11-3: Inherited permissions are shown as grayed-out boxes with check marks in the Permissions for users pane of the Security tab.

Object Auditing

Do you want to know who is accessing objects, such as files and folders? Office 2007 won't do this automatically for you, but you can define a policy setting that will automatically check users accessing certain objects. The object must have its own system access control list (SACL) specified, as follows:

1. Go to the object's Advanced Properties.

2. Select Auditing.

3. Enter names.

4. Click OK.

5. Select a permission for the audit by choosing Successful or Failed in the Access pane of the Object tab (as shown in Figure 11-4).

6. Click OK.

Too much auditing can literally crash a system because it slows the system down and creates large amounts of audit data, so give careful thought to how much auditing you turn on and who it's for.

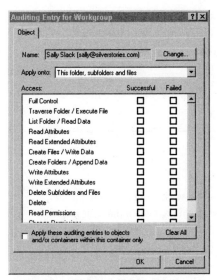

Figure 11-4: Object auditing can help you monitor who is accessing objects. The choice of Successful or Failed in the Access pane establishes conditions for the audit.

Controlling User Access by Configuring Permissions

We've already talked a great deal about permissions in this book, but there are still more aspects to consider as you assign permissions. In this section, we go into detail about how you can control user access by granting, changing, or denying permissions for individuals and groups. Some things to remember before we get started:

■ File and folder permissions can only be set on drives formatted to use NTFS.

▧ Only owners or administrators — or those granted permission by the owner or administrator — can change permissions.

 ▧ A group or user with Full Control for a folder can create or delete files and subfolders within that folder regardless of permissions protecting the files and subfolders.

 ▧ New users and groups will have the following permissions by default: Read & Execute, List Folder Contents, and Read.

File and Folder Permissions at a Glance

You are probably familiar with the six primary folder permissions (Full Control, Modify, Read & Execute, List Folder Contents, Read, and Write). Did you know there are 14 special permissions affiliated with these primary permissions? Table 11-1 outlines the special permissions, and Table 11-2 shows which primary permission a special permission belongs to. You should note that anyone granted Full Control on a folder can delete any files within that folder — regardless of the permissions protecting it.

Table 11-1   Special Permissions — Windows XP

Permission	*Description*
Traverse Folder/Execute File	For folders: Traverse Folder allows or denies moving through folders to reach other files or folders, even if the user has no permissions for the traversed folders. This permission takes effect only when the group or user is not given the Bypass traverse checking default.
List Folder/Read Data	List Folder allows or denies viewing file names and subfolder names within a folder. Read data allows or denies viewing data within a file.
Read Attributes	Allows or denies viewing the attributes of a file or folder. (Attributes are defined by NTFS.)
Read Extended Attributes	Allows or denies viewing the extended attributes of a file or folder (defined by programs rather than NTFS).
Create Files/Write Data	Create Files allows or denies the creation of files within a folder. Write Data allows or denies making changes to a file and overwriting existing content.
Create Folders/Append Data	Create Folders allows or denies the creation of folders within a folder. Append Data allows or denies making changes to the end of the file but *not* changing, deleting, or overwriting existing data.
Write Attributes	Allows or denies changing the attributes of a file or folder (as defined by NTFS).

Table 11-1　Special Permissions — Windows XP *(Continued)*

Permission	Description
Write Extended Attributes	Allows or denies changing extended attributes of a file or folder (as defined by individual programs).
Delete Subfolders and Files	Allows or denies the deletion of a subfolder and files, even if the Delete permission has not been given.
Delete	Allows or denies deleting the file or folder. Note: Regardless of Delete permission status on a file or folder, you can still delete it if you have Delete Subfolders and Files permission on the parent folder.
Read Permissions	Allows or denies reading permissions of the file or folder.
Change Permissions	Allow or denies changing permissions of the file or folder.
Take Ownership	Allows or denies taking ownership of the file or folder.
Synchronize	Allows or denies different threads to wait on the handle for the file or folder and synchronize with another thread. Note: This only applies to multithreaded, multiprocess programs.

Table 11-2　Special Permissions Associated to Primary Permissions (Full Control, Modify, Read & Execute, List Folder Contents, Read, Write) — Windows XP

Permission	Full Control	Modify	Read & Execute	List Folder Contents	Read	Write
Traverse Folder/Execute File	✓	✓	✓	✓		
List Folder/Read Data	✓	✓	✓	✓	✓	
Read Attributes	✓	✓	✓	✓	✓	
Read Extended Attributes	✓	✓	✓	✓	✓	
Create Files/Write Data	✓	✓				✓
Create Folders/Append Data	✓	✓				✓
Write Attributes	✓	✓				✓
Write Extended Attributes	✓	✓				✓
Delete Subfolders and Files	✓					
Delete	✓	✓				
Read Permissions	✓	✓	✓	✓	✓	✓
Change Permissions	✓					
Take Ownership	✓					
Synchronize	✓	✓	✓	✓	✓	✓

Caution

In Table 11-2, List Folder Contents and Read & Execute apply the same special permissions. But be careful! These permissions are inherited differently in each case. List Folder Contents is inherited by folders only; Read & Execute is inherited by both folders and files. Read & Execute is always present when you view file or folder permissions.

Setting, Viewing, Changing, or Removing File and Folder Permissions

Now that you see how permissions work within Office 2007, basic permission setting activities will seem really simple.

1. First locate the file or folder you want to work with. Right-click it.

2. Click Properties.

3. Select the Security tab. (See Figures 11-2 and 11-3.)

To set permissions for a new group or user (one that does not appear in the Group or user names boxes) from the Security tab:

1. Click Add.

2. Enter the names as prompted in the Select Users, Computers, or Groups window. (See Figure 11-5.)

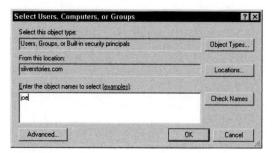

Figure 11-5: Clicking Add on the Security tab allows you to add new users, computers, or groups in this window.

3. Click OK.

To change or remove permissions from existing groups or users from the Security tab:

1. Click the name of the group or user.

2. Select Allow or Deny in the Permissions for Users box *or* Click Remove.

Changing inherited permissions works a little differently. Were the check boxes shaded when you viewed the permissions of an object? If so, then the object has inherited permissions from a parent object.

Let's talk about parent/child objects for a moment. A *parent* object *is one in which another object resides*. A *child* object *is the one that resides within* another object. For example, a parent object can be a folder that is created. Files within that folder are child objects. Now, to get just a little more detailed, child objects can also be parent objects. Turning the example a bit differently, a parent object can be a folder, a child object can be a folder within the parent folder and — at the same time — can hold files within it that are now child objects, which now makes the original child object a parent folder. See Figure 11-6 for a little visual help on this concept.

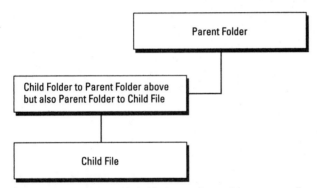

Figure 11-6: Parent and child object relationships can get a bit confusing. Take your time when trying to determine where an object fits in the permission categories.

You can tell which folders and subfolders a permission is applied to and where the permissions were inherited from by reviewing the Permissions tab on the Advanced dialog box. To open this dialog box:

1. First locate the file or folder you want to work with. Right-click it.

2. Click Properties.

3. Select the Security tab.

4. Click Advanced.

To make changes for these objects, you first need to decide whether to make changes to the parent object or the child (the file or folder that inherited the parent object's permissions). If you make changes at the parent level, the child object will simply inherit the changes.

If you don't want to change the parent object, you can do one of two things in the object you are working with: Override the inherited permission by selecting the opposite permission (allow or deny) showing, or clear the inherited parent permissions. Remember: Deny *always* takes precedence over any other permission!

To clear the inherited parent permissions, click the Advanced button on the Security tab, as shown in Figure 11-7. This takes you to the Permissions tab, where there are two check boxes at the bottom of the window. Deselect the check mark from Inherit from parent the permission entries that apply to child objects. Include these with entries explicitly defined here. Now, make permission changes or remove users or groups as desired. Just remember, the object will no longer inherit permissions from the parent object, so consider this carefully before you clear these permissions.

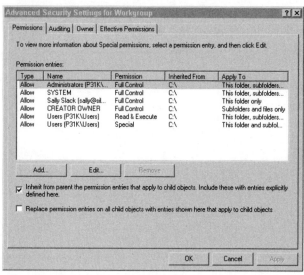

Figure 11-7: Clearing inherited permissions is as easy as removing a check mark in the Inherit from parent box.

Caution

Clearing inherited permissions is permanent!

Managing Project Data

Office 2007 simplifies how people work together, and actually offers many ways to do that. While we can't cover everything in one chapter, we can give you brief overviews of two data management options you can consider.

Understanding Information Rights Management

A good way to manage project data with Office 2007 is to take advantage of the new features in document and records management. For example, users and administrators can restrict permissions to content with information rights management (IRM). By using this feature, you can restrict sensitive information from being forwarded, copied, or printed; that restriction remains with the document, workbook, or presentation no matter where the information goes. That's because the permission restriction is stored within the object itself. The restrictions can be applied by user, by document, or by group.

Users that attempt to open the restricted object must connect to a licensing server, which will require them to download a use license. The process verifies users' credentials via information about their e-mail address and permission rights and is required for every restricted file, so that's something to consider if you decide to implement IRM. Don't worry, information actually contained in the document is never sent to the licensing server.

In order to use IRM, you need Windows Rights Management Services Client Service Pack 1. If you receive a file that has been rights-managed through the use of IRM, Office 2007 prompts you to download the Services Client if you don't have it.

SharePoint Server 2007

One nice aspect of Office 2007 is that SharePoint Server 2007 can be integrated into its applications quickly and easily. If you haven't used SharePoint Server before, consider using it now.

With it, people can connect to documents, calendars, contacts, or tasks. Users on your network will be able to manage their project data more effectively with its new or enhanced features:

- **Automated workflows:** Users can select workflows from within an Office application, launching an automatic e-mail and Outlook task for reviewers. A full workflow history is maintained so both users and IT administrators can track the step.

- **Slide libraries:** Users can link PowerPoint 2007 slides and related documents to SharePoint for updating and automatic synchronization.

- **Search Center:** Users can index and find information that resides with other users.

- **Knowledge Network:** Users (typically managers) can perform searches for employees skills and other variables, plus determine who has useful networking relationships.

- **My Site:** Personal sites for employees. Administrators can regulate viewing of selected public content, among other networking enhancements.

Another thing that SharePoint Server 2007 can do is help you manage your document processes, too. In Word 2007, the document information panel lets you change a document's editorial status. When the document is saved back to the server, the new status is updated as well.

Summary

Throughout this chapter, you've learned about key pieces of setting up user access — from owners and permissions to configuring permissions to ideas for managing project data. You should now have a good background for organizing and configuring an environment where documents are shared and distributed. This information is important for systems and network administrators but also helpful for average users. Knowing these system-related aspects will help you maintain effective and organized files in your system as you work with the Office 2007 suite.

Chapter 12

Collaborating Options

If the stock market in Japan drops, investors in the United States know it immediately. When a hostile takeover bid is made in Los Angeles, business people in Paris learn about it within hours. Communication can occur so quickly across so many time zones that the once-futuristic concept of a global community has now become reality in many ways.

This reality made it imperative that the goal of collaboration — to keep coworkers, partners, and customers synchronized through communication and information sharing — was a primary focus in Office 2007. In this chapter, we'll take a look at how the Office 2007 system can help you meet collaborative challenges. It does this through integrated communication and extended collaborative workspaces. While you may not currently need all of the methods described in this chapter, it's good practice to know what they are and how to access them; who knows what the future holds for you?

In this chapter, we explore the aspects of integrated communication including online display status, unified messaging, Web conferencing, and instant messaging. We also briefly explore extended collaborative workspace options such as SharePoint Services Technology, Office Groove 2007, shared note-taking, and configurable workflows.

Note

Most of what you see in this chapter requires you to also have SharePoint Services Technology, SharePoint Server 2007, Exchange Server 2007, or upgraded versions of Office 2007, such as Professional Plus or Enterprise Edition. As a result, this chapter focuses primarily on the options available to you instead of step-by-step processes.

Understanding Integrated Communication

"Call me." "Send me an e-mail." "Ping me." With all the communication tools available today, it's sometimes overwhelming to remember who wants which method of communication. Call someone who prefers instant messaging, and you'll get a curt "Next time, just ping me." E-mail someone who prefers the phone, and you may not get a response for days.

The beauty of Office 2007 is that it really does make it easier to connect with people. It has what Microsoft calls "intelligent integration," which is a fancy way of saying that you can quickly tell whether another person is on the phone, at his or her computer, in a meeting, and — best of all — the method of communication that person prefers.

Knowing Who Is Online

Knowing who is available at the precise moment you need help or information is a terrific communication tool. With Office 2007, the most common way to determine whether someone else is online at the same time you are is with Outlook 2007.

To enable the display of a person's online status in Outlook 2007:

1. Go to Tools.

2. Select Options.

3. Choose the Other tab.

4. Place a check mark in the Person Names box next to Display online status next to person name.

5. Click OK.

The next time the two of you are on a compatible instant messaging program (MSN Messenger, Office Communicator, Windows Live Messenger, or Windows Messenger) at the same time, you will see your contact's status as you view that person's e-mails within Outlook. Their status will instantly show up as a green circle next to their name in Outlook e-mail messages, as shown in Figure 12-1. If the green dot is there, you can start a real-time message to that person directly from Outlook without switching to an instant messaging application. Here's how:

1. Right-click on the person's name.

2. Select Reply with an Instant Message.

Indicates Juliann's online status

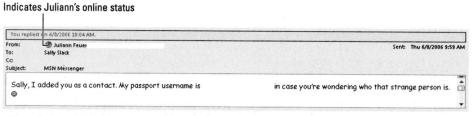

Figure 12-1: Outlook 2007 helps you collaborate by showing you the online status of your contacts from within an e-mail. In this example, the green circle next to Juliann's name shows she is online.

You can do something similar in Word 2007, too. When you're working on a document, you can see the people associated with the document along with information about their availability status. If someone is available, you can initiate a conversation. For more information on this option, read Part V of this book, "Working with Word."

Taking Advantage of Unified Messaging

If you are on Exchange Server 2007, you can take advantage of a cool new collaboration option: having voice mail and faxes delivered to your Office Outlook 2007 Inbox. This may sound like something you've heard of before, but users of earlier versions of Outlook, Outlook Web Access, and Exchange Server are limited to receiving mail as a standard e-mail sound file attachment (*.wav or *.wma). They also do not have voice mail configuration options available within Outlook.

In Office 2007, Unified Messaging works much more easily. Unified Messaging allows you to play a voice message either through Microsoft Windows Media Player in an Outlook mail form or message list, or on the telephone. Plus, you can configure individual voice mail settings. This feature is great for collaboration because those trying to reach you don't have to try and figure out which method is best. They can choose the communication method best for them, while you receive their message in the format that works best for you. For step-by-step details on setting up this feature, read Part VIII of this book, "Keeping in Touch with Outlook."

Web Conferencing

You'll notice in Outlook 2007 that there is no longer an option for turning a meeting request into an online meeting. That's because Microsoft Exchange Conferencing, Windows Media Services, and NetMeeting are no longer supported by Microsoft; Microsoft wants you to use Office Live Meeting as a replacement due to its improved functionality.

Office Live Meeting is a hosted Web conferencing service that uses your PC, Internet connection, and a telephone. It is not part of the Office 2007 system but has options that allow you to schedule and conduct meetings directly from Microsoft Office programs (such as Outlook, PowerPoint, Excel, Word, Visio, and Project) as well as Microsoft Windows Messenger. It's available as a download at www.microsoft.com.

If you upgrade to Office Professional Plus 2007, Office Communicator 2007 is automatically included to give you instant Web conferencing capabilities. Office Communicator 2007 is cool because it integrates with nearly all the programs in the Office 2007 system, which makes it easy for you and others to collaborate during a Web conference. If you have Microsoft Office Home and Student, or are on Office Enterprise 2007, you can take advantage of shared note-taking in Office OneNote 2007 and add a new twist to the Web conferencing concept. More details about shared note-taking are explained later in this chapter.

Using Instant Messaging

Instant messaging is here to stay. There are so many different messaging options available, it's impossible to review them all in this book. And, while Microsoft has four different messaging options you can take advantage of (Windows Messenger, Windows Live Messenger as shown in Figure 12-2, MSN Messenger, and Office Communicator), only one is part of the Office 2007 system: Office Communicator 2007. It is automatically included with Office Professional Plus 2007 and Office Enterprise 2007. The other three can still be used with Office 2007, but Office Communicator 2007 is unique in its integration capabilities, chief of which are listed here:

   ▪ Integrates with several programs in Office 2007: Outlook, Word, Excel, PowerPoint, OneNote, Groove, and SharePoint Server.

- Offers voice and video along with instant messaging, without having to open new windows or starting other programs.

- Allows you (in some situations) to communicate with people using other instant messaging services such as MSN Messenger, Yahoo! Messenger, and AOL Instant Messenger.

- Integrates presence information from sources such as your calendar or out-of-office message so others know when and how you're able to communicate.

- Works with existing address books and corporate directories so you can find anyone in your contact lists, see their availability, and instantly communicate.

Don't want to upgrade just for Office Communicator 2007? To download and use Windows Messenger, Windows Live Messenger, or MSN Messenger, go to www.microsoft.com. You'll still be able to take advantage of basic online status and messaging features with Office 2007 programs.

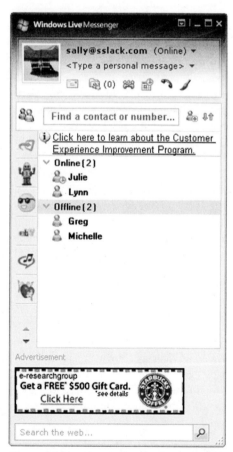

Figure 12-2: Instant messaging programs allow you to take advantage of online status and messaging features within Office 2007. Windows Live Messenger is shown here.

Exploring the Extended Collaborative Workspaces

Business has changed, and along with it business teaming concepts have changed. Today, a project team might have four people on-site and six off-site, with each of the six in a different geographic location. Between coordinating disparate time zones (ever tried working on a team with members in New York, Sydney, and New Delhi?) and managing cultural differences, communication and collaboration can be pretty challenging.

Yet the 24/7 working concept has taken hold in large enterprises, and smaller ones are starting to see how they can join forces with others around the globe to compete on a larger scale. By basing the Office 2007 system on the Windows SharePoint Services technology, Microsoft has come up with some new twists in collaborative workspaces. In this section, we explore team site extranets, using Office Groove 2007 for workspace creation, and shared note-taking.

Using SharePoint Services Technology and SharePoint Server 2007

In the previous chapter, we briefly discuss SharePoint Server 2007. But there are actually two SharePoint terms you will hear about and it's important to understand the differences between them. In simple terms, Windows SharePoint Services technology is actually part of Windows Server 2003 and uses a browser-based workspace technology to help people collaborate, while Office SharePoint Server 2007 is an actual suite of server-based applications that connects sites, people, and business processes. Depending on how your IT department is set up, you may or may not have either or both of these items.

You may have heard the term "SharePoint site" at some point. That's because SharePoint Services lets teams create Web sites for information sharing and document collaboration — its resources include portals, team workspaces, e-mail, calendar viewing, presence awareness, and Web-based conferencing. Once created, these sites can be easily searched and alerts are sent to tell people when existing documents and information have been changed or new documents added. In addition, all of a site's content can be read and edited within Office 2007 programs. An example of this is shown in Figure 12-3.

Both SharePoint Services and SharePoint Server 2007 have capabilities for document storage and management, along with search, workflow, rights management, and administration features. SharePoint Server 2007, however, acts as an extension for SharePoint Services by offering additional management and organizational tools. A nice feature of SharePoint Server 2007 is its search capabilities. In particular, there are new functions to help you search for people and expertise, an indexing feature, and business intelligence capabilities that allow employees to share, control, and reuse business information across an organization.

Tip

If your organization owns Windows Server 2003 licenses, it has the rights to also use Windows SharePoint Services. Check with your IT department to find out whether you can take advantage of it.

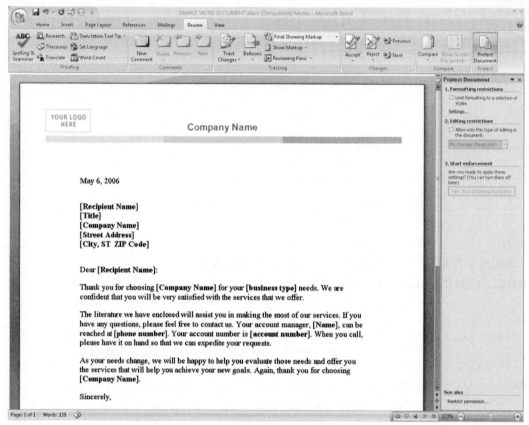

Figure 12-3: In Word 2007, SharePoint sites make it easy to collaborate with others by using a Web-based format for information sharing and document collaboration. This example shows the options available for document management when working in a Word 2007 document on a SharePoint site.

Using Office Groove 2007

When mobile workers need to work together, connectivity can sometimes be a problem. Security can be an issue as well, and time zones can really put a damper on person-to-person conversations. But what if you weren't connected and could still collaborate with others? What if security, time zones, and other pesky issues could be reduced or eliminated? You will need to upgrade to Microsoft Office Enterprise 2007, but, once you do, you will have access to Office Groove 2007 (shown in Figure 12-4), a collaborative environment that puts all team members, communications, tools, and information into one location accessible from each team member's computer. One person can be in an airplane, another can be on the ground — it doesn't matter because the workspace is stored individually on computers and later synchronized.

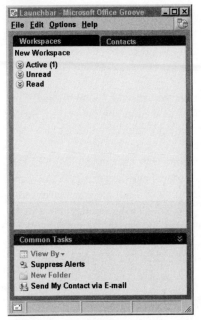

Figure 12-4: Office Groove 2007 is a collaborative tool that uses workspaces to share information among people in different companies and locations.

The only requirement is that participants have Office Groove 2007 installed on their computers — not a problem if your IT department has licensed it. Three types of workspaces are included; you choose the one that fits your needs and then invite others to join it:

- **Standard workspace:** Includes Files and Discussion tools. Other tools can be added if needed.

- **File sharing workspace:** Synchronizes a selected Windows operating system file folder and its contents across participating computers.

- **Template workspace:** Allows you to choose from several options designed for different project requirements, such as calendar or sketchpad.

When invitees accept a Groove invitation, an exact copy of the workspace is sent to their desktop. Invitees do not need to be on your network — in fact, you can share workspaces with people in other companies and locations without servers or IT assistance. Built-in encryption helps ensure data is protected as it travels the globe; a nice bonus is that Office Groove 2007 supports 278 different languages.

To invite people to a file sharing workspace:

   1. Double-click the file-sharing workspace on the Workspaces tab of the Groove Launchbar.

2. Click Invite Someone in the Synchronization Tasks pane.

3. Select recipient and role options in the Send Invitation dialog box.

Understanding Shared Note-Taking

If you haven't tried Office OneNote 2007 to help with collaboration, you should. As mentioned earlier this chapter, it's available with Office Home and Student 2007 as well as the Office Enterprise 2007 suite. It can also be downloaded from Microsoft as a standalone program if you don't have one of these Office 2007 suites.

Think of OneNote 2007 as a digital notebook that lets you include not just written content but audio, image, and video content as well. It works on desktops, laptops, and tablet PCs. Some very cool features let you create shared workspaces for group brainstorming and initiate live sharing sessions, which allow you to share notes with others in real-time. The live sharing sessions are sort of like a virtual meeting binder with a whiteboard attached; team members can edit drawings, photo images, text, and handwriting. In the live sharing sessions, each person gets a copy of the shared notes as part of his notebook. Figure 12-5 shows you how simple the OneNote interface appears.

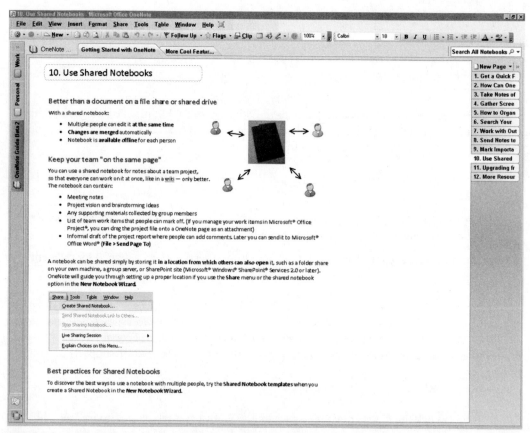

Figure 12-5: Office OneNote 2007 can help you work with others in a team format using a shared notebook concept.

If you don't have time to work in real-time with others, you can still collaborate through the use of a shared notebook on a file server or a SharePoint site. Members of the team can contribute information and ideas on their schedule; OneNote 2007 manages the changes for you and stores a local copy of the shared notebook to each user's computer.

When used in conjunction with SharePoint Services, the content of these notebooks then becomes searchable by others in the organization. OneNote 2007 continually indexes information so that searches are returned quickly and the search includes not just text, but audio and video recordings as well. You can also publish your notes in a Web page format to place them on a file share, Web site, or a SharePoint Services site.

To create a new shared notebook in a SharePoint library, go to the Share menu and click Create Shared Notebook. When the New Notebook Wizard dialog box opens as shown in Figure 12-6, take these steps:

1. Enter a name for the shared notebook.

2. Choose a color for the notebook cover, if desired.

3. Select a default template, if desired, in the From Template list.

4. Click Next.

5. Click Multiple people will share the notebook under Who will use this notebook?

6. Click On a server (SharePoint, network share, or other shared location).

7. Enter the Web address of the SharePoint library you want to use under Path. (Click Browse to find the SharePoint site and library if you need to.)

8. Leave the check box selected next to Create an e-mail with a link to this notebook so that I can send to other people.

9. Click Create.

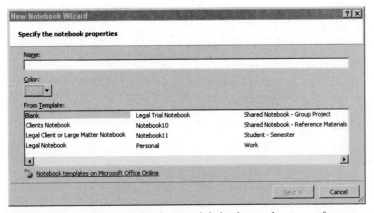

Figure 12-6: The New Notebook Wizard dialog box makes it easy for you to share your notebook with others.

Configurable Workflows

People are sometimes the biggest obstacle to getting a job done in a timely manner. It's not that they *mean* to hold things up, but procrastination does seem to be a common middle name for some. Here is one way you can take control with Office 2007 and keep your project moving along.

When used in conjunction with SharePoint Server 2007, Office Word 2007 lets you create workflows to better manage your content and track approvals — within your document. These workflows are great for making certain that everyone follows the right steps in document management. For example, if you send an expense report to your boss, you can designate that she must approve it before it can be sent on to other management for final approvals. Workflows appear at the top of a Word document when they are being used. For more details about using Office 2007 features that are available with SharePoint Server 2007 only, please go to www.microsoft.com.

Summary

This chapter provided an overview of integrated communication features offered in Office 2007; features include online display status, unified messaging, Web conferencing, and instant messaging. These features make it easier than before to connect with other people by allowing you to determine the best way to reach them, as well as giving you instant information about the person's online status.

Microsoft Office 2007 can also be used to provide collaborative workspace options when used in conjunction with SharePoint Services Technology, Office Groove 2007, Office OneNote 2007, and SharePoint Server 2007. It's important to note that not all users of Office 2007 can take advantage of every feature — your organization may not use or provide the applications mentioned in this chapter. If it does, however, take advantage of the features available to you. They will make collaborating with others a much more enjoyable part of your day.

Part V

Working with Word

Chapter 13

Performing Common Tasks in Word

M icrosoft Word 2007 has a completely new look and feel. At first glance, you might feel a little overwhelmed by all of the changes. Don't. Take a deep breath and keep reading because
all of the common tasks that you've completed in the past can still be done in this new version. And
it's actually a little easier once you get a handle on how to navigate through the new interface. For
example, all of the most frequently used functions are right there in the open, so if you want to
change styles, add pictures, or embellish your documents, you won't lose precious time finding the
commands.

The key word here is easier. The new interface makes it much easier to accomplish complicated
tasks that used to take forever to complete. A new point-and-click design puts complex, formerly
hard-to-find features like linking to live data, collaborating, and creating main mail merges right in
plain sight. But as good as they are, the changes do take some getting used to.

Exploring the Interface

The first thing you'll notice when you open the new Word 2007 is that it looks nothing like previous
versions of Word. Everything, from the background to the toolbars, looks different. Many of the
functions that you know and love are the same, but that's just about all.

The new design should facilitate your workflow by making it possible for you to quickly find the
functions that in the past were often buried deeper than Davy Jones's locker, preview and change formats with the click of a button, and manage files better with new file formats, sharing capabilities,
and digital rights management tools. In short, Word has finally been designed with the user in mind.
So, yes, you may have a short learning curve, but in the end it's all worth it.

Word's New Look

Word's new look is a little overwhelming the first time you see it. Gone are the drop-down menus
that were so confusing that even the most accomplished Word users spent far too much time fum-
bling around, looking for the right option in the right menu.

Word now features a set of tools along the top of the window called the Ribbon. This Ribbon,
shown in Figure 13-1, is a visual, tabbed system that makes the most frequently used options available to you at the click of a button.

Smart Tabs

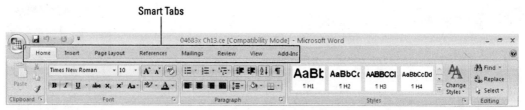

Figure 13-1: The Ribbon contains all of the options that used to be hidden in drop-down menus.

The Ribbon is designed with eight contextual tabs (also called smart tabs), indicated in Figure 13-1, that represent the major functions of Word. They include Home, Insert, Page Layout, References, Mailings, Review, View, and Add-Ins. You may also have a Developer tab, which gives you access to tools like the Macro recorder and Visual Basic Editor.

If you don't see the Developer tab, you can add it by going to File → Word Options → Personalize. Then select Show Developer Tab in the Ribbon option and click OK.

Note

You could spend days looking for the File menu in Word 2007. It's very cleverly disguised as the Office Button in the top-left corner of the page, as illustrated in Figure 13-2. Click the icon to find the File menu commands, including New, Open, Convert, Save, Save As, Print, Prepare, Send, Publish, and Close. There are also two buttons on this menu: Word Options and Exit Word.

You'll notice a few other changes in the appearance of Word. The first is the background color. The change in colors is consistent across all of the Office products. The blue — called Windows XP (blue) — is easier on the eyes than the black-and-white color scheme of past versions of Word, but that's about the only function that it serves. (Although this author finds the color much more comforting than black and white.) However, if you're one of those people who don't care for blue, you can switch to a black view. Here's how:

1. Go to File → Word Options and select Popular (the default view).

2. On the Color Scheme drop-down menu, select the desired color, in this case black.

3. Click OK and the background color of your document is changed. The black option is a much more extreme view and will appeal to those of you with a more adventurous bent.

The other change you'll notice is that the horizontal and vertical rulers are missing. As with other versions of Word, you can use the ruler or not. The difference is that now it's much easier to turn it on and off. You'll find the control for the ruler on the right side of the page just above the scrollbar, as indicated in Figure 13-2.

Office button/File menu   Ruler controls

Figure 13-2: Some of the features of Word are harder to find than others, for example, the ruler controls are just above the scrollbar on the right.

Tip
There's more than one way to find the rulers. You can also access them on the View tab. They're in the Show/Hide section of the Ribbon. Place a check mark in the Ruler box, and they appear on your page.

The last major change in the appearance of Word is the toolbar at the bottom of the page. Remember how you had to go to Tools → Word Count to figure out how many words you had in a document in the past? Now it's right there on the left side of the toolbar (it's called a live word count), all the time. You'll also find a page count next to it, right alongside the macro recording button. Several menu buttons live on the right side of this toolbar: Print Layout, Full Screen Reading, Web Layout, Outline, and Draft. There's also a new slider in the right corner. This slider lets you zoom in or out on the page.

Exploring New Tools and Features
The driving factor behind the considerable changes to Word is to make it more usable — to make it easier for you to design professional looking documents quickly so that you spend more time writing and less time trying to format the document. To that end, the design team at Microsoft included several new tools and features to make document design easier and to improve document management.

- **Galleries:** Having the ability to choose from a set of document designs without having to go through several menus to achieve the design saves a lot of time. This new feature in Word makes it easy for you to design professional looking documents, but if you need more control over your designs, you still have menu options for better customization.

- **Live Preview:** Wouldn't it be great to be able to preview a style before you actually make the change? With Live Preview you can. Simply move your pointer over the style that you're considering and your document morphs to show you a preview. If you don't like the style, move on. If you do like it, simply click the style name and it will automagically be applied to the entire document.

- **Building blocks:** The problem with copying and pasting content from one document to the next is that it introduces the potential for errors. In this version, Word introduces document building blocks, predefined blocks of content that can be applied to a document with the click of a button. You can use content blocks that are built into the application or you can create your own content blocks (like copyright notices) to suit your organizational or personal needs.

- **Improved graphics capabilities:** One of the most exciting new additions to Word is the SmartArt graphics capability. This tool lets you quickly insert document illustrations such as Venn diagrams, pyramids, cycles, and targets. A new charting feature also makes it easy to create charts and graphs from existing data in Excel spreadsheets.

- **Document Inspector:** The Document Inspector is a new tool that's designed to help protect you from unintentionally exposing private or inappropriate information to others. When activated, the tool checks for comments, tracked changes, metadata, XML, and hidden data that should be removed from the document. With two clicks, this information is located and can be removed from your document.

- **Digital signatures:** Digital signatures are used more frequently now than they ever have been in the past. The digital signature feature of Word allows you to quickly insert a digital signature into any document.

- **New file formats:** Several new file formats are introduced in Word 2007 to help you manage your documents better. Some of the new file formats (and their file-name extensions) are a file format for macro-enabled documents (.docm), the default format for Word documents (.docx), a file format for templates (.dotx), and a file format for macro-enabled templates (.dotm).

- **Equation Builder:** Creating documents that include mathematical equations has always been a headache, but this new version of Word has a pill for that pain. The Equation Builder makes it easy for you to quickly add equations to your documents.

- **Integration with SharePoint Server 2007:** Finally it's easier to move documents through the review and approval process. Integration with SharePoint Server decreases the amount of time and frustration involved in moving a document through these frustrating processes.

Many of the features that you've used in Word in the past are still available to you. But the designers at Microsoft took the time to really listen to what users need from the program, and they've built many of those features into this new version of Word. All the new elements can be confusing and difficult to find, but, given some time, great guidance, and a little practice, it won't take you long to get comfortable with the new interface and features. When you are comfortable with it, you'll find that designing and creating professional, high-impact documents is much easier than it has ever been in the past.

Customizing the Interface

Every person works differently and every project has different requirements. You need to be able to customize Word's interface to meet your needs. And you can.

1. Select File → Word Options to be taken to a dialog box like the one shown in Figure 13-3

2. From this dialog box, you can change and customize the interface and behavior of Word to meet your specific style and needs.

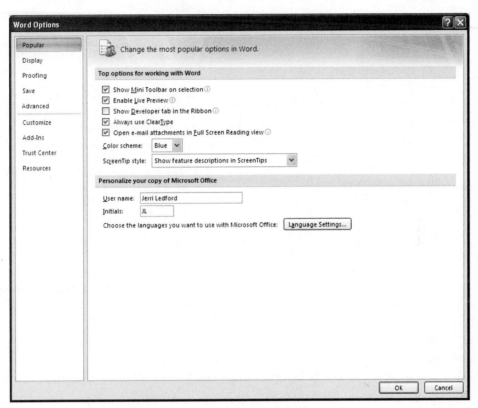

Figure 13-3: Customize Word using the Word Options dialog box.

In the Word Options dialog box there are several customization options:

■ **Popular:** Use the Popular screen to change the look and feel of your Word program. Here you can add or remove tabs from the Ribbon, change the color of your Word skin, enable or disable certain functions, and change your preferences for saving Word documents. You can also change your user name, initials, and language settings.

■ **Display:** On this screen, you can change how your documents are displayed on the computer and in print. From this menu, you can make changes to your display options, formatting marks, and printing options.

■ **Proofing:** Manage your correcting and formatting options from here. Those options include autocorrection settings, spelling correction options for both Word and Office, and grammar correction options.

■ **Save:** Manage how (and where) your documents are saved. Saving options include backup information, draft locations, checkout options, and fidelity preservation for document sharing.

■ **Advanced:** All of your advanced functions can be found on this screen. Set options for editing, displaying editing elements or document content, accessibility, and compatibility using this menu. There are also additional options including print, save, preserve fidelity, and general options.

■ **Customize:** Use the Customization screen to change what's included in your Quick Access toolbar and to create or change keyboard shortcuts. The Quick Access toolbar is located on the top-left of the page, next to the Office file menu and tab contents. This toolbar lets you quickly access some of the most used functions of Word such as Save, Print, and Undo.

■ **Add-Ins:** View and manage your add-ins from this screen. For example, some programs place an icon on your Office toolbars to allow quick access to those applications. These are called add-ins and this section is where you can remove or change the properties of those add-ins.

■ **Trust Center:** This is one of the new features of Word. The Trust Center is where you select options for the protection of your documents and the security of your PC. You'll find access here to advanced Trust Center settings that include managing publishers, locations, add-ins, ActiveX controls, macro settings, document Message Bar settings, and privacy options.

Caution

It's not recommended that you change any of the options in the Trust Center. These options are preset to the most secure settings for your protection. Changing the settings could result in putting your personal information at risk.

■ **Resources:** Additional resources located here are links to Office Online, Office activation, updates, the diagnostics program, contact information for Microsoft, and security and privacy information and policies.

At the time this book was written, there are only three skin colors to choose from, and although they're pretty cool, they probably won't appeal to everyone. It's likely just a matter of time before Microsoft or independent developers offer new skinning capabilities, so this is a minor annoyance. The ability to add buttons to the Quick Menu is a nice feature, as is the addition of Trust Center Controls and the much easier to locate Add-Ins or to tabs menu. The fact that Microsoft has improved the appearance of Word (and Office) is a big step forward, but more important are the many improvements in functionality. What Word lacks in aesthetics, it more than makes up for in functionality.

Adding Flair to Your Documents

The driving factor behind this new version of Word is the ability to create documents quickly and easily. With that in mind, the Office team added several features designed to make creating professional documents as easy as clicking a button. Well, it's not quite that easy, but it's certainly not as hard as it was in previous versions of Word. New theme, style, and graphics capabilities give you the tools you need, and if you need more versatility than the Ribbon offers, there are still toolbars that let you go beyond the basics.

Enhancing Documents with Fonts and Headings

Typography has to do with the various fonts and typefaces that are used in creating both print and electronic documents. How a font or typeface is created determines how easily it can be read, how it appears on the page or screen, and how it appears in print. There are teams of people that spend all of their time — sometimes for years at a time — designing and perfecting the fonts that you see in your Word program.

Word 2007 features six new fonts: Calibri, Cambria, Candara, Corbel, Consolas, and Constantia. Each of these fonts is designed to work well both in print and on-screen, but each performs differently in a different environment. For example, Consolas is designed for use in programming environments and Cambria is best used for on-screen reading.

In addition to the new fonts, there's a new way to apply text styles to your document, as well. On the Home tab, there's now a Style Set option (in addition to options for colors and fonts). As shown in Figure 13-4, the default text styles are grouped to allow you to enhance your documents without having to manually change every heading and block of text within the document.

Figure 13-4: Style Sets, colors, and fonts within a document can easily be changed by selecting a different style.

To preview how a style might appear in your document, place your pointer over the style name. The headings and text in the document will temporarily change to reflect the new style, as shown in Figure 13-5. Don't worry, it won't change permanently until you click on the style name. You can examine how all of the styles look without ever changing the first letter of your text.

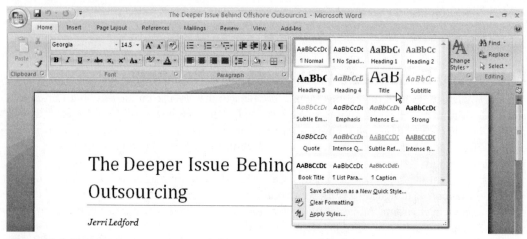

Figure 13-5: Placing your cursor over a style lets you preview a style before committing to it.

One thing you need to know about the style preview, however, is that in order for it to work properly you need to be using proper (and consistent) heading and text styles throughout your document. If you simply type a heading as bold or italics, it will only change as much as the body text changes, so you won't get a true image of what the headings in the document will look like.

Figure 13-6 shows that once you change styles, then the headings menu will automatically change to reflect the new style that you're using.

Figure 13-6: The headings menu automatically updates to reflect a change in styles.

Linking to Live Data from Charts, Diagrams, and Tables

One of the truly useful features of Word is the ability to link to data between documents. That includes sharing information between Word and Excel or PowerPoint as well as other Office programs.

The cornerstone of sharing between applications is the crown jewel of Office — the SmartArt graphics tools. These tools allow you to insert colorful, meaningful diagrams into your documents, as shown in Figure 13-7.

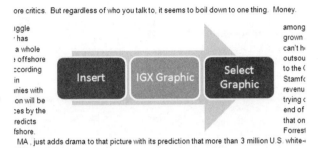

Figure 13-7: Insert diagrams into documents using the SmartArt graphics tools.

SmartArt graphics are a series of designs that illustrate processes or relationships visually. To use SmartArt graphics, select the Insert tab and then click the SmartArt Graphic button. You're taken to a dialog box where you can select the diagram that you want to use. Once you select the graphic that you want to include, you're taken to the Design tab. Use the tools on the Design tab to change layout, construction, colors, and styles for your graphic.

Charting and diagramming is also different in Word 2007. Using the Chart button on the Insert menu, you can insert a chart into any document that contains information from any spreadsheet you've previously created, as shown in Figure 13-8.

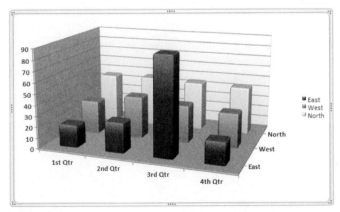

Figure 13-8: Use the Chart function to insert charts into your documents that contain data from Excel spreadsheets.

To insert a chart in a document, go to the Insert tab and click the Chart button. In the Create Chart dialog box, select the graphical chart representation that fits your needs, and click OK. The chart is inserted into your document, and then the default spreadsheet is opened for editing. Change the data in the spreadsheet to reflect your own data. The changes are immediately reflected in the chart.

Back in your Word document, when the chart is inserted into your document, you'll be taken to the Chart Tools smart tabs where you can change the design, layout, and format of your charts.

Inserting tables into your documents is equally as easy.

1. Place your cursor where you want the table to appear and then go to the Insert smart tab.

2. Click the Table button, and the Insert Table dialog box appears, as shown in Figure 13-9.

Highlight boxes with pointer to create chart   Live Preview

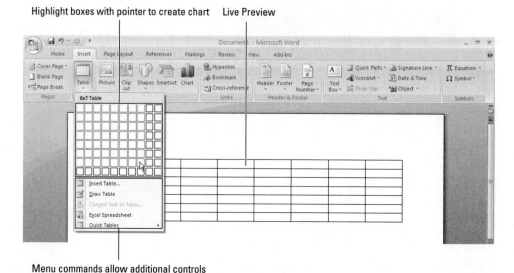

Menu commands allow additional controls

Figure 13-9: Insert tables into your documents using the Insert Table dialog box.

There is more than one way to insert a table. You can either drag your pointer over the small squares in the dialog box until your table is the size that you desire, or you can click the Insert Table command, and another Insert Table dialog box appears. This dialog box, shown in Figure 13-10, is one that you should be familiar with.

Figure 13-10: The Insert Table dialog box shown here was also used in previous versions of Word.

On the Table menu, you'll also find the option to draw a table or insert an Excel spreadsheet. There's also a Quick Table option that places a preformatted table into your document so you don't have to go through all of the headaches of formatting the table. If you choose not to use the preformatted tables, however, you can format any table that you insert into your document from the Table Tools Design smart tab that appears when you click inside a table.

Inserting Pictures and Drawings

No document is complete without the right illustrations to highlight the text. Word 2007 features the ability to insert pictures using the same options as previous versions of Word. And now there's also the option to add captions to your pictures with the click of a button.

To insert a caption:

1. Add your picture to the page, and make sure it's selected.

2. Go to the References tab and select Insert Caption.

3. A dialog box like the one shown in Figure 13-11 appears.

Figure 13-11: Provide the information for your figure captions in the Caption dialog box.

4. Add the required information to the dialog box and then click OK and the caption is inserted below your picture.

What's a little different in this version is the ability to insert drawings in your document. These aren't exactly what you think of when you think of drawings. Instead, this is where you can create your own grouping of shapes, with colors, shadows, and other effects that you design.

To create your own drawings:

1. Go to Insert → Shapes and select New Drawing Canvas from the bottom of the menu.

2. Select the shapes you want in your drawing and choose your formatting options from the Format tab that appears.

Embellishing Your Documents with Easy Effects

If you don't already appreciate the new design of Word, you will before you finish this section. Probably the most useful, and most exciting, new features of Word involve the ability to embellish your documents.

The ability to insert a cover page in your document is one of the best new features of Word. You'll find this option on the Insert tab, as shown in Figure 13-12. The cover page is a decorative top page for any document that you create, and Word has several nicely designed cover pages for you to choose from.

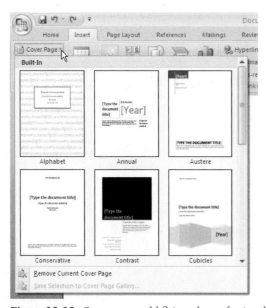

Figure 13-12: Cover pages add flair and a professional element to your documents.

Themes are a returning aspect of Word. The theme options are located on the Page Layout tab, and give you packaged options for colors that work together. Combining themes with Styles enables you to create a customized document design package; then creating a professional document is as simple as adding text and graphics.

One final effect that you might find useful is the Watermark. A watermark is a light background image over which the contents of a page are placed. In earlier versions of Word, adding a watermark was difficult because finding the correct commands and designing the watermark were time-consuming tasks. Now all you have to do to add a watermark to your documents is click a few buttons.

1. The Watermark option is located on the Page Layout tab. Select Watermark.

2. The menu shown in Figure 13-13 appears.

3. Select the watermark that you want to use and click OK. The watermark is inserted into the background of your document.

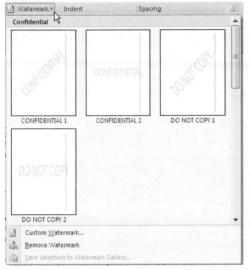

Figure 13-13: The Watermark menu lets you select from a variety
of predesigned watermarks to apply to the background of your document.

Inserting Special Characters

In many situations, a special character or set of characters is an important element within a document. For example, different countries use different currency symbols; on an English-language keyboard made for the United States, foreign symbols might be difficult to find. To make accessing these symbols easier, there's now a Symbol menu on the Insert tab.

To insert a special symbol into a document, all you need to do is select it from the list of available symbols. Currently there are 28 sets of symbols available in Word 2007, including currency symbols, some foreign languages, and mathematical operations. There's also a list of special characters such as copyright symbols and em spaces from which to choose.

Along the same lines, Word now also has an equation option. As Figure 13-14 shows, the Equation option allows you to insert the most frequently used equations in your text without having to waste precious time to find all of the correct symbols to do it.

Two other options fall loosely under the definition of special characters that you'll find useful. They are Quick Parts and the Signature Line. Quick Parts can be accessed on the Insert tab; these are selections of commonly used text, such as fields or page numbers, that you can insert with the click of a button rather than having to copy and paste the element each time you wish to enter it in a document. And the Signature Line is a quick tool represented by an icon to the right of the Quick Parts menu that can be used for creating a place for others to sign a document. For example, if you're creating a contract, use the signature-line command to quickly add a signature line to the document instead of having to fight with lines and tabs to get the lines spaced and placed properly.

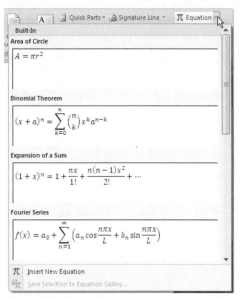

Figure 13-14: Use the equation menu to quickly insert any of the most commonly used equations into your documents.

Getting Things Organized

Organization within documents is essential to creating documents that have a clear, understandable purpose. It also helps to make those documents easier to read. There are several tools available to you to make creating an organized document easier.

Functions like bullets and numbers, tabs, and correction tools ensure that your document is uniform and as professional as you can make it. Keep reading to learn about how these elements are presented in Word 2007.

Using Bullets, Numbers, and References

Bullets and numbers have always been an element of Word. And in the past, they weren't too difficult to find — unless you needed to change the standard formatting of these elements. Then you could spend half a day just locating the commands you needed to make changes.

As part of improving the usability of Word, bullets and numbers are now found right on the Ribbon in the Home tab. Using these elements is as easy as clicking on the button that represents either bulleting or numbering and then selecting the options that you want to use.

If the style of bullet or numbering that you need isn't located in these predefined styles, then you can create your own style by selecting the Define New command from either menu. For example, if you choose to create a new bullet, select the bullet menu and then click on Define New Bullet. You're taken to the Define New Bullet dialog box where you can select the symbol, picture, or font that you want to use for a bullet. In that dialog box, you'll also find an option for defining how you want the bullet to be aligned.

In the same general category as bullets and numbers are references. All of the Word reference capabilities can be found on the References tab.

- **Footnotes:** Define footnote styles and insert footnotes into your documents using the Footnotes commands.

- **Citations:** Add sources or placeholders for sources using the Citations commands.

- **Bibliography:** Creating a bibliography is now much simpler. Use the Citations and Bibliography menus to manage bibliography entries.

- **Table of Figures:** Creating a table of figures means keeping up with all of the figures that you place in a document. That's not too difficult if you have only a few figures, but when there are dozens, this could be an onerous task. If you use the figure caption functions in Word, however, it's now as easy as clicking the Insert Table of Figures button, which is located in the Captions section of the tab, to create a complete figure table.

- **Cross Reference:** Click the Cross Reference button to add a cross reference to your document.

- **Mark Entry:** Create cross referencing or indexing points using the Mark Entry command, which is located in the Index section of the tab.

- **Insert Index:** To create an index in previous versions of Word, it almost felt like you needed a master's degree in library science with a minor in computer science. Use the Insert Index command in Word 2007 to quickly create an index for your document.

- **Mark Citation:** Mark a citation within your text using this command.

- **Table of Authorities:** Creating a table of authorities used to be a largely manual process. Now you can use the Table of Authorities dialog box to easily create a table of authorities for your document.

There are more tools for document creation available in Word 2007, but many of the tools that were available in previous versions of Word are also there. In the past, it was a matter of being able to find the commands and capabilities that you needed. Now those capabilities are much easier to find and to use, so you'll be using advanced features of Word in less time than it takes to pour your first cup of coffee.

Setting Tabs

Remember when the document ruler was briefly mentioned at the beginning of this chapter? Well, it's time to revisit that ruler, because that's where you're going to set your tabs.

Setting tabs in Word 2007 works just like it did in previous versions of Word; it's just a matter of finding the place to do it.

To set your tabs:

1. Expand the ruler by clicking on the ruler indicator at the top of the scroll bar on the right side of the page. This action expands both the horizontal and the vertical rulers. Once you have expanded your rulers, you'll notice there's a small box at the top-left corner of your work area. That box, as indicated in Figure 13-15, is your tab selection box.

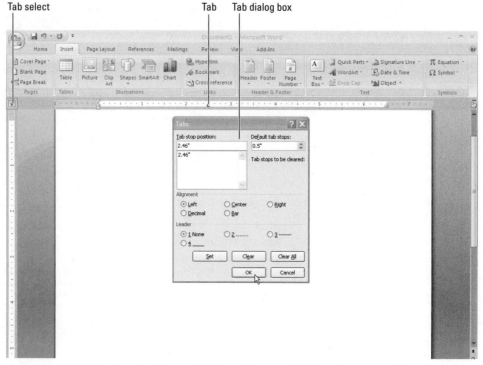

Figure 13-15: The horizontal ruler stays hidden unless you click the ruler command to expand it.

2. If you click the box, it will rotate between Left Tab, Middle Tab, and Right Tab.

3. To change the tab settings on your document, all you need to do is double-click to the left, in the middle, or to the right of the horizontal ruler. A small indicator, like the ones seen in the small box in the left corner, appears.

4. Click and hold the indicator and drag it to where you want the tab to stop.

5. You can double-click to add as many tabs as you need or use the Tabs dialog box to set tab properties, as indicated in Figure 13-15.

See, it's not so different from the way you've set tabs in the past. At least, once you figure out how to get to the ruler it's not so different.

Using Grammar and Spell Check

One of the difficulties with the new Ribbon menu system of Word 2007 is that at first it's difficult to find functions that you've been using for years. The proofing tools — spelling and grammar check among them — are some of those functions. Once you get a feel for the Ribbon navigation system of Word, though, it makes perfect sense where you'll find them.

The Grammar and Spell Check function can now be found in the Review tab of the Ribbon under the Proofing menu.

Working with Data

Word 2007 gives you a variety of options for working with data. Some of those options we've already covered including inserting various elements such as a table of figures or an index. In this buffet of usefulness that the developers at Microsoft have given us, however, there are still more tools to help you view data in different elements of a document.

Summarizing Documents

There are several ways to summarize a document. The table of figures or index are two of them. But an additional way is by using a table of contents. Creating a table of contents for your document is much easier now than it has ever been in the past.

To create a table of contents:

1. The Table of Contents menu is located in the References tab.

2. As shown in Figure 13-16, when you click on the Table of Contents button, you're shown a series of options for how you want your table of contents to appear.

Figure 13-16: The Table of Contents menu gives you options for the visual design of your table of contents.

3. Select one of the options and Word automatically creates a table of contents for you.

4. Make sure your cursor is where you want the table of contents for the document to be, because it will place this element into the document wherever your cursor happens to be.

You can create your table of contents at the beginning of your document creation, before you've put any text into the document, then as you add headings, you can click the Update Table button to update your table of contents to include the information that you've added to the document over time.

There are also some advanced table of contents options. One option allows you to create links in the table of contents that will jump readers to the different headings within a document. Another aligns all of the page numbers properly. And a third allows you to choose a format other than the one you're using for your document.

Creating Outlines

Outlines are valuable tools for monitoring the contents of a document, especially when there are dozens — or hundreds — of pages of information. But creating an outline from an existing document can be a royal pain. Word now has a feature, however, that makes creating an outline as simple as clicking a button.

The Outline command is location on the View tab. When you click the Outline button the document that you have open is switched to the Outline view, as shown in Figure 13-17. Don't stress the view change. You can switch it back by clicking on the Close Outline View button.

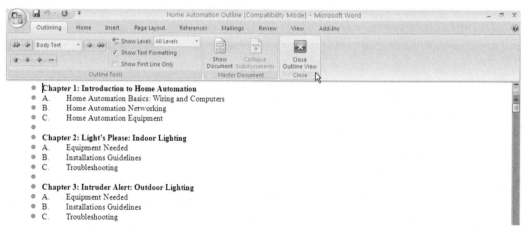

Figure 13-17: The Outline view lets you see an outline for your document based on the headings within the document.

You'll notice that the Outline view automatically switches you to a tab labeled Outlining. From this tab you can control how many headings are shown in your outline, how much text is shown in the outline, and you can even move headings up or down in the text if you feel they're in the wrong place. Use caution when moving headings, however, because the text following the headings is not moved with them.

Obtaining Research

On the Proofing menu (which can be found on the Review tab) there is an option named Research. This option helps you to find the research materials that you need while you're creating a document. Need statistics on the number of broadband users in the United States? The Research pane, shown in Figure 13-18, is the place to find it.

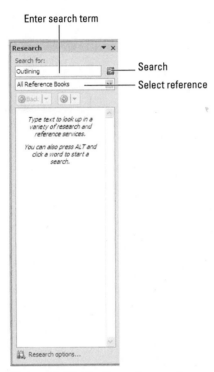

Figure 13-18: The Research pane gives you options for finding research materials to support your document.

When you open the Research pane, you should see a search box and below it a drop-down menu where you can select the reference book you want to search. Select a reference (or the All Reference Books option) and then click the green arrow to perform a reference search.

There's also a Research options link in the Research pane. This link lets you customize the resources that are used during research activities. You can also use this link to set parental controls on the research service and to remove research references that are dated.

Working Collaboratively

There are always projects that require collaboration on various documents. When you're collaborating on a document, there's always the risk of having something go wrong and losing part of the information. Microsoft has addressed some of those collaboration issues in the newest version of Office. Of course, some of your favorite collaborative features are still available, but you may have to look a little to find them.

Tracking Changes

Tracking Changes is one of the most useful tools during collaboration. The Track Changes feature of Word makes it possible for one document to be used or reviewed by several people. Each person who makes changes to that document with Track Changes on is assigned a color, and all of the changes or comments that they make in that document are made in that color. Then the person who is controlling the document can accept or reject changes as they see fit.

Word 2007 still has all of these features, and you'll find them in the Review tab. This is a good example of how Word has been redesigned to be easier to use. Instead of having to dig into a drop-down menu to find the Track Changes options or to activate the Track Changes toolbar, all of your collaboration options are located on this one tab. They're easy to find and using them requires only a point and click.

Comparing and Combining Document Files

Two more useful collaborative features are the ability to compare shared documents (Figure 13-19) and the ability to combine multiple documents. Both of these options can be found in the Compare menu on the Review tab. Click the Compare menu and then you can select two documents to combine as shown in Figure 13-20.

Figure 13-19: Select two documents to compare.

Figure 13-20: Select two documents to combine.

Mailings

Mail merge. The very term strikes dread in the hearts of even the best Word users. The Mail Merge function of Word has always been difficult to use in the past. Fortunately, Microsoft's developers finally realized that mail merge is much more difficult than it needs to be and (hallelujah) they've finally created a version that is user friendly. Of course, the other mailings tools are still available, and they're easier to find now, too.

Creating Mailings

How many letters do you write in any given day? Wouldn't it be great if you could automate that process a bit? Word 2007 has some great new features that help you do just that. No longer do you have to search high and low to find what you need, either. Everything you need to create mailings, prepare envelopes and labels, and perform mail merges is right on the Mailings tab.

When you first navigate to the Mailings tab, you'll notice that only four of the buttons on the tab are active. The other tabs become active as you perform mailings tasks, but for now, let's focus on Envelopes and Labels.

In past versions of Word, the Envelopes and Labels option was buried in the Tools menu. Now they're right there on the Ribbon. Easy to get to and they work just like they have in the past. Click one of the buttons, fill in your address or label information, and click Print or Add to Document. There's no steep learning curve with these functions.

Starting Mail Merge

Fortunately, there's no real learning curve with Mail Merge, either. To begin a Mail Merge, click the Start Mail Merge button on the Ribbon. A menu appears with several options for you to choose from.

- **Letters:** Write letters to be used in Mail Merges.
- **E-mail Messages:** Create e-mails to be used in Mail Merges.
- **Envelopes:** Create envelopes.
- **Labels:** Create labels.
- **Directory:** Create a Mail Merge Directory.

■ **Normal Word Document:** Create a Word document that's not specifically designed for Mail Merges.

■ **Step by Step Mail Merge Wizard:** A wizard interface that walks you through creating a Mail Merge.

You can choose to create your Mail Merge manually or use the wizard. The wizard walks you through six steps, the result of which is your final Mail Merge document. If you've never had experience with creating a Mail Merge, this wizard will make your life so easy you'll wonder why Microsoft didn't come up with this idea sooner. In fact, it did. It just wasn't nearly as uncomplicated in past iterations.

Write and Insert Fields

The Write & Insert Fields menu is another new feature in the Mailings menu that should make your life a little easier. As you can see in Figure 13-21, the options on this menu help you to quickly see what are merge fields and to make changes to your merge document without making you develop the ability to leap tall buildings in a single bound.

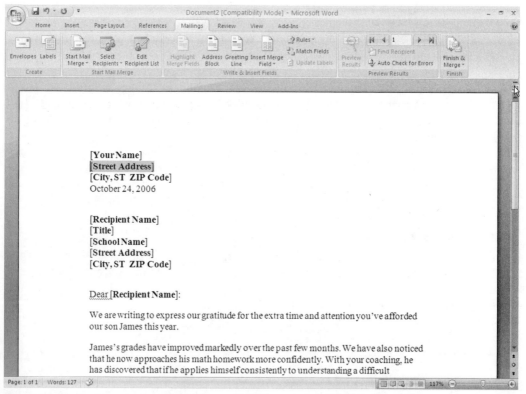

Figure 13-21: The Write & Insert menu becomes fully functional when there's an active document open in the Word window.

The first button on the Write & Insert Fields menu is the Highlight Merge Fields button. Click it to see the merge fields in your document highlighted. You can use this feature to know what you shouldn't change or what you should format properly for the merge during the creation process.

Next is the Address Block button. This function lets you create the format and location of the addresses that you want to include in your Mail Merge. Once you've used the Address Block option to format your address, Word will insert addresses from your merge list.

The Greeting Line button works the same way the Address Block button works. You select the formatting, Word supplies the changing text.

Insert Merge Field is the option you use to quickly add a merge field to your document. As shown in Figure 13-22, you can select from a list of over 25 fields including names, address components, and e-mail addresses.

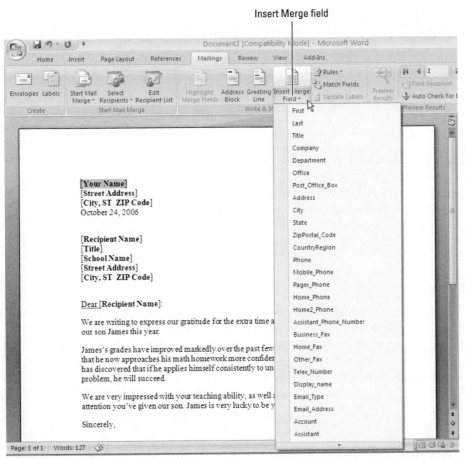

Figure 13-22: Use the Insert Merge Field menu to add additional merge fields to your document.

Finally, there are three additional options on this menu. The Rules option lets you set rules for your mail merge. So, you can merge or skip records and filter the ones you want included or ignored during your mail merge.

The Match Fields option lets you tell Word what a field you have designed corresponds with. Maybe you've set up your contacts so that the field title Work refers to the contact's business phone number. Use the Match Fields command to tell Word how your titles translate into the Mail Merge application.

The Update Labels button does exactly what you might expect; it's a command to update labels that you may have created. This is a useful feature if you change your Mail Merge database after you set up your labels.

All of these operations are point-and-click. They make it much easier for you to build and make changes to a Mail Merge application.

Previewing Results

Once you've created your mailing, it's always a good idea to preview the results to ensure there are no mistakes in it. The Preview Results options let you see what your merged documents will look like and they let you find specific recipients (for changes or removal). You can also autocheck for errors in your mailing.

These features help you save time and prevent possibly embarrassing errors in your Mail Merge documents.

Finishing Documents

When you've created your Mail Merge mailing and checked for errors, then it's time to finish and merge the documents. When you click the Finish & Merge button on the Mailings tab you're given the option to edit individual documents, print your merged documents, or create the merged e-mails.

Summary

There are so many great features in Word 2007 that it's hard to do them all justice. This chapter could go on forever, but that wouldn't do you any good at all, now would it? A few more features of Word should be covered, but we're going to get to them in the next chapter. For now, you've learned about many of the major feature and function changes and additions in Word 2007. You should feel comfortable working through the Ribbon and all of its associated tabs, and you should have a good understanding of how to use these new features. In Chapter 14, we'll hit the rest of Word's new features.

Chapter 14

Exploring Additional New Features in Word

Document formatting is at least half of creating great, professional looking documents. We can't give you the ins and outs of writing in a way that moves readers and provides information in an easy-to-digest style. That is well beyond the scope of this book. (There are many good books on the subject, however, if you need a refresher course.) But we can give you insight on the tools that make creating those documents a snap. You'll see that using formatting options, the Document Inspector, Quick Parts, the document information panel, and the floaty will make creating professional documents easier, faster, and more efficient than ever before.

Using the Floaty

Floaty — there's a word with a whole cadre of visual implications. A floaty could be that small bobber on a fishing line. "Dad, my floaty keeps disappearing under the water."

It could be those floatation devices that you put on your child before going swimming. "Sweetie, you have to wear your floaties if you're getting in the pool."

Maybe it's referring to those little spots that seem to float in front of your eyes when you're staring at nothing in particular. "Doc, I see floaties."

And we won't even discuss the floaties that children leave behind when they're sharing your drink.

All of these things could be considered floaties, but they have nothing to do with Word. The floaty that we're referring to here is something entirely different. This floaty is actually called the Mini Toolbar. It's a small, unobtrusive toolbar that pops up when you select text within a document, and it's affectionately earned the name of "Floaty" because it floats around, appearing only where you're currently working. The purpose of the Mini Toolbar is to make formatting faster and easier to accomplish. It's a shortcut if you will, that keeps you from having to move your pointer all the way to the top of the page and switch tabs to format a section of selected text.

Accessing the Mini Toolbar

Finding the Mini Toolbar the first time can be a little tricky. Unless you've never selected text before, you've probably stumbled on it at one time or another, but you may never have noticed it. That's because, as you can see in Figure 14-1, it barely shows up at all when you first select a section of text to work with; it's nearly translucent.

Mini Toolbar appears when you select a portion of the text

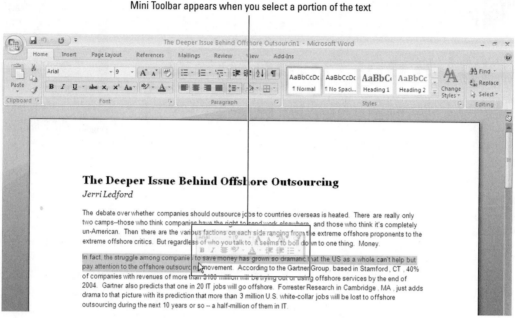

Figure 14-1: The Mini Toolbar appears translucent when you select a portion of text.

To get a better look at the Mini Toolbar place your pointer over it. It will darken, making it easier to see (and use), as shown in Figure 14-2.

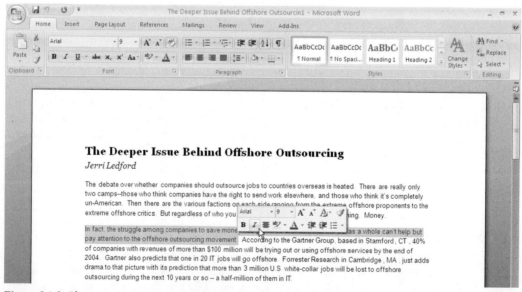

Figure 14-2: Place your pointer over the Mini Toolbar to make it darken.

The best part of the Mini Toolbar is that if it's something you don't want to use, it will disappear completely when you move your pointer away from it. And it won't come back for the remaining duration of your current text selection. So it's not popping back up on top of your text, driving you crazy while you're trying to work. But just because you may choose not to use it doesn't mean you've turned it off. It will come back the next time you highlight a text selection.

Applying Formatting from the Mini Toolbar

Now that you know how to get to the Mini Toolbar, how do you use it to format your text? The simple answer is in the same way that you've always used formatting commands to format text. When you select a portion of your text and the Mini Toolbar appears, then all you need to do is select the formatting option that you want, and the text is changed accordingly. The options on the Mini Toolbar include the following:

- **Font:** Changes your font style or size.

- **Increase Size:** Increases the size of the selected text.

- **Decrease Size:** Decreases the size of the selected text.

- **Change Quick Styles:** Takes you to the Quick Styles selection tool so that you can change styles quickly.

- **Format Painter:** Lets you select formatting from the selected text to apply to a different text selection.

- **Bold:** Emphasizes text with bold formatting.

- **Italics:** Emphasizes text with italics formatting.

- **Centering:** Centers the selected text. If the text is in the middle of a paragraph, this option formats the whole paragraph.

- **Highlight:** Highlights the selected text.

- **Text Color:** Changes the color of the selected text.

- **Decrease Indent:** Decreases indent for selected text.

- **Increase Indent:** Increases the indent for selected text.

- **Bullet:** Enables you to choose from bullet list options for the selected text.

The purpose behind the Mini Toolbar is to save you some time. For example, if you're working on the Mailings tab, you don't want to have to flip back over to the Home tab to format a section of the text in a document you're working on. The Mini Toolbar makes it easier for you to make those formatting changes without jumping from one place to another.

Other Formatting Options

If you're a keyboard formatter and not a mouse formatter, you might find the mouse controls — even something as useful as the Mini Toolbar — to be a little cumbersome. Microsoft anticipated this and made Word 2007 backwards compatible with existing keyboard shortcuts. So, all those shortcuts you've memorized over the years will still work for you. Additionally, there are a few new shortcuts that might make your life a little easier. And the good news is, you don't have to memorize them to use them.

This new shortcut feature can be found by pressing the ALT key on your keyboard. When you do, all of the ALT commands for the tab that you're working in appear, as shown in the accompanying figure.

Press the ALT command key to access the function

Press the ALT command key on the keyboard to access the desired function.

Once the commands appear on the screen, you can use them to perform most of the functions that you would ordinarily perform with a keyboard.

Getting Information from Super ToolTips

ToolTips are a mainstay of Office. In older versions of Office, you could place your pointer over a command or button and the name of that command or button would appear below it in a small box. That's a ToolTip. But what if you put those ToolTips on steroids? What could you do with them then?

The Office team asked that same question, and the decision was to make ToolTips more useful for users. What Office 2007 uses for ToolTips now is called a Super ToolTip. This is a ToolTip, like the one shown in Figure 14-3, that not only shows you the title of the command, but also additional information on how to use that particular option.

Each Super ToolTip includes the title of the command, a brief description of how it can be used, and in some cases, a picture. The purpose behind the picture is to give you a visual representation of how a tool will change your document or some element of you document.

You may still have to use Office Help from time to time, and if you do, some ToolTips list the commands used to find out more in Help. But for the most part, these Super ToolTips should cut down on the time you spend jumping from your document to the Help section.

Super ToolTips provide more information
than previous versions of ToolTips did

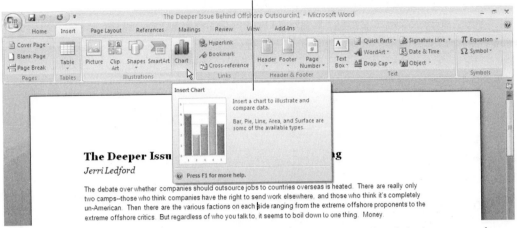

Figure 14-3: Super ToolTips cut down on the amount of time you spend searching help documents to learn how a feature works.

Using the Document Inspector

How many times in the past have you completed a document only to find that there was some hidden element still in it that turned up later at the most inopportune time? Here's a good example. We heard recently about a gentleman who was trying to convert a Word document to a PDF document. During the conversion, the PDF document was rendering with unexplained line breaks in the text.

This guy spent hours trying to figure it out. Finally, he turned to a group of peers for suggestions, all of which involved a very long, drawn-out process of removing and then reinserting all of the formatting in the document. Given that the document was well over 100 pages in length, that proved to be an arduous task.

In the end, the culprit turned out to be some hidden line breaks in the Word document that were throwing the formatting for the PDF document off.

What if this poor guy could have used some feature of Word to find and remove the unwanted page breaks? He would have saved a lot of time and one seriously massive headache. That's what the Document Inspector is supposed to do.

This new feature of Word reviews your document, searching for unwanted items — like comments, revision, document information, headers and footers, and other unwanted information — that it can then remove. It's part of a group of document finishing tools included in Word 2007. You can find the Document Inspector by going to File Button → Prepare → Inspect Document, as shown in Figure 14-4.

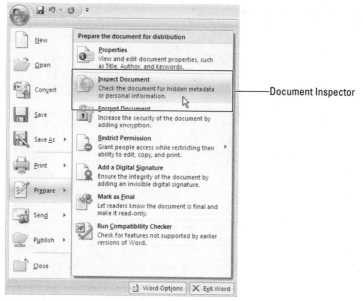

Document Inspector

Figure 14-4: The Document Inspector searches for and removes unwanted items from your document.

What You Can Find

Figure 14-5 shows the dialog box for the Document Inspector. As you can see, you have the option to search your document for various items, including:

- Comments, Revisions, Versions, and Annotations
- Document Properties and Personal Information
- Custom XML Data
- Headers, Footers, and Watermarks
- Hidden Text

Using the Document Inspector, you can find and remove these items, some of which could potentially threaten your security or the security of your organization. Additionally, removing unwanted items helps to prevent future issues with content such as the one mentioned earlier in this section.

What You Can Get Rid Of

The Document Inspector searches your document for the items that you've chosen to search for (and you can select or deselect any of those items), shows a report, as Figure 14-6 illustrates, that tells what in those categories has been found, and gives the option of removing the found items. Unfortunately, the Document Inspector may find items you don't want removed and the report doesn't show details about what is found. Use caution when selecting the Remove All option.

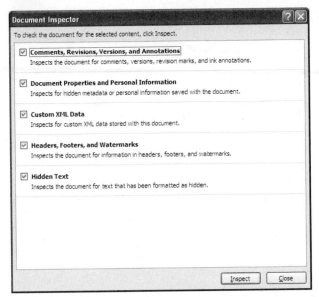

Figure 14-5: The Document Inspector saves you from unwanted surprises in the future.

Figure 14-6: The Document Inspector tells you if there are elements that should be removed from your document.

Note that once you tell the Document Inspector to fix anything it finds that should be removed, you can reinspect the document to double-check.

Caution

Be aware that some of the items that the Document Inspector removes from your document will be unrecoverable. You should always save a copy of your draft document and check it thoroughly before replacing it with a future draft.

Document scrubbing is becoming more and more crucial as organizations and individuals learn more about identity theft, hacking, corporate espionage, and all the other bad things that can happen if the wrong data is released into the world. The Document Inspector is a tool that helps you protect yourself and your organization.

Using Quick Parts

One very interesting new piece of Word 2007 is a function called Quick Parts. How often do you repeat the same formatting — for example, page numbering or inserting a specific field or title — for a specific section of a document? Even though you spend only a few seconds on it each time, those seconds start to add up.

But if you could create or select from a group of parts that were already created and formatted, not only would document creation go easier, but you'd save a little time. That's the promise of Quick Parts.

Quick Parts are small snippets of formatting or text that you use repeatedly in the documents that you create every day. You'll find the Quick Parts option in the Text section of the Insert tab on the Ribbon.

Word 2007 is already equipped with some Quick Parts. From the Quick Parts toolbar you can access the following options:

- **Document Property:** Lets you insert properties such as Author, Category, Comments, Keywords, Status, Subject, and Title.

- **Field:** Allows you to quickly insert a field into your document. When you select the Field option you're taken to the Field dialog box, shown in Figure 14-7. In that box, select the field you want to insert in your document.

- **Building Blocks Organizer:** Lets you manage and edit the Building Blocks in the Quick Parts section. As you can see in Figure 14-8, there's already a considerable list of available Building Blocks, but you can edit and add to those according to your needs as you're creating documents.

- **Save Selection to Quick Part Gallery:** If you're working in a document that already has building blocks that you would like to apply to another document, you can save those documents to the Quick Part Gallery using this option. Simply highlight the part you want to add to the gallery and then select Save Selection to Quick Part Gallery from the Quick Parts menu. Also remember to select descriptive options for the new Building Block. Then the next time you want to apply that building block to a document it's only a click away.

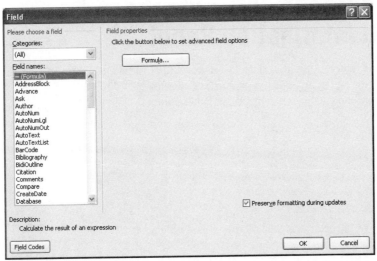

Figure 14-7: Choose the field you want to insert in your document from the Field dialog box.

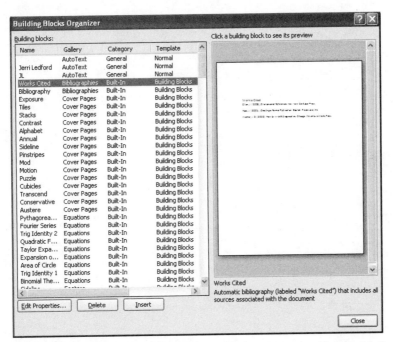

Figure 14-8: The Building Blocks Organizer lets you organize and edit Quick Parts.

Quick Parts are designed to make document creation faster and easier. If you use a lot of repetitive elements in the documents that you create, store them in the Quick Part Gallery for faster access.

Managing Documents with the Document Information Panel

One additional feature that you might find useful in Word 2007 is the Document Information Panel. This feature lets you manage how your documents are handled by Word. To find the feature, go to the Developer tab and then click on the Document Panel option, as shown in Figure 14-9.

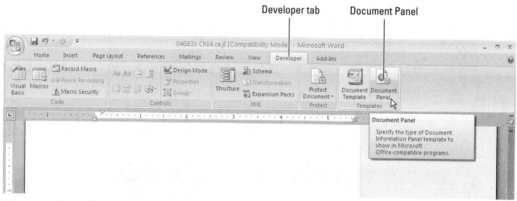

Figure 14-9: The Document Information Panel is located on the Developer tab.

Using the Document Information Panel, shown in Figure 14-10, you can specify a custom information template for your document.

Figure 14-10: The Document Information Panel lets you specify a custom template for your document.

This is not the same kind of template that you would expect if you were formatting your document. This information template works for the classification of documents and gives you the ability to add information such as Author, Title, Subject, Keywords, Category, Status, and Comments, as Figure 14-11 illustrates.

Click for Advanced options

Figure 14-11: Use the Document Information Panel to tag documents with specific search information.

There are also some advanced features available on the Document Information Panel. If you use the drop-down menu shown in Figure 14-11, you can select the Advanced option. This option opens a dialog box, like the one shown in Figure 14-12.

Figure 14-12: Use the Advanced Option to add more detailed information about a document.

In the dialog box that opens there are several tabs to which you can add or view information:

- **General:** The General tab shows general information about the document, including the file name, document name, size, location, and dates of creation and modification.

- **Summary:** Using the Summary tab, you can summarize the document for searching and storage including entering information such as Title, Subject, Author, Manager, Company, Category, Keywords, Comments, Hyperlink Base, Template used, and you also have the option of saving a Preview Picture of the document.

- **Statistics:** The Statistics tab is especially useful if you're working on document creation in a group environment. This tab shows you information such as when the document was created, when it was modified, when it was last accessed, when it was last printed, who it was last saved by, what revision number the document is, and the total editing time that's gone into the document. There's also a Statistics box that shows the number of pages, paragraphs, lines, words, characters, and characters including spaces are in the document.

- **Contents:** The Contents tab lets you include specific content from the document in the Document Information Panel.

- **Custom:** The Custom tab is probably one of the most useful tabs in this dialog box. On this tab, you can set customized tagging and information fields that reflect the needs of your organization. For example, you can choose to add a client field to your document that will allow you to search for documents by client. Fill in the information in the required fields and click Add and the new field is added to your document.

Once you've set the tagging features that you want your document to have, then you can choose to have them applied to your document every time it is opened and on the initial save so that the information stays up to date.

Summary

Word offers many features that are designed to give you more control and to work faster in your existing environment. The Mini Toolbar gives you the most common formatting tips, right where you need. And additional formatting options are nearby.

Don't worry if you forget what everything does, either. The new Super ToolTips in Word 2007 make it easy for you to identify the buttons and commands on the toolbar. Even the Document Information Panel is designed with your needs in mind.

This new feature of Word is designed to save you time when it comes to using metadata to tag your documents. The world of metadata is complex, and you probably don't want to go into a lot of detail about it in this book. However, if you want to learn more about metadata tagging, there are many great books on the topic.

Part VI

Presenting with PowerPoint

Chapter 15
Performing Common Tasks in PowerPoint

Chapter 16
Exploring Additional New Features in PowerPoint

Chapter 15

Performing Common Tasks in PowerPoint

Microsoft PowerPoint 2007 has a whole new look and feel. At first glance it looks very similar to Word 2007. But there are a few differences. All of the common tasks that you've completed in the past can still be done in this new version, but additional features like the Slide Library make it easier than ever to create and use effective, professional presentations.

The key word here is easier. In this chapter, you'll learn about creating presentations, working with objects and animations, collaborating, and sharing — all with the new PowerPoint interface. The new interface makes it much easier to accomplish complicated tasks that used to take forever to complete. A new point-and-click design puts features that you had to search for in the past right in plain sight when you need them. And new tools for creating and using graphics let you link your PowerPoint presentation to other data sources, too.

Exploring the Interface

Of all the changes Microsoft made to the Office 2007 programs, the changes to PowerPoint 2007 are the most exciting. Previous versions of PowerPoint were not at all user-friendly. Many of the functions were lost in drop-down menus or hidden on toolbars, making it difficult to create the presentations you envisioned.

The changes to PowerPoint 2007 are similar in appearance and function to the changes in Word 2007. Drop-down menus and toolbars have been replaced by the Ribbon navigational structure that follows the order in which Microsoft has learned that users most commonly perform tasks.

The result is a program that is much easier to use. You no longer need to waste time floundering around the different menus looking for a specific function. All functions, tools, and commands are now very visual and contextual. When you insert a graphic into your presentation, the appropriate menu appears and all the tools you need to create a professional image are just a mouse-click away.

Understanding PowerPoint's New Look

The new interface that you explored in Word 2007 is back in PowerPoint 2007. The Ribbon navigational structure has replaced the drop-down menus of the past. You'll also find the Quick Access Toolbar at the top of the window, near the Office Button, and the slide sorter is on the bottom-right corner of the page. These controls are illustrated in Figure 15-1.

File menu   Quick Access Toolbar

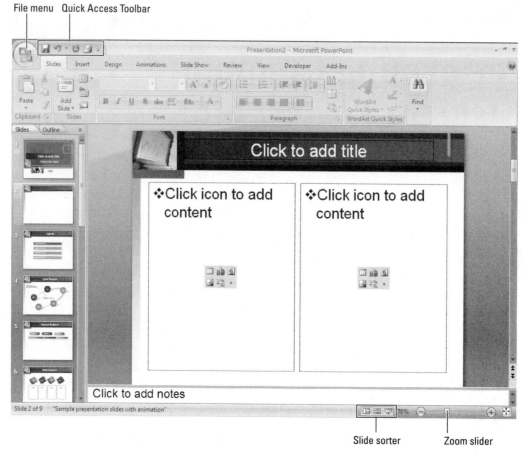

Figure 15-1: Intuitive navigation is one of the new features of PowerPoint 2007.

New Tools and Features

There are a host of new tools and features available in PowerPoint. For example, when you open the program you're automatically taken to the Home tab where you have a single blank slide available and buttons located in the Ribbon to add more slides.

By studying users' habits, Microsoft has discovered that this is usually the first task that users undertake when they open PowerPoint. The remaining tabs are arranged in the order in which they are most frequently used.

Here are some additional new features and tools:

- **Quick formatting options:** You have several formatting options in PowerPoint. The Home tab gives you the controls that you need to quickly create and format slides. From the Insert tab you can add a variety of graphics, and from the Design tab you can quickly change the look and feel of your presentation.

- **Contextual menus for tables and charts:** Contextual menus put everything in context, so if you're working with graphs or charts, appropriate menus appear for those functions. If you're reviewing your document, you're taken to an appropriate menu for that. PowerPoint puts the tools you need in front of you when you need them.

- **Layout and theme options:** Apply existing layouts and themes or create your own with a few mouse-clicks. And using the Live Preview option, you can view these changes before you commit to them.

- **Animation and effects:** Animation and effects have never been easier to apply to your presentations. Use the Animations tab to quickly add animation and effects to your presentation, and if you don't find what you're looking for there, create your own.

- **New presentation options:** The new presentation options in PowerPoint make the program more useful than it's ever been. If you've ever wished you could run a presentation on multiple computers, you're in luck. Now, using the options in the Slide Show Set Up, you can set your presentations to be viewed on multiple monitors or you can change the way the presentation is viewed: as presented by a speaker, as viewed by an individual, or as browsed at a kiosk.

- **Graphics tools:** The graphic tools in PowerPoint are more powerful than ever. When you add a graphic to your presentation, menus that help you design and format your graphic automatically appear. When you've finished formatting your graphics, the tabs disappear so they aren't cluttering your Ribbon. Don't worry, though. Getting them back is as easy as double-clicking on the graphic.

- **Publishing options:** Another new feature in PowerPoint is the ability to publish presentations to a slide library, package them for disk, and publish to a SharePoint server. These publishing options give you more control than ever for using your presentations in a way that works with your needs.

- **Finalization tools:** Finalization tools help you increase the security of your documents. Add digital signatures, inspect the document, or restrict permissions using the Finalize option on the File menu.

All of the new features of PowerPoint are designed with one purpose: to make it quick and easy for you to create powerful, professional presentations. You can draw from a library of prepared slides or create your own custom slides. Templates make it easy to create a presentation on the fly, and you'll find that creating your own templates is easier then ever before. It's all part of the plan to make it easier for you to use PowerPoint to achieve professional results.

The new tools and features are also much easier to find, because they're no longer buried out of sight. Live Preview lets you see results before you commit to them. Want to insert a chart in your presentation and use data from an existing Excel spreadsheet to populate it? It's easy to do using PowerPoint's graphics tools. And it's all part of the grand (re)design: Make it easy to use.

Customizing the Interface

Changing the PowerPoint user interface is about the same as changing the user interface in Word, but you'll find that some of the options are different. Some of the customization you can do is aesthetic, but some functional customization is available, too.

As with Word, customization starts in the File menu, which is located behind the Office button, as shown in Figure 15-2.

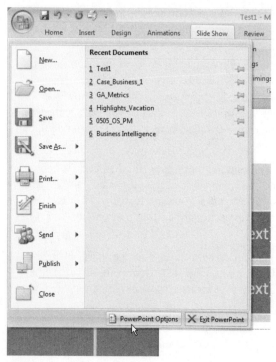

Figure 15-2: Select PowerPoint Options to customize the PowerPoint user interface and other options.

The customization options in PowerPoint include the following:

▪ **Popular:** Use the Popular menu to change the look and feel of your PowerPoint program. Here you can add or remove tabs from the Ribbon, change the color scheme of your PowerPoint skin, enable or disable certain functions, and change your user name, initials, and language settings.

▪ **Proofing:** Manage your correcting and formatting options from here. Those options include autocorrection settings, spelling correction options for all Office programs, and spelling options for PowerPoint.

- **Save:** Manage how (and where) your documents are saved. Saving options include backup information, draft locations, and fidelity preservation for document sharing.

- **Proofing:** Manage how AutoCorrect behaves in Publisher and in Office.

- **Advanced:** All of your advanced functions can be found on this screen. Set options for editing, displaying editing elements or document content, accessibility, and compatibility using this menu. There are also additional options that occur in other menus as well. Those include Print, Save, Preserve Fidelity, Grammar, and General Options.

- **Customization:** Use the Customization menu to change what's included in your Quick Access Toolbar and to create or change keyboard shortcuts. The Quick Access Toolbar is located on the top-left of the page, next to the Office Button. This toolbar lets you quickly access some of the most used functions of PowerPoint such as Save, Undo, Repeat, and Quick Print.

- **Add-Ins:** View and manage your add-ins from this screen.

- **Trust Center:** This is one of the new features of Office. The Trust Center is where you select the options for the protection of your documents and the security of your PC. You'll find options here for advanced Trust Center settings that include managing publishers, locations, add-ins, ActiveX controls, macro settings, document Action Bar settings, and privacy options.

Caution

It's not recommended that you change any of the options in the Trust Center. These options are pre-set to the most secure settings for your protection. Changing the settings could result in putting your personal information at risk.

- **Resources:** Additional resources are located on this page of the PowerPoint Options dialog box. These aren't customization links but instead are links to Office Online, Office activation, updates, the diagnostics program, contact information for Microsoft, and security and privacy information and policies.

If you don't happen to be one of the people that likes the Windows Blue that's the default background color for all of the Office programs, you can change it.

1. Go to File → PowerPoint Options.

2. In the PowerPoint Options window that appears, select Personalize.

3. Click the Color Scheme drop-down menu, as shown in Figure 15-3.

4. Select the desired color and click OK.

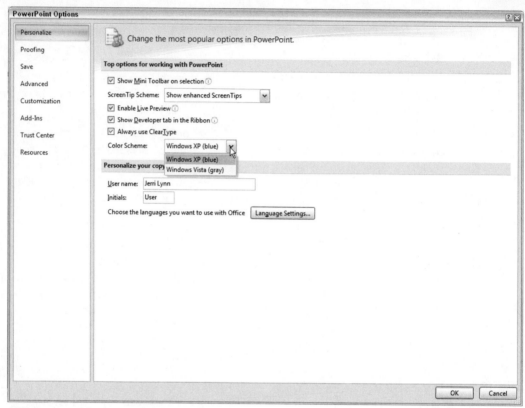

Figure 15-3: Change the background color of PowerPoint using the PowerPoint Options menu.

Note

The ability to switch between the blue, gray, and black color schemes in Office makes for a change of pace if you get bored working in the same environment; you should know, however, that when you change the background color in one program, you change the background color in all Office programs.

It's not a customization feature, but the View toolbar, shown in Figure 15-4, lets you change the way you see the PowerPoint presentation that you're working on. This toolbar is located in the lower-right corner of the PowerPoint window, and gives you the ability to quickly switch between normal view, slide sorter view, and slide show view. The zoom slider is also located in this menu along with the control that lets you fit the presentation to your current window size.

Figure 15-4: Change the view of the presentation using the View toolbar.

Creating Presentations

The new interface for PowerPoint seems drastically different on the surface, and to some extent, it is. However, it's a good different. It's easy to acclimate yourself to the changes, and once you get comfortable with them you'll be ready to begin creating great presentations.

Creating a presentation is much more streamlined in PowerPoint 2007 than it was in previous versions of PowerPoint. When you open the program, a single slide is shown; this slide is the basis for a new presentation. You can use that single slide and build upon it, or if you prefer you can choose one of several new templates, use existing templates, or build your own templates. PowerPoint is flexible and backward compatible, so you won't lose everything you did in the past.

Choosing a Presentation Template

The fastest way to create a new presentation is to use an existing PowerPoint template. As with previous versions of PowerPoint, a few templates come installed with the program. Additional templates can be downloaded from the Microsoft Office Web site, and PowerPoint 2007 makes that even easier than in the past. Presentation options give you the flexibility to create your own presentation from a single blank slide, or to use new templates or templates from previous versions of PowerPoint.

To create a presentation from a template:

1. Go to File → New.

2. The New Presentation dialog box appears, as shown in Figure 15-5. Select a presentation option: blank presentation, a PowerPoint 2007 template, or an existing template from a previous version of PowerPoint.

3. Click Create.

Figure 15-5: The New Presentation dialog box contains all the template options for creating a new presentation.

Microsoft improved the usability of downloading templates in this version of PowerPoint, too. As Figure 15-6 shows, online templates now appear in the New Presentation dialog box. You can browse these templates without having to open a Web browser and navigate to the Microsoft site. And downloading them is easy. Select the template you want to download and click Download. When the download completes, the presentation (or slide) opens and you can save it to your computer or begin using it to create a new presentation.

Figure 15-6: Online templates are shown in the New Presentation dialog box.

Note

To view templates that are located online, make sure you have an active Internet connection. If your Internet connection is not active, you'll see the option to use templates from online, however, when you try to access them you'll receive an error message.

Using Slide Libraries

One other option that you have for creating a presentation is to use a deck of slides, or a single slide from several decks from a local slide library. A slide library is a group of presentations that have been saved to your SharePoint server for use across the organization. Any presentation can be saved as part of a slide library.

Slide libraries cut down on the amount of content that you have to recreate. Rather than repeatedly creating the same slides, you can store them in the slide library and then pull one slide or a whole presentation into a new presentation. And you can link the slides in your presentation to their copies on the server so that any changes made are reproduced to the copy of the presentation that you're using.

Slide libraries are managed by SharePoint Server 2007, so if you don't have SharePoint installed, the slide libraries won't be available to you.

Formatting Text

Whether you're using a template to create your presentation or creating a presentation from a blank slide, there may come a time when you want to change the text on all the slides within the presentation. Maybe you're using a presentation that was created and run through two test groups before you began using it. Your test groups liked the presentation, but the most common suggestion from both groups was to make the text more readable.

1. Place your cursor within the text, anywhere in the presentation.

2. Go to the Design tab.

3. Select the Theme Fonts drop-down menu, as shown in Figure 15-7.

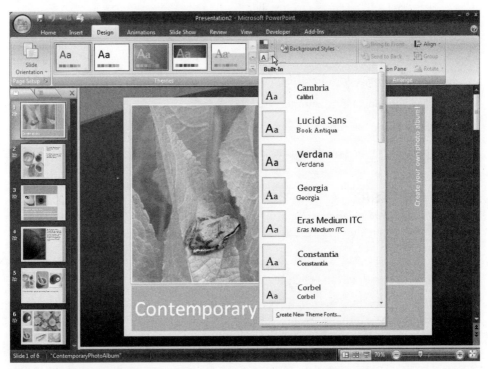

Figure 15-7: Use Theme Fonts to change the fonts within an entire presentation.

4. Choose the font that you want to apply to the presentation. When you put your mouse pointer over a font, the Live Preview function shows you how fonts will look in your presentation before you commit to them.

USING FORMATTING TOOLS

The appearance of the text in your presentation has to perform a specific function; it has to convey information without being distracting. To do this, you may need to use multiple formats within a single presentation. Fortunately, all of the formatting tools that you've used in the past are still available to you.

The main font menu on the Home tab is your all purpose formatting menu. This menu gives you all of the standard options, such as font type, font size, bold, italics, and underline. But what if you need something that's not standard?

In that case, there are two places to where additional formatting tools are available. The first is on the Home tab. In addition to the standard formatting options, you'll also find a WordArt menu on this tab. The WordArt menu gives you the option to add and edit WordArt in your presentation.

There's also a Paragraph menu on the Home tab. This menu allows you to use formatting options such as bullets and numbers, paragraph styles, fill colors, and line spacing to format the text on your slides.

Another option is the Text menu on the Insert tab. On this tab there's a Text menu that gives you several additional options for adding and formatting text:

- **Text Box:** Add a text box to any slide.
- **Header & Footer:** Add headers and/or footers to the slides in a presentation.
- **WordArt:** Select a WordArt style to apply to selected text.
- **Date & Time:** Insert the date and/or time into a slide.
- **Slide Number:** Insert a number into a slide.
- **Symbol:** Add a symbol to text on a slide.
- **Object:** Insert an object (such as a PDF document) into your presentation.

ADDING A TEXT BOX

If you're creating a presentation using blank styles, you can either use predesigned slides, or you can add text boxes to your slides as needed.

To add a text box:

1. Go to the Insert tab and click Text Box.
2. Then you can draw the text box position and width. The height is automatically defined by what you type into the text box.

One more formatting feature that you might find useful is the Drawing Tools Format menu that appears when you insert a shape that contains text into your presentation. This menu appears automatically. On the Drawing Tools Format menu there are several text formatting options that you've seen before and one that you haven't. This option, shown in Figure 15-8, is the Text Effects menu.

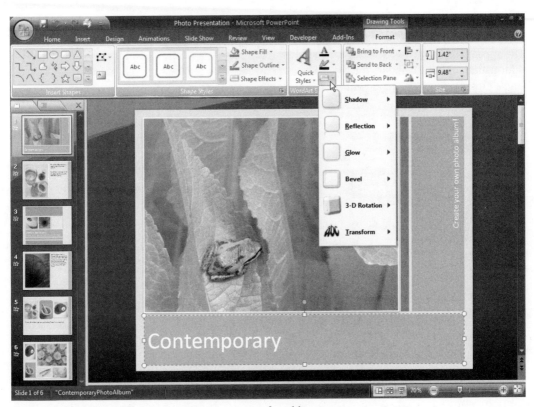

Figure 15-8: The Text Effects menu gives you options for adding interest to your text.

The Text Effects menu gives you options for changing the effects of text within an object or shape. Choose from Shadow, Reflection, Glow, Bevel, 3-D Rotation, and Transform.

ADDING BULLETED LISTS

One of the more interesting new features in PowerPoint is what you can do with bulleted lists. Adding a plain bulleted list is easy enough; click the bulleted list button on the Paragraph menu. But PowerPoint now offers exciting options that you can use in place of bulleted lists. You might never use plain bulleted lists again.

Probably the most interesting of the bulleted list functions is in diagramming. You'll learn more about diagrams later in this chapter, but for now you should know that you can either create a list-type graphic (called SmartArt), as shown in Figure 15-9, or you can create a bulleted list first and then convert it to a diagram.

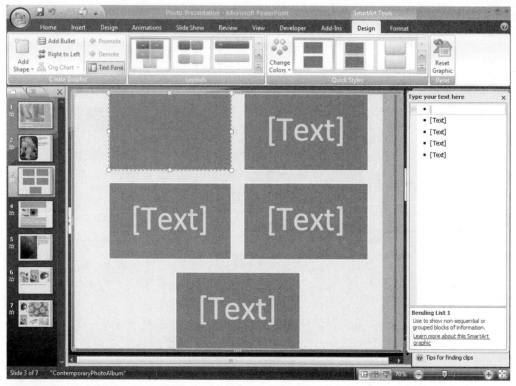

Figure 15-9: Plain bulleted lists are out. Bulleted lists made fancy with graphics and effects are a new hot feature of PowerPoint 2007.

Working with Objects

Objects are what make PowerPoint presentations interesting. Text can be placed on any document, but objects — graphics — really come alive on a PowerPoint presentation. Want to get the point across to your sales team that sales figures are up or down? Show them. Don't just give them numbers, give them pictures that will stick with the entire sales team every time they consider making a call or approaching a new customer.

Working with objects in previous versions of PowerPoint wasn't easy. If you could find the object you wanted to include in the presentation, customizing it to meet your needs was time consuming, frustrating, and sometimes impossible. PowerPoint 2007 makes including these elements in your presentation easier and more eye-catching than they have ever been in the past.

INSERTING IMAGES AND CLIP ART

Standard fare for documents and presentations of all types are images and clip art. PowerPoint 2007 is no exception.

To insert a picture or clip art into your presentation:

1. Go to the Insert tab.

2. Select Picture or Clip Art.

3. Select the image you want to insert and click Insert.

4. The image is inserted into the presentation and, as shown in Figure 15-10, the Picture Tools Format menu tab appears.

Figure 15-10: Insert a picture or clip art and the Picture Tools Format menu tab appears.

5. Use these tools to format, change, and arrange the picture or clip art.

You can also use these directions to insert a table or shapes into your presentation. And, as with other objects, when you add these elements into your presentation, the contextual menus appear so you can change, update, rearrange, or format the elements.

ADDING SOUNDS

Sound, when used sparingly, adds a nice element to your presentation. For example, if you want to get the audience's attention at the beginning of a presentation, you can add an upbeat audio track to the title slide. The audio track will alert attendees that the presentation is about to begin.

You can also record your own audio to add to a presentation. However, recording your own audio track requires that you have a microphone attached to your computer.

If you want to add audio to your presentation, follow these steps:

1. Select the slide to which you'd like to add the audio file.

2. Go to the Insert tab and select the Sound command.

3. As Figure 15-11 shows, you'll be given four options for adding audio to your presentation.

4. Select the audio option desired.

Figure 15-11: Select the type of audio file that you would like to attach to the slide.

Once you select an audio option, the menu or dialog box appears for that option. Each option is slightly different. For example, if you select Sound from file, you're taken to a dialog box that allows you to select the sound (stored on your hard drive) that you want to include. But if you choose to insert a recording, the Recording dialog box appears.

After you select the sound that you want to include in your presentation, you may also be prompted to set the attributes of the sound. One of the options that you may be prompted to choose is whether the sound should start on a click or automatically.

You'll also be taken to the Sound Tools Options tab. From this tab you can set additional attributes for the sound you've inserted, including whether the sound should loop or play just one time and what volume the sound should be.

Note

When you insert a sound into your presentation, a small icon that looks like a speaker may appear on the slide. This icon indicates that there is a sound clip attached to the slide. To hide that icon, right-click it and select Send to back. The icon will then be placed behind other elements on the screen. This is most effective when the icon is sent behind a picture or textbox that will completely hide the icon.

WORKING WITH ANIMATIONS

Another element that makes PowerPoint presentation interesting is animation. Without animation, a presentation is nothing more than a boring set of slides. However, when you add animation, then you have slides that come together in pieces, that perform some automated function automatically, or that appear on a click, as you're discussing the elements of the slide.

Here are the steps to add or change the animation on a slide:

1. Navigate to the slide to which you want to add animation.

2. Click the Animation tab, shown in Figure 15-12.

3. Select the animation that you want to add to the slide.

You can also add animation to elements within a slide rather than to the whole slide by clicking on the element that you want to animate and then selecting an animation effect for the element.

Note

Animation for each slide, whether it's the whole slide that's animated or an element on the slide, is indicated by a small star shown next to the slide in the slide preview. If you click the star, the animation is previewed in the Design view.

In some cases, the animation that you want to include in your presentation isn't predesigned. If that's the case, you can create custom animation by selecting the object or slide that you want to animate and then choosing the Custom Animation option. The dialog box shown in Figure 15-13 is displayed.

Click star to preview animation   Animation tab

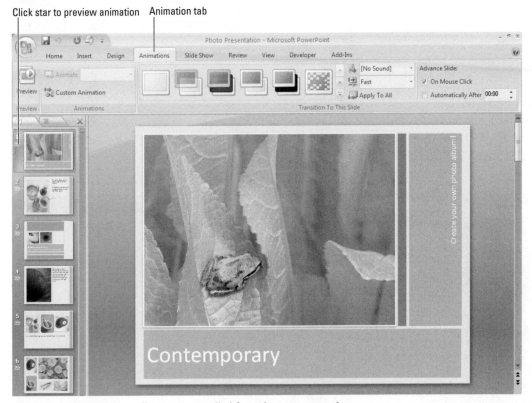

Figure 15-12: Animation effects are controlled from the animation tab.

Figure 15-13: The Custom Animation dialog box allows you to
set the elements of animation that you want to include in a slide or object.

Using the Custom Animation options you can add animation or remove it, set it to start on a click or automatically, and set the speed of the animation or reorder it (for multiple elements of animation).

One last animation feature that you may want to be aware of is the Transition Animation. Transition animation is the animation that occurs when you move from one slide to another. You can have slides fly in, fade in, or one of several other options. The Transition Animation menu is located on the Animation tab.

When you add custom animation, the animation is indicated in the Design view by numbers on each slide or element where the animation takes place, as shown in Figure 15-14. The numbers indicate the order in which the animation will occur. You can also select transitions for individual elements to occur simultaneously by selecting With Previous from the Start menu.

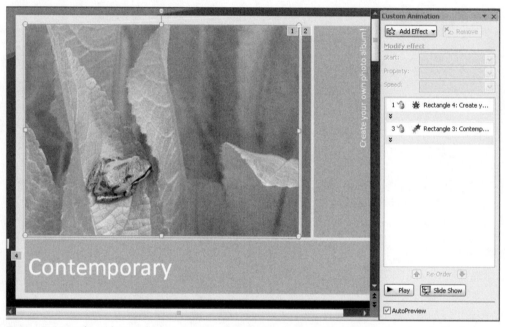

Figure 15-14: The order in which animation takes place is indicated on the slide in numerical order.

Working with Diagrams and Charts

Diagrams and charts give you the ability to quickly convey complex information in an easily understandable, visual way. Complex information is often better displayed visually because it makes it easier for the audience to understand. In previous versions of PowerPoint, adding charts and diagrams, especially useful charts and diagrams, was no easy task.

PowerPoint 2007 makes those difficulties relics of the past. Adding a diagram or chart in this new version of PowerPoint is much easier to do.

Creating Diagrams

Diagrams show how processes, cycles, and relationships work. These elements are useful when you're trying to illustrate how information fits into these processes, but in the past there was no easy way to add a diagram to your presentation.

Adding them to presentations created in PowerPoint 2007 is much easier than before, however. All it takes to add a diagram to your presentation now is for you to select the slide into which you want to insert the diagram, click the Insert tab, and then select the diagram that you want to add to the slide from the SmartArt menu.

When the diagram appears, as shown in Figure 15-15, add your own text to complete the visual image.

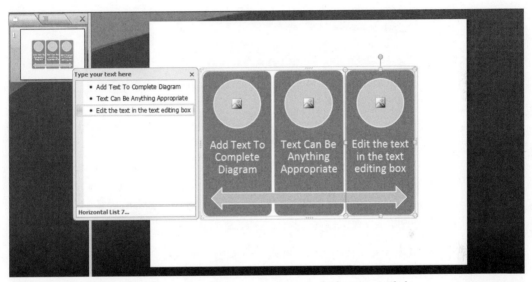

Figure 15-15: Complete the diagram by adding your own text in the boxes provided.

If the diagram you've added has a small picture icon in it, then you can also add pictures and clip art to the diagram to customize it. Further customization of colors and effects can be added from the Design tab. Use themes to consistently change colors, add backgrounds, and create visual appeal in your diagrams.

Creating Charts

Creating charts works in much the same way that creating diagrams works. The difference is that charts generally draw from numerical information rather than text information. To insert a chart into your presentation:

1. Select the slide on which you would like the chart to appear.

2. Go to the Insert tab and select Chart.

3. The Create Chart dialog box appears, as shown in Figure 15-16. Then click OK.

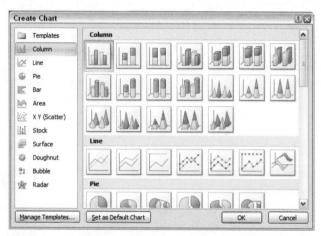

Figure 15-16: Select the chart type that you want to insert in the presentation.

4. The chart is inserted into your presentation and a sample Microsoft Excel worksheet containing information that populates the chart appears.

5. Enter the information that you want to include in the chart, and then save and close the Excel workbook.

6. Now your chart is complete and you can reformat it in whatever manner works best with your presentation.

Once you've created the chart, the Chart Tools tabs appear. They are Design, Layout, and Format. Use these tabs to change and customize the chart that you've just created. You can also use them to change, update, or add to the data source for the chart.

Collaborating and Sharing

In many organizations, the creation of a PowerPoint presentation isn't a single person job. More often, several people or teams are involved in the creation of a presentation or one person creates the presentation but someone (or a group of people) must sign off on it before it can be shown to an audience. That's where the collaboration and sharing tools in PowerPoint come in handy.

These tools work similarly to the collaboration and sharing tools used in Word, though there are some minor differences. Ultimately, however, these tools help make the collaboration and approval process much faster and easier to complete.

Tracking Changes

Tracking changes is one of those functions that's available in Word but that works differently in PowerPoint. To track the changes on your presentation as it makes its rounds through the collaboration and approval process, go to the Review menu. From this menu, you have access to proofing tools, but there is also a limited set of tracking capabilities.

Users can add comments to the presentation to help with the editing process, and if changes are made to the original, they can be integrated with the existing version of the presentation. If you happen to be the person reviewing the changes, you'll also find tools to accept or decline any changes that were made to the presentation.

Merging Presentations

One final capability that you might find useful, especially if you're using SharePoint Server 2007, is the ability to make changes across multiple versions of a presentation. That's accomplished with the file library. As long as copies of any slide or presentation in a slide library are linked, then changes to the original (and to the copies if specified) are synchronized in the copies or the original. This helps to ensure that everyone who might be using the presentation has the same version, which cuts down on confusion and reduces your risk for presenting faulty information.

Summary

PowerPoint 2007 is the tool that you've been waiting for. The new tools, features, and capabilities of PowerPoint make it easy to quickly and easily create PowerPoint presentations. These presentations can be anything from a vacation photo album to a complex presentation that includes charts, diagrams, and animation.

The new design of PowerPoint makes everything point-and-click easy. And that's a feature we've been waiting for, for a very long time.

Chapter 16

Exploring Additional New Features in PowerPoint

One of the steps that Microsoft took when designing and creating the new Office programs was to look at the way that people work and what they do with each program. For example, were you ever asked to participate in a survey or to report an error in Microsoft? If so, the information that you submitted was used to improve the way that programs like PowerPoint perform.

In the last chapter, you saw many of the improvements to the Office program. But there are more. As if the options that you've already reviewed weren't enough, the Office design team packed even more into the program. For example, you can convert a list to a diagram in just two clicks, and you can create custom layouts without much more effort than that. PowerPoint 2007 also gives you the option to package your presentations for distribution on CD. These are features that make life easier in a lot of ways, as you'll see in this chapter.

Converting Lists to Diagrams in Two Clicks

You learned about diagrams and charts in Chapter 15, but there just wasn't room to include information about one of the coolest features of PowerPoint 2007: using a list to create a diagram in just two clicks. Honest, it's really that simple. Here's how:

1. Create a slide in your presentation. You can use just about any layout that includes text capabilities to create the slide.

2. Right-click anywhere within the list area.

3. From the list that appears, highlight Convert to SmartArt, and as shown in Figure 16-1, the SmartArt options appear.

4. Click the thumbnail that represents the SmartArt diagram that suits your presentation; it will automatically be inserted on your slide in place of the list that you originally created, as shown in Figure 16-2. The text list is also opened automatically so you can change any of the points included in the original list.

Select thumbnail to convert list   Highlight to show SmartArt options

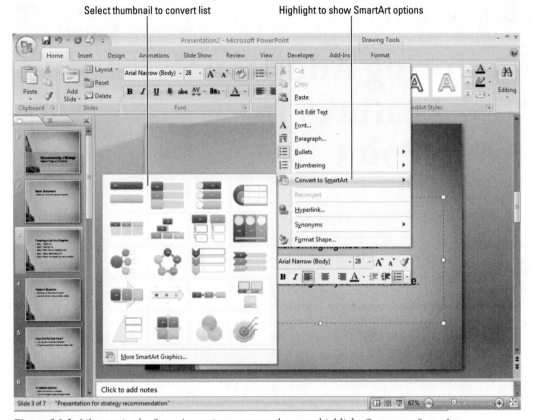

Figure 16-1: Like magic, the SmartArt options appear when you highlight Convert to SmartArt.

Note

One limitation of the SmartArt feature that you should be aware of is the tendency of PowerPoint to automatically convert all of the text outside of the title area of your slide into SmartArt diagrams. Even if you highlight only the lines that you want converted to SmartArt, the program will still convert all of the text, highlighted and unhighlighted, and merge it into the SmartArt diagram.

Once you have inserted the SmartArt diagram into your slide, you are automatically taken to the Design tab where you can change the diagram layout and style or change the colors of the diagram with a few mouse clicks. Live Preview is also available from this tab, making it possible for you to preview your results before you commit to them.

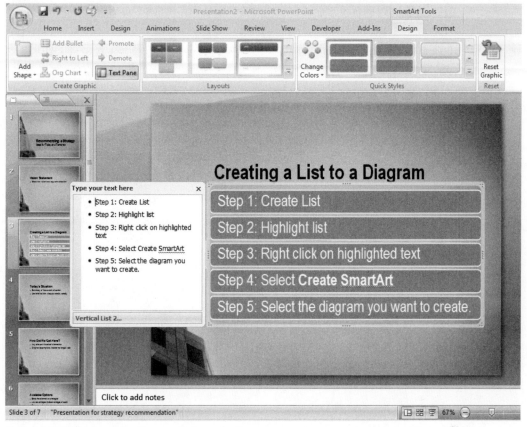

Figure 16-2: The SmartArt diagram replaces the list you created.

Creating and Saving Custom Layouts

Microsoft goes to work well in advance of releasing a new product to put together templates and document layouts for use with the final product. Even so, when the product is released it's impossible to include every layout and template that you might need. Every organization has different requirements. And with different requirements comes the need for custom layouts.

To make PowerPoint (and other office programs) as usable as possible, PowerPoint gives you the capability to create custom layouts that suit your needs. However, if you tried to figure this out without some help, you could spend days on it and still not locate the right commands. The names have changed, and with the change in controls, you may not recognize the controls that you need.

No worries. Here's how it's done.

1. Either in an existing presentation or in a new slide, click the View tab, and then select Slide Master from the Ribbon.

2. You're taken to the Master View, and the Ribbon and tabs change to reflect the tools you'll need to create your custom slide.

3. Click Insert Slide Master to add a new master slide to your presentation. A screen with several master-slide layouts appears; select the slide you want to work from. Don't worry if there are elements in the existing masters that you don't want; you can remove them by right-clicking the border of the element (also called placeholder) and selecting Cut.

4. To design your custom layout, select Insert Placeholder, as shown in Figure 16-3. Then select the placeholder that you would like to insert on the slide and define the area on the slide where you want to insert the placeholder by dragging your mouse across the desired area on the slide template.

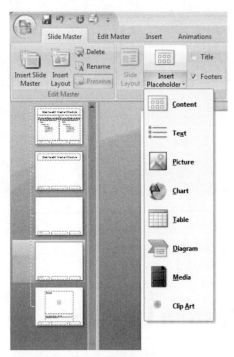

Figure 16-3: Insert placeholders on your custom slide to complete the desired layout.

5. You can also toggle titles and footers on and off by placing a check mark in or removing it from the box next to these options. When you've finished laying out your slide, click File and select Save As → PowerPoint Presentation, and then add the name of the file and use the Save type as drop-down menu to select PowerPoint Template.

When you've finished with your custom slide, remember to select Rename and give it a meaningful name that will help you locate the slide when you need it. To return to your original document, all you need to do is click Close on the Slide Master tab.

Then you can add your custom slide to any document by selecting the Insert tab. Click Add Slide → Reuse Slide, and then navigate to and select the custom slide that you've created. It can be reused any number of times in any number of presentations. If there is a specific slide layout that you use regularly, this is the fastest way to ensure that it's always available to you.

Note

When you add a custom slide to an existing presentation, the presentation theme is automatically added to the slide. If you prefer to have a different theme, you'll have to change it manually.

Creating and Saving New Text Effects

In some documents, you may want to change the text effects throughout the document. In the past, that meant highlighting text and making the changes. Today, it's easy to do.

Today you can change the way text looks all the way through the document with the click of a button. All you need to do is highlight the text you want to change and then use the Text Fill, Text Outline, and Text Effects buttons to make your changes. Once the changes are made, you can save the document to keep from losing your new formatting.

To apply new formatting to your entire document:

1. Go to the Design tab.

2. In the Themes section of the tab, select the Theme Fonts drop-down menu to make the changes that you desire, or click Create New Theme Fonts.

3. Make your selections and enter a name for the new theme fonts.

4. Click Save. Now you have a font theme you can apply to any document.

PowerPoint is full of powerful, easy-to-use options that were very difficult to find in the past. These new options take a little getting used to, but once you figure them all out, it's easy to create professional, effective PowerPoint presentations in less time than ever before.

Packaging for CD

One additional feature of PowerPoint 2007 that you might find useful is the ability to package your presentation to be burned to CD. Storing your presentation on CD makes it easy to share and archive. But in the past, burning a presentation to CD was less than user-friendly. Today, even with charting and graphics that included imbedded information from other sources, you can save a CD-ready file, or burn your presentation to CD with the click of a button. Here's how.

1. Once you've completed your presentation select File and then click Publish → Package for CD.

2. The Package for CD dialog box appears.

3. Select the desired options: name your CD, select any additional files that you want to save, and then click the Options button. (Don't worry about embedded files; the program handles that.)

4. In the Options menu, you can select the Presentation Type, select the Include these files options, and set Security and privacy.

5. When you've made your selections, click to either save the finished file or burn it to CD, and you're done.

Summary

The simplicity that's inherent in the new PowerPoint 2007 program is a great improvement over previous versions. Adding visual appeal with SmartArt elements and creating custom layouts is a snap. PowerPoint 2007 even has new tools that allow you to quickly create reusable elements that will speed the time it takes to create new presentations. When your presentation is complete, packaging it all together to burn on disk makes distribution easy. That's the point of the new PowerPoint design — ease of use. In no time at all, you'll have your presentations created and ready to distribute. All with a few clicks of the mouse.

Part VII

Managing Data with Excel

Chapter 17
Performing Common Tasks in Excel

Chapter 18
Exploring Additional New Features in Excel

Chapter 17

Performing Common Tasks in Excel

Excel 2007 has plenty of welcome changes for just about everyone. It's easier to navigate, and analyzing, managing and sharing your information is a lot less complicated with this version. Considering Excel is rarely anyone's favorite program (except for financial-oriented folks!), the improvements might actually entice more people to use the program. That's a good thing, because Excel really is a useful program for anyone who works with large amounts of data.

In this chapter, we'll show you the new interface and look at the changes in managing functions, formatting worksheets, creating tables, sorting and filtering, importing and exporting, and working with data by using PivotCharts and other chart elements.

Exploring the Interface

If you have used other programs in Office 2007, then you won't be surprised by the new look of Excel 2007. The File menu has been replaced with the Office Button on the upper-left of your screen, just as in the other Office 2007 programs. With earlier versions of Excel, it was possible to set Options from the Tools menu. Now, most of those options are located within the Office Button. Click on its button and at the bottom-right, select the Excel Options button.

The navigation pane on the left, as shown in Figure 17-1, offers you an assortment of options:

- **Popular:** Click Popular and you'll see this is where you can change popular items such as color scheme, font, and whether to show a Mini Toolbar for selected items.

- **Formulas:** Click Formulas to change formula calculation, performance and error handling options such as enabling Excel 2007 to automatically calculate formulas in a workbook, and enabling error checking functions. (A word to the wise: Be sure Formula AutoComplete is checked.)

- **Proofing:** In the Proofing option, you can set up AutoCorrect options and spelling correction items.

- **Save:** In the Save option, you can set your defaults for the format you prefer to save files in, for AutoRecover timing, and for off-line editing options.

- **Advanced:** For online editing options, go to the Advanced option. You'll find Cut, Copy, Paste, Display, and other preferences there.

- **Customize:** The Customize option is fairly complex; you can customize your Quick Access Toolbar from here (more about that in this chapter) and there are dozens of options to choose from.

The next three options (Add-Ins, Trust Center, and Resources) are helpful and worth looking through, but aren't necessarily items you will need on a regular basis.

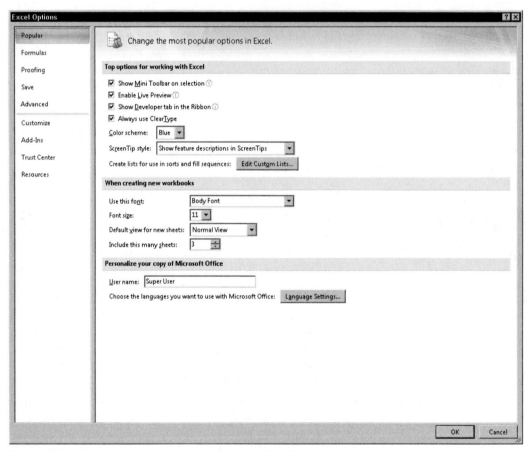

Figure 17-1: Excel Options are now accessed through the Office Button.

Beyond the Office Button, you will notice that the menus and toolbars have been replaced with a horizontal tabbed layout called the Ribbon. This design makes Excel easier to use because it lets you quickly find and work with the commands you need. For anyone who grew weary of trying to figure out how to accomplish a common task in earlier versions of Excel, one look at the Ribbon (the strip across the top of the screen) will make you feel more confident about handling those same tasks in

Excel 2007. One of the ways it does that is by providing you with only the most commonly performed tasks up front, then by adding options for you as you develop your worksheet and workbook. The Ribbon is key to this process — it is responsive to your selections and shows you only the options you need for the current status of your work.

Exploring the Excel 2007 Ribbon

The Ribbon was designed with task management in mind: Commands are organized into logical groupings under activity tabs. Essentially, this means that instead of digging through buried menus, you can see at a glance the options available to you. As you use the Ribbon, pay attention to how the commands you've seen before are now grouped together in a more logical fashion. As you notice that, you'll start to see how Excel 2007 will be easier to use than previous versions.

The first thing to notice are the eight tabs across the top of the Ribbon. Each of these houses commands that Microsoft identified as the ones most commonly used as basic tasks are performed. The tabs listed here are shown in Figure 17-2:

- Home
- Insert
- Page Layout
- Formulas
- Data
- Review
- View
- Add-Ins

Figure 17-2: Eight tabs across the top of the Ribbon represent core tasks performed in Excel. If your version shows the Developer tab, then you have selected that personalization option. It is not a standard default option.

Figure 17-3 shows how each tab holds groups of related items, which are really just the commands you use to perform tasks. So, for example, select the Home tab and you'll see seven groups: Clipboard, Font, Alignment, Number, Styles, Cells, and Editing. Within each of those groups are command buttons, boxes, and menus. If you want to change the font within a worksheet cell to italics, for instance, you would select the cell and text you wish to change, select the Home tab, and select the Italics button. Some commands have a down arrow: these arrows represent more menu items to choose from.

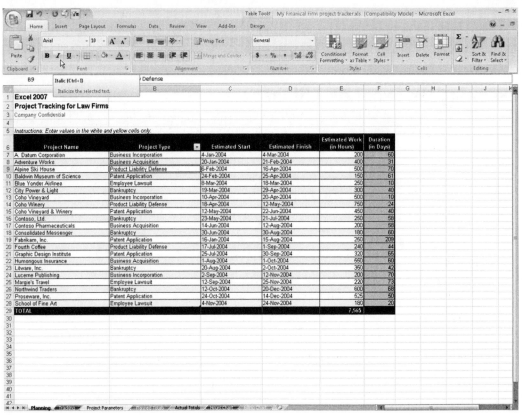

Figure 17-3: Each tab holds groups of related items with the commands most often used. In this example, the Font group is shown with the Italics command highlighted.

As you use the Ribbon, you will notice that it is responsive to the actions you take. Some commands are not shown until you take the action required to see them. For example, if you don't have any shapes in your worksheet, you don't need to see all the formatting options for shapes. But once you place a shape into your worksheet (go to the Insert tab, choose a shape from the Shapes Group, and insert it into your worksheet), you will see a new tab appear: Format. In it are the Groups and Commands needed to format a shape. As long as that (or any other) shape remains in your worksheet, you will have the Format tab available. These tabs that appear only when you need them are called Contextual Tabs; they appear only in the context of what you have asked Excel 2007 to do.

Notice, though, that when you move to a different worksheet that does not have a shape in it, you do not have the Format tab available. That's because the Ribbon "knows" that this new worksheet has no shape inserted and therefore no reason to muddy up the waters with the Format tab. Try playing around with various commands inside the tabs and you'll find other items that work in the same way.

The Dialog Box Launcher is another new item to watch for. As an example, look for it in the lower-right corner of the Alignment group (it's not in all groups, by the way) on the Home tab and click the arrow as shown in Figure 17-4. You will see a task pane appear that provides more formatting options for your worksheet cells.

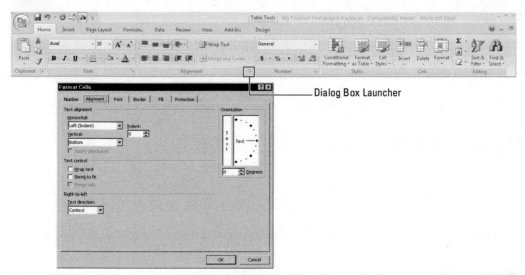

Figure 17-4: The Dialog Box Launcher is located in the bottom-right corner of a group. As shown here, this option brings up a dialog box with more command options for the Alignment group.

Need more room to work in your worksheet? Double-click a tab and the Ribbon will minimize. Double-click again and it will reappear.

Tip

When selecting text within a worksheet, a faint outline of a font selection box appears just above it. This is called the Mini Toolbar. Pull your cursor to the selection box and it will appear in full detail. This feature allows you to change the font quickly without having to go to the Home tab and use the Font group commands.

Customizing the Interface

As with other Office 2007 applications, Excel 2007 has a Quick Access Toolbar located at the top-left of your screen, just above the tabs next to the Office Button. The point of this toolbar is to provide a place to quickly access the commands you use the most when using Excel; it's customizable because not every person works with Excel in the same way.

Standard commands on the Quick Access Toolbar are Save, Undo, and Redo. Add the commands you want at your fingertips to the Quick Access Toolbar by finding and right-clicking the command you want. Click Add to Quick Access Toolbar. Alternately, if you add a command that you later decide you don't need on your Quick Access Toolbar, right-click the command on the toolbar and click Remove from Quick Access Toolbar. For example, let's assume you use the Filter command often. Go to the Data tab, right-click Filter, select Add to Quick Access Toolbar. Now, the Filter command appears in your Quick Access Toolbar as shown in Figure 17-5.

Figure 17-5: The Quick Access Toolbar shown here lets you customize Excel 2007 by placing the commands you want at your fingertips.

You can also move the Quick Access Toolbar to a location below the Ribbon if you don't like where it's located. Click the down-arrow on the bottom-right of the Quick Access Toolbar and select Place Quick Access Toolbar below the Ribbon.

Using New Tools and Features

We told you Excel was easier to use this time around, and there are some new tools that make this simplicity possible. Here is a quick glance at several; others are explained in greater detail in this chapter:

- **Quicklaunch:** Allows you to select from a list of data sources instead of trying to remember the names of servers and databases.

- **Connection manager:** Allows you to view all connections in a workbook, as well as reuse the connection or substitute it with another one.

- **Resizable formula bar:** Prevents formulas from covering other data in your worksheet.

- **XPS format:** Allows you to save and share your workbook in a format that is easy for other people to print or view online.

- **Improved filtering and sorting:** Lets you arrange worksheet data in new ways to find answers you need.

- **Quick access to Excel templates:** Allows you to instantly access template categories for Excel 2007 when creating a new workbook.

Formatting Worksheets

If you work with massive amounts of data, you'll be glad to know that Excel 2007 can keep up with you. With Excel 2007, workbooks are limited only by available memory and system resources. Depending on the language version of Excel 2007 that you have installed, you can have up to 250 number formats in a workbook, 170 adjustable cells in Solver, more than 65,000 pages, and up to 10,000 filter drop-down lists. Linked sheets and scenarios are limited by available memory only, although scenarios summary reports will list only the first 250. Excel 2007 now also supports up to one million rows and sixteen thousand columns on every worksheet, with columns now ending at XFD instead of IV. Even better, you can format worksheets with a lot less hassle now. In this section, we look at some of the most commonly performed tasks and how they are handled in Excel 2007.

Inserting, Deleting, or Formatting a New Column or Row

In the Home tab, go to the Cells group as shown in Figure 17-6. Choose the action you want (Insert, Delete, or Format) and click the down arrow for the menu of options. You'll see that Format offers you the most choices, while Insert and Delete offer simple commands involving rows, columns, cells, and sheets. Under Format, you can change the height and width of cells, hide and unhide rows and columns, rename, move, or copy sheets, and add security protections to your sheet. Don't forget to title your rows and columns!

Figure 17-6: Under the Home tab, the Cells group offers many options for formatting your worksheet. This example shows the menu you will see when selecting the Format option.

Creating a Table

Locate the spreadsheet you want to work with and select the data you want formatted into a table, then follow these steps to create a table:

1. Go to the Insert tab and select Table from the Table group, as shown in Figure 17-7.

Click Table

Figure 17-7: Creating a table is quickly accomplished from the Insert tab; be sure to select Table and not PivotTable.

2. A Create Table window appears; click OK. The range of data you selected appears in this window.

3. Check My Table Has Headers. A window appears advising you that your header text will now be static text. Click Yes and you can continue formatting the table. Click No and Excel stops the process so you can start again.

    If you do not want your header information changed to static text, remove the check mark from My Table Has Headers the next time you begin the process. Removing the check mark will allow your table headers to display names you can change.

Notice that once you have completed this command, your table columns have headings and AutoFilter has been applied by default. If you wish to remove the AutoFilter, you must turn off the table headers. Removing table headers also removes any other applied filters.

Want to remove an Excel table by converting it to a range of data? Click anywhere in the table, then, under Table Tools, go to the Design tab and click Convert to Range in the Tools group. Oh — in case you have been looking for the Excel list feature, note that it still exists but has been renamed Excel table.

Caution

The name of a new table header cannot be determined by a series fill adjacent to the new column if the table headers are not displayed.

FORMATTING A TABLE

Now that you have inserted a table, the Design tab appears. This tab offers five groups to help you find the commands to format your table:

- Properties
- Tools
- External Table Data
- Table Style Options
- Table Styles

Apply a table style you like as shown in Figure 17-8. Under Table Style Options, you can make some quick adjustments by placing or removing check marks in the items available. For example, selecting Totals Row automatically adds a row at the end of your table to display a total for the column. Play with these options a bit and you'll see how easy it can be to make your rows and columns quickly stand out.

Figure 17-8: The Design tab makes it easy for you to format tables almost any way you want. Here, you can see all the groups and commands available.

In the Tools group, you can further customize and edit your table. For example, to convert a table to a range of data, click Convert to Range. To check columns for duplicate information or remove duplicate rows, select Remove Duplicates. This is also where you can select Summarize with Pivot to easily arrange and summarize your data.

INSERTING A PIVOTTABLE

PivotTables are a great way to interactively explore data to find answers, patterns, and trends. You can use them to build standard reports, too. On the Insert tab, select PivotTable. In the dialog box, select the table, range, or external data source you want to use, as well as where you want the PivotTable to be located.

Placing fields into your report is the same as with earlier versions of Excel; just select the item to add from the PivotTable Field List with a check mark as shown in Figure 17-9 or by dragging them to where you want. By default, Excel 2007 places numerical data fields into the Values field list and other fields into the Row labels field list. The new item to take a look at is the lower portion of the PivotTable Field List. With the instruction to "Drag fields between areas below," this region lets you move pieces of your report between Report Filter, Row Labels, Column Labels, and Values. It also stops you if moving something doesn't make sense for your report.

Here are some nice improvements over previous versions in Excel 2007's PivotTables:

- You can undo almost any action when creating or rearranging a PivotTable.

- Plus and minus drill-down indicators show you whether parts of a PivotTable can be expanded or collapsed.

- Sorting and filtering is easier.

- Conditional formatting can be applied by cell or by intersection of cells.

- Predefined or custom styles can now be applied to PivotTables.

Figure 17-9: When working with PivotTables,
you can drag fields or select them with a check mark.

Inserting and Formatting a Worksheet

To the right of the worksheet tabs is the Insert Worksheet button but it can also be accessed via the Home tab by going to the Cells group, clicking the arrow in Insert and clicking Insert Sheet. Once created, the actual worksheet tab appears at the bottom of the spreadsheet.

A right-click on a worksheet tab brings up a menu that offers both theme colors and standard colors when you select Tab Color from the menu. Select the color you want. You can also perform this task by using the Home tab, selecting the Cells group, clicking the arrow on Format, pointing to Tab Color, and selecting the color you want.

Using Key Tips

If you prefer using the keyboard instead of the mouse, you will be interested in another new feature that involves what were previously known as keyboard shortcuts in earlier versions of Excel. Now, keyboard shortcuts have a new name: Key Tips. There are two big advantages that Key Tips have over earlier keyboard shortcuts:

- There are shortcuts for every single button on the Ribbon.

- The new shortcuts often require fewer keystrokes.

Press ALT inside a worksheet and you will see Key Tips appear for all Ribbon tabs, the Quick Access Toolbar and the Office Button (see Figure 17-10). Press the key for the tab where you want Key Tips displayed and they will appear for all commands on the tab you have chosen.

Don't fret if you have an affinity for CTRL keyboard shortcuts; those still work just like they always have. If it didn't begin with CTRL, however, there is a new one to get used to.

Figure 17-10: Old keyboard shortcuts have been replaced by Key Tips, with the exception of CTRL shortcuts.

Exploring Page Layout View

Page Layout view shown in Figure 17-11 is a new feature as well. This is similar to the Print Layout view in Office Word and provides page margins at the top, sides, and bottom of your worksheet. You can turn the rulers on and off as needed by selecting the View tab and clicking Ruler in the Show/Hide group.

PAGE LAYOUT VIEW OPTIONS

In Page Layout view, you can also adjust your worksheet before printing it. Click the Page Layout tab and you'll see five groups that will help you finalize printing options for your worksheet:

- Themes
- Page Setup
- Scale to Fit
- Sheet Options
- Arrange

Choosing Page Setup will allow you to set margins, choose portrait or landscape views, confirm page size and print areas, set page breaks, and set up page tiles. No matter which one you choose, what you see on the screen is what will print.

Page Layout view (see Figure 17-11) also allows you to add headers and footers by using the Design tab and lets you see each sheet in a workbook in the view that works best for that sheet. See "Setting Headers and Footers," the following section in this chapter, for more information.

Ruler

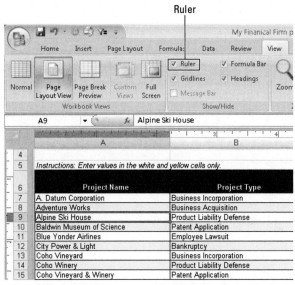

Figure 17-11: The new Page Layout View highlighted here means you don't need Print Preview to make adjustments to your worksheet before printing, plus it gives you new design options. Note, for example, the rulers that can now help perfectly size your worksheet.

SETTING HEADERS AND FOOTERS

The new Page Layout view makes it easy to add headers and footers to a worksheet. (See Figure 17-12.)

1. Click the View tab and select the Workbook Views group.

2. Click Page Layout View.

3. Select Click to add header at the top of your worksheet. As you do click in that box, a new tab called Design appears with a variety of Header and Footer tools and elements. For our purposes, we typed in the header December Sales Report.

Figure 17-12: The Design tab provides several options for creating headers and footers in Excel 2007.

Note

If you do not see the Click to add header box, your worksheet has hidden white space. Place your cursor between the worksheet and the ruler until you see the double arrow option to Show White Space. Select this option to display the header box.

As Figure 17-12 shows, now it's up to you to decide how to structure your headers and footers with all the options available in the Design tab. In the header and footer areas, there are three text boxes that aren't really visible until you click in the blank space. In Figure 17-13, you can see that the date command (shown in actual command format) has been added to the left-hand portion of the header, with the title in the middle (added previously), and the current time on the right (shown as it appears in final copy). We added the date and time by simply placing the cursor in the section of the header where we wanted the item shown and selecting the command from the Ribbon. The date was added by selecting the Current Date command and the time was added by selecting the Current Time command. You can add other elements simply by selecting the ones you want from the Header and Footer elements group. Choose from the following:

- Page Number
- Number of Pages
- Current Date
- Current Time
- File Path
- File Name
- Sheet Name
- Picture

Figure 17-13: Both the header and footer areas are divided into three sections to help you set up evenly spaced elements.

Notice that when you are working in the header, the Ribbon shows the Go to Footer command so you can quickly move through the document. When working in the footer, that command changes to Go to Header.

Caution

Different screen resolutions will change what you see when working with Excel 2007. A minimized screen or a screen set to 800 × 600 pixels can limit your view of Ribbon groups to group name only, rather than showing all the commands in the group. Click the arrow in the group button to display the commands if you can't see them.

Working with Functions

Working with functions isn't as intimidating with Excel 2007 as it used to be. Select the Formulas tab, and you'll immediately see a variety of items at your fingertips designed to make it easier to write functions, and audit and calculate information.

Creating Equations

Excel 2007 is perfect for working with numbers and mathematical equations. Where these two items are concerned, you need to know how to enter and use simple formulas in order to use Excel 2007 effectively. In this section, we'll go over the basics.

Formulas will appear in the formula bar above the worksheet anytime you select a cell that contains a result. If you can't see the formula bar, go to the View tab and select Formula Bar in the Show/Hide group.

To create a simple formula using addition, division, multiplication, or subtraction, type in an equals sign, use the mathematical sign you need (+,-,*,/) and press Enter. So a simple formula would look like these:

- =2+2 (add)
- =2-2 (subtract)
- =2*2 (multiply)
- =2/2 (divide)

To use a cell reference in a formula, type **=(cell number)+(cell number)** inside a cell. So, if you want to add the values of cell 4 with cell 7, type **=C4+C7**. You can also accomplish this task by typing the equals sign, clicking the first cell, typing the plus sign, and clicking the second cell. Table 17-1 shows common cell reference formulas.

Table 17-1   Cell Reference Formula Examples — Excel 2007

To refer to the values in	*Use this cell reference format*
A cell in column B and row 5	B5
The cells in column B, row 5 and column C, row 12	B5,C12
The range of cells in column B and rows 9 through 50	B9:B50
The range of cells in row 5 and columns A through T	B5:T5
The range of cells in columns A through T and rows 9 through 50	A9:T50

To add values in a row or column, use the Sum function, as follows:

1. Click a cell to the right of a row of values or below a column of values.

2. Go to the Home tab and click the Sum command in the Editing group.

3. Press Enter.

You can also find the Sum command in the Function Library group under the Formulas tab — click AutoSum.

Want to just copy a formula instead of constantly reentering it? Use the fill handle. You'll find this handy little handle when you click in a cell containing the formula you want to copy and place the cursor over the lower-right corner of the cell. A black cross appears. Drag the fill handle over the cell or cells to which you want to copy the formula, release the mouse button and voilà! Your formula has been copied.

You can simplify formulas by using prewritten functions. These prewritten functions are located in the Home tab (in the Editing group) and the Formulas tab (in the Functions Library). Select the arrow on the AutoSum button and choose a function from the list. To see more functions, check out all the buttons in the Function Library under the Formulas tab.

Tip

Are your results not automatically updating? Go to the Formulas tab and click Calculation Options in the Calculation group, then select Automatic.

Using Formula AutoComplete

The Formula AutoComplete feature was mentioned briefly earlier in this chapter. This feature lets you write formulas and functions involving arguments and refer to named ranges and tables within formulas by offering automated assistance that helps you fill in the formula to ensure accuracy. This feature is great for helping minimize typing and syntax errors.

When you begin to type in a formula anywhere that a formula can be entered — even in the middle of an existing nested function or formula — a drop-down menu appears on the Formula bar to help you. As you move through the options the automated feature offers, you will also see an explanation of the formula appear to help you make the correct decision for your worksheet.

Try this out by typing the equals sign and a first letter in your worksheet or on the Formula Bar. As you see in Figure 17-14, the menu and information automatically display. Choosing a formula inserts it into your worksheet. If you don't want anything Formula AutoComplete is displaying, you can always type in whatever you want to complete the formula.

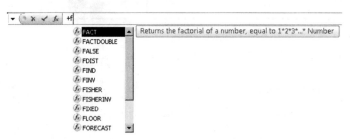

Figure 17-14: Formula AutoComplete is a new feature that helps you enter
the correct formulas every time.

To turn off Formula AutoComplete, click the Office Button, click Excel Options, and then click Formulas. Under Working with Formulas, clear Formula AutoComplete.

Working with Function Arguments

There are dozens of functions that can be used in a spreadsheet, too many to list in this book. But a key feature that you will probably want to take advantage of is the Function Wizard. With Excel 2007, you can nest up to 64 levels of functions. The Function Wizard shown in Figure 17-15 will help you set up these nested functions.

1. Click the cell where you want to enter the formula, then click Insert Function, located in the Formulas tab in the Function Library. You can search for a function or simply select one in the window that appears. Once you have chosen a function, enter the arguments needed.

2. Click Collapse Dialog next to the argument you want in order to enter cell references as an argument, then click Expand Dialog to open the dialog box again.

3. Enter another function by adding it to the argument box you want. Notice that the functions you selected in previous steps are displayed in the Function Arguments dialog box.

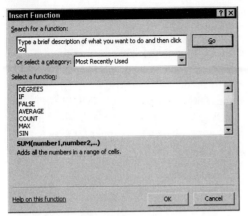

Figure 17-15: Shown here is the Formula Wizard. Selecting this option on the Formulas tab can help you quickly insert functions.

Managing Data

Excel 2007 helps you manage data — two kinds of data, actually — text and numbers. It doesn't matter what kind of data you manage as long as it falls into one of those categories. As you start typing, remember that pressing the Tab key on your keyboard will move you one cell to the right and pressing Enter will move the selection down one cell. As an organizational tip, try to remember to title your worksheet rows and columns. Your readers will thank you, especially if your worksheet has a lot of information in it.

Database Basics

Databases are the organized method for storing data. Office 2007 allows you to retrieve information from nine different places:

- Third-party providers

- Text file databases

- Paradox

- dBase

- Oracle

- Microsoft Access 2007, FoxPro, Excel 2007, SQL Server Analysis Services

The ability to retrieve this information means that you can pull data into Excel 2007 without having to retype it, plus the data can be automatically refreshed in some circumstances.

Importing and Exporting Data

In Excel 2007, the word *import* means making a permanent connection to data that can be refreshed. You can import data from a variety of places; go to the Data tab and click From Other Sources, for example. You'll see several options. Using the Data Connection Wizard or Microsoft Query here are great ways to access external data sources that have already been defined, but you can also choose to create connections to SQL servers or Analysis Services cubes and open or map an XML file in Excel. Don't be afraid to explore the Get External Data group (see Figure 17-16) a bit to get a good feel for how you can quickly obtain information from a variety of sources; Excel 2007 makes it easy to grab information from the Web, Access 2007, text documents, and existing connections.

Figure 17-16: The Get External Data group offers many choices for importing data into Excel 2007 worksheets.

Microsoft Query allows you to select specific data from a database by creating a query — a simple question you ask about the data that is stored externally. Maybe you want to know about specific product sales in a certain country, for example; you can choose the columns of data that you want and import just those columns with Microsoft Query. To use Microsoft Query for data import into Excel, you need to set up a data source to connect to your database.

To set up a data source:

1. Go to the Get External Data group on the Data tab, click From Other Sources, and select From Microsoft Query.

2. Choose either the Databases tab (if you want data for a relational or text file database, or an Excel list) or the OLAP Cubes tab.

3. Double-click New Data Source and follow the prompts when that dialog box is displayed.

Once you set up a data source through Microsoft Query, you can use it whenever you want to without having to retype all of the connection information.

Note

You may need to obtain and install a Microsoft Office–compatible ODBC driver if the external database you want to access is not supported by Microsoft Query. Contact the owner of the database you want to access for driver and installation instructions.

You can refresh external data either manually or automatically. To automatically refresh an external data range every time a workbook is opened:

1. Click a cell in the external data range.

2. Go to the Connections group on the Data tab, click the arrow next to Refresh All, and select Connection Properties.

3. Click the Usage tab and place a check mark in the Refresh data on file open box. Refreshing data in multiple external data ranges is simply a matter of clicking the arrow next to Refresh and clicking Refresh All.

To refresh data in an imported text file:

1. Go to Connections in the Data tab.

2. Click the arrow next to Refresh All and click Refresh.

3. In the Import Text File dialog box, select the text file and click Import.

To remove the data connection from an external data range:

1. Click the worksheet containing the information.

2. Click the arrow next to the Name box on the formula bar, then click the name of the external data range where you want the connection removed.

3. Go to the External Table Data group on the Tools tab and click Unlink. Everything will look the same on your worksheet, but the connection will be deleted.

By the way, you can still easily copy data from Access 2007 into Excel 2007. Copy the information in Access, then in Excel go to the Clipboard group in the Home tab and click Paste. To bring Access data into Excel that can be refreshed, click the cell where you want to place the data. Click From Access in the Get External Data group on the Data tab, locate and double-click the Access database you want in the Look in list. The Select Table window allows you to click the table or query you want to import; click OK. Once those steps are complete, you need to decide how you want to view the data. Make your selections in the Import Data dialog box and click OK.

To export data from Excel 2007 into Access 2007, see Part IX, "Managing Data with Access."

Sorting and Filtering Data

With the worksheet sizes that Excel 2007 can accommodate, it's a good thing it has improved sorting and filtering options. The AutoFilter drop-down list can display more than 1000 items, you can filter data by color or date and select multiple items to filter, and you can now sort data by color up to 64 levels.

To sort data in a worksheet, go to the Sort & Filter group on the Data tab. Highlight the cells that contain the information you wish to work with and choose either the quick buttons to sort largest to smallest or smallest to largest or chose the larger Sort button. If you choose the larger button, a Sort Warning appears if Excel 2007 believes additional information could be sorted. When it appears, you have the option to either expand your selection or continue with the current selection. See Figure 17-17.

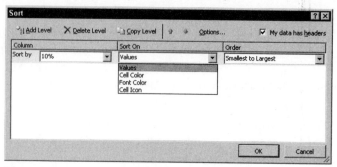

Figure 17-17: A Sort dialog box offers you different options depending on the information you have chosen to sort.

In this case, we sorted by revenue of 10% and by color; the resulting sort shows as indicated in Figure 17-18.

Project Type	General Partner	Business Lawyer	Defense Litigator	Intellectual Property Lawyer	Bankruptcy Lawyer	Administration Staff	Total
Business Incorporation	10%	40%	0%	0%	0%	50%	100%
Business Acquisition	10%	40%	0%	10%	0%	40%	100%
Product Liability Defense	20%	0%	50%	0%	0%	30%	100%
Patent Application	10%	0%	0%	60%	0%	30%	100%
Employee Lawsuit	20%	10%	40%	0%	0%	30%	100%
Bankruptcy	10%	20%	0%	0%	40%	30%	100%
Blended Rates							

Figure 17-18: This completed sort shows that the General Partner column was sorted first by amount of revenue (10%) and then by color coding.

Filtering by using AutoFilter makes it very easy to find and work with data because the filtered data displays only the rows that meet the criteria you specify. AutoFilter lets you create filters in three ways: by a format, by a list of values, or by criteria. Careful! You can choose one option for each range of cells or a column table but that's it; they are mutually exclusive.

To filter data in a worksheet:

1. Go to the Sort & Filter group on the Data tab.

2. Click on a range of information in your worksheet and select the Filter command.

3. A drop-down arrow appears in the header row of the table. Select the arrow and a drop-down menu appears as shown in Figure 17-19, providing you with basic sorting options as well as filtering options.

You can also perform this command from the Home tab; go to the Editing group and select Sort & Filter, then click Filter.

To learn how to sort and filter in a PivotChart, see the following section, "Charting Data."

Figure 17-19: This is an example of a filter menu that appears when a filter is applied to a range of information.

Creating Criteria

You can establish criteria for filtering numbers, dates, and text in your worksheets instead of using Excel's criteria.

To create filter criteria for numbers:

1. Select a cell or range of cells containing numeric data and filter it.

2. Click the down arrow in the column header and select either a specific command or Custom Filter from the Number Filters menu as shown in Figure 17-20.

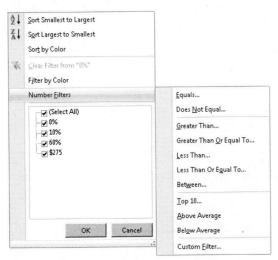

Figure 17-20: Choosing Number Filters from the Filter drop-down menu allows you to set specific criteria for your filter.

Tip

Custom Filter gives you all the specific commands to choose from. For example, to filter by a lower number of 2 and a higher number of 300, enter those numbers in the Custom Filter dialog box.

Creating criteria for text is very similar to creating criteria for numbers — just slight differences in the menu options. To create filter criteria for text, select a cell or range of cells containing alphanumeric data and filter it. Click the down arrow in the column header and select either a specific command or Custom Filter from the Text Filters menu.

To create filter criteria for dates, you need to decide whether you want a common filter or a dynamic filter. A dynamic filter is one where the criteria can change when the filter is reapplied; a common filter is based on static criteria called comparison operators. Comparison operators are the signs used in comparisons such as = (Equal to) or > (Greater than).

To create a common filter:

1. Select the cell or range of cells containing the date data.

2. Filter it by selecting the down arrow.

3. Point your mouse to Date Filters and select one of the commands or click Custom Filter. In the Custom AutoFilter dialog boxes that appear, enter a time or date either manually, by using the list, or by using the Calendar button.

To create a dynamic filter instead, click a predefined date command and click OK.

Note

All date filters are based on the Gregorian calendar, and fiscal years and quarters start in January of the chosen calendar year.

Charting Data

Creating professional charts is not the cumbersome task it used to be in Excel. With Excel 2007, achieving a polished look doesn't take long and your charts will also behave predictably when you use them in other Office 2007 programs. There are no new chart types available with Excel 2007; it's the creation method that has been streamlined.

Charting Basics

To insert a chart, highlight the worksheet information you want on the chart. Then go to the Insert tab and select a chart type from the Chart group. Once you do that, you'll notice that the Design tab appears, with layout and style options for you to choose from. Don't be afraid to experiment! This is where you can learn how to make your charts look as if you had hired a top-notch graphic designer; you can apply special visual effects (think 3-D enhancements, glow, shadows, etc.) and, if you like a certain chart, you can set it as a default that can be pulled from your templates folder in the future.

Charts typically have two axes: horizontal and vertical; although 3-D charts have a third axis called the depth axis. This depth axis allows data to be plotted along the depth of the chart. Not all charts display axes the same way, however, and some charts have just one axis (radar charts) or none at all (pie and doughnut charts). Keep these differences under consideration as you decide which chart to use; just because a chart looks cool doesn't mean it's the right one to display your data.

To add a title to a chart, click the chart. Under Chart Tools, you will see the Design, Layout, and Format tabs. Go to the Labels group in the Layout tab and click Chart Title. Select Above Chart or Centered Overlay Title and when the Chart Title text box appears, just type in the text you want.

If you want to add titles to the horizontal or vertical axes on a chart, go into the Labels group in the Layout tab and click Axis Titles. Decide whether you are changing a primary or secondary axis, and whether it is horizontal or vertical, then choose the option you need. You can also add a title to a depth (series) axis in here if you have a 3-D chart. When the Axis Title text box appears for whichever option you have chosen, type in your text.

Creating PivotCharts

If PivotTables are a great way to interactively explore data to find answers, patterns, and trends, then PivotTable Charts are a great way to visually share the information you uncover. We talked earlier about PivotTables and how to create one.

To create a PivotChart, which incorporates the information from a PivotTable and turns it into a visual chart:

1. Go to the Tables group on the Insert tab.

2. Select the down arrow under PivotTable.

3. Click PivotChart. The process will seem similar to creating a PivotTable, except that once you have chosen the table or range and where you want the PivotChart placed, an actual chart appears on your worksheet.

4. Click on the PivotChart and a PivotChart Filter Pane appears. (If it doesn't, go to the Analyze tab and select PivotChart Filter in the Show/Hide group.) This pane allows you to filter fields and choose from a variety of sort options.

5. Use the PivotTable Field List drag fields option and pull a value over to the Report Filter section; watch what happens to the PivotChart. It automatically changes in reaction to the drag-and-drop action you just took. See Figure 17-21.

Figure 17-21: PivotCharts are a great way to visually show the information you have uncovered while using a PivotTable. The sorting and filtering options let you quickly and easily change the look and feel of the chart as needed.

Formatting Chart Elements

There are three different methods you can use to select a chart element for formatting.

- You can use the mouse by clicking on the chart element you want to select. As you rest the pointer over the element, Excel 2007 displays the element name and the element will be clearly marked with a red border.

- You can go to the Current Selection group on the Format tab and click the arrow next to Chart Elements. Then simply select the chart element you want.

- You can use the keyboard to select a chart element. After you have selected a chart sheet, use the keyboard strokes as shown in Table 17-2.

Table 17-2   Cell Reference Formula Examples — Excel 2007

To	Use this key
Cancel a selection	ESC
Select the next group of elements	UP ARROW
Select the previous group of elements	DOWN ARROW
Select the next element within a group	RIGHT ARROW
Select the previous element within a group	LEFT ARROW
Select the next object or shape	TAB
Select the previous object or shape	SHIFT+TAB

Now that you know how to select chart elements, you can format those elements (chart area, plot area, legend, data labels, axes, or data series). Select the chart element and go to the Format tab. Choose one of the following options:

- To format text by using WordArt, go to the WordArt Styles group and select Text Fill, Text Outline, or Text Effects. Choose the formatting options you like.

- To format the shape of an element, go to the Shape Styles group and choose formatting options from either Shape Fill, Shape Outline, or Shape Effects.

- To format any other chart element, click Format Selection under Current Selection and choose the options you want.

Summary

In this chapter, you learned about key changes in the new interface and explored changes in managing functions and working with data. As you work with Excel 2007, remember that the Ribbon is intuitive; the more you work with it, the more options that will display as you need them. You can also arrange the Quick Access Toolbar with the items you use the most so that tasks are easy to perform. Basic information about formatting worksheets was explained in this chapter; new features and tools allow you to format more quickly than before. In the next chapter, we'll explore in more detail other new features and aspects of Excel 2007 that will help you get the job done quickly and effectively.

Chapter 18

Exploring Additional New Features in Excel

In the previous chapter, we discussed key changes in Excel 2007's new interface and explored changes in managing functions and working with data. Some of Excel 2007's new features were also touched upon, but in this chapter we'll take a more in-depth look at other new features that you should know about. Specifically, we'll discuss Formula AutoComplete, new things you can do with charts and chart templates, tips for better printouts and working with larger workbooks, and how to obtain and use free Excel templates.

Creating Formulas with Ease

Formulas in Excel 2007 haven't changed. They still contain any or all of these items: functions, references, operations, and constants. And Excel 2007 still uses four types of calculation operators to create formulas: Arithmetic, comparison, text concatenation, and reference.

Did you know that the order in which you enter these calculators in a formula can affect how Excel 2007 returns a value? Here's how it does that: A formula in Excel 2007 always begins with an equals sign (=), which tells Excel that the following characters are part of a formula. Then, Excel calculates the formula from left to right and follows the specific order you have entered the formula; it follows the calculation order first, then ranks operators in the order shown in Table 18-1, then by how parenthesis are placed in the formula. If you want to change the order of evaluation, simply enclose in parentheses the part of the formula that should be calculated first.

To help you with formulas, Excel 2007 offers a new feature: Formula AutoComplete. It is designed to provide automated assistance when working with formulas in Excel 2007. In Chapter 17, we discussed the basics of how this feature works. It's a default feature that can be turned off via the Office Button, but we suggest you try it for awhile before ditching it. Unless you are an expert with formulas, you'll find this feature exceptionally useful. That's why we felt it worth mentioning again.

Table 18-1   Precedence of Operators in Formulas in Excel 2007

Description	*Operator*
Reference operators	:
Space	(single space)
Comma	,
Negation	- (as in -1)
Percent	%
Exponentiation	^
Multiplication and division	* and /
Addition and subtraction	+ and -
Connect two strings of text	&
Comparisons	=<> <= >= <>

This feature works by offering a drop-down menu on the Formula Bar as you type in a formula, as shown in Figure 18-1. You can choose from the options provided on the menu or continue to fill in your own formula. As you scroll down the menu, detailed screen tips tell you exactly what the formula does so you can make a smart choice.

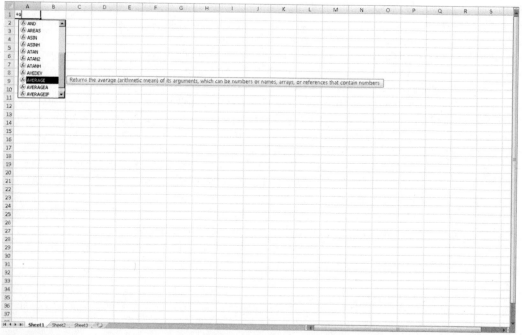

Figure 18-1: Excel 2007 offers a new feature called Formula AutoComplete to help you complete formulas accurately and quickly. A drop-down menu offers you instant formula choices.

Once you've settled on a formula, it's easy to enter that same formula into a range of cells, by the way. Just select the range to be calculated, type in the formula and press CTRL+ENTER. Try this:

1. Type random numerical values into cells B1 through C5.

2. Highlight cells D1 through D5.

3. Type **D1:D5** in the Name box (to the left of the Formula Bar.)

4. Type **=SUM(B1:C1)** in the Formula Bar.

5. Press CTRL+ENTER. Watch as Excel enters the formula into each cell in the range you specified.

You can use Formula AutoComplete with keystrokes, too. To turn the feature on or off, press ALT+DOWN ARROW.

Note

Pressing ALT+RIGHT or LEFT ARROW works as well on some systems.

Table 18-2 shows which keys will help you navigate the drop-down list.

Table 18-2	Keystrokes to Navigate the Formula AutoComplete Drop-Down List — Excel 2007
Select	*To Perform this Action on the Drop-down List*
HOME	Select the first item on the list.
END	Select the last item on the list.
UP ARROW	Move up one item.
DOWN ARROW	Move down one item.
RIGHT ARROW	Move one character to the right.
LEFT ARROW	Move one character to the left.
PAGE UP	Move up one page and select a new item.
PAGE DOWN	Move down one page and select a new item.
ESCAPE	Close the drop-down list.

Note

Even when you use Formula AutoComplete, you must type the closing parenthesis for a function, closing quotation mark for an MDX text string, or the closing bracket for a table reference.

Another new feature in Excel 2007 is the ability to resize the formula box as shown in Figure 18-2. If the size of the formula box is hindering you, just resize it to where it works best for you. When you do this, the active cell will always stay visible on the worksheet. You can resize the formula box in one of three ways:

■ Click the chevron button at the end of the formula bar to instantly expand it to three lines or collapse it to one line.

■ Move your cursor over the bottom of the formula box until the cursor changes to a vertical double arrow and then collapse or expand the box as much as you want. Releasing the mouse button or pressing ENTER sets the size.

■ Move your cursor over the bottom of the formula box until the cursor changes to a vertical double arrow and double-click the vertical double arrow to automatically fit the formula box to the number of lines of text in the active cell (up to the maximum height allowed).

Figure 18-2: Now you have the ability to resize the formula bar so you can read the entire formula.

Moving or copying formulas in Excel 2007 isn't really a new feature, but the way you do it is new. To move a formula:

1. Highlight the cell containing the formula to be moved.

2. Go to the Home tab and click Cut in the Clipboard group.

3. Paste the formula and its formatting by clicking Paste in the Clipboard group.

    OR

    Paste the formula without formatting by clicking Paste → Paste Special → Formulas in the Clipboard group.

To copy a formula:

1. Highlight the cell containing the formula to be copied.

2. Go to the Home tab and click Copy in the Clipboard group.

3. Paste the formula and its formatting by clicking Paste in the Clipboard group.

    OR

    Paste the formula without formatting by clicking Paste → Paste Special → Formulas in the Clipboard group.

Exploring New Charting Options

Some cool new chart options are available in Excel 2007 because, with this version, charts are now drawn with OfficeArt. As a result, almost anything you can do with an OfficeArt shape can be done to an Excel 2007 chart: 3-D, shadows, whatever. Additional improvements include clearer lines and the use of ClearType fonts that enhance readability. Plus, new maximum limits mean you can include more charts, links, and data than ever before.

With Excel 2007, you can reuse charts you create by saving the chart as a chart template (*.crtx) in the chart template folder. Then, the next time you create a chart, you can pull the chart template just like any other built-in chart type. You can even save your chart as a default chart type if you like. These chart templates differ from user-defined custom charts in earlier versions of Excel because they are true chart types and can be used to change the chart type of an existing chart.

To save a chart as a chart template:

1. Click on the chart.

2. On the Design tab, click Save As Template in the Type group.

3. Select Charts in the Save In box and type in the name you want for the template.

4. Click Save.

To apply a chart template, you have two options: you can create a new chart based on the template you already created or you can simply use the template.

1. To use a chart template or create a new chart based on the template, go to the Insert tab, and select any chart type in the Charts group.

2. Click All Chart Types.

3. Click Templates and choose the chart template you want, making modifications as needed.

Excel 2007 has another new key charting feature that should be noted: the ability to share charting between Excel, Word, and PowerPoint. Previously, Word and PowerPoint used charting features supported by Microsoft Graph. You could see the Excel charts and modify them somewhat in Word and PowerPoint, but the entire process was cumbersome and awkward. Now, Excel, Word, and PowerPoint all use the same chart tools, making it easier to work between the three applications.

To paste an Excel chart into a PowerPoint presentation while maintaining a link to the Excel data, take these steps:

1. In Excel, select the chart.

2. In Excel, go to the Home tab and click Cut in the Clipboard group.

3. In PowerPoint, click the location where you want the chart inserted.

4. In PowerPoint, go to the Home tab and click the arrow under Paste in the Clipboard group. Click Paste.

Now, when you update the data in the Excel 2007 file, the chart in PowerPoint will be updated as well.

Note

To change the data in the chart, you must make the changes in the linked worksheet because the worksheet is a separate file and not actually saved within the PowerPoint file.

To actually embed data from an Excel 2007 chart into your PowerPoint presentation, you will start within the PowerPoint presentation:

1. In PowerPoint, click the location where you want the chart inserted.

2. In PowerPoint, go to the Insert tab and click Chart in the Illustrations group.

3. In PowerPoint, click a chart in the Create Chart dialog box and click OK. Excel opens and displays dummy data on a worksheet.

4. In Excel, replace the dummy data by selecting the cells you want and typing in the new information.

5. In Excel, click the Office Button and click Save Copy As.

6. In Excel, select a folder or drive in the Save In list displayed in the Save As dialog box.

7. In Excel, type a new name for the file in the File Name box and click Save.

8. In Excel, click Close on the File menu.

The Excel worksheet is used as the actual chart data sheet for Word and PowerPoint, which allows you to use Excel's formulas, filtering, sorting, and even external data sources in your chart in those programs.

Tip

When copying charts from Excel to Word or PowerPoint, the Excel worksheet data can either be embedded in the new application or left in Excel. Embedding it into Word or PowerPoint increases the size of those other documents.

Getting Better Printouts

Fine-tuning your worksheet pages before printing them for the world to see is pretty easy with Excel 2007. The Page Layout view (View tab, in the Workbook Views group) was specifically designed to make printing your worksheets simple and fast. The first thing to do is choose the paper size you will be using in the Page Layout view.

Letter size (8.5 inches by 11 inches) is the default page size in Excel 2007. To change this, go to the Page Layout tab in the Page setup group and click Size. Now, choose the size of paper you will be using. You can also select envelope sizes here.

Excel 2007's ruler default is to display default units specified in the regional settings under the Control Panel. However, you can change these units to millimeters, inches, or centimeters. To change the default:

1. Select the worksheet you want to work on and then go to the Page Layout view.

2. Click the Office Button and select Excel Options.

3. Go to Display in the Advanced category and select the unit measurement you desire in the Ruler Units list.

Now that you have the measurements set the way you like, you should set your page margins to ensure they will print according to your printer's specifications.

1. In your selected worksheet, go to Page Layout view again.

2. In the Page Setup group, click Margins.

3. Now, choose Normal, Narrow, or Wide. Notice that each of these choices shows you the exact dimensions that will be used. You can also choose Custom Margins to create your own measurements. The header and footer margins will automatically adjust according to the page margin chosen.

If you want gridlines, row headings, and column headings to appear in your printout, you will need to take some action; these are not printed automatically. On your selected worksheet, go to Page Layout. In the Sheet Options group as shown in Figure 18-3, choose one of the following options:

- Clear or select the View check box under Gridlines to hide or display gridlines.

- Select the Print check box under Gridlines to print gridlines.

- Clear or select the View check box under Heading to hide or display row and column headings.

- Select the Print check box under Headings to print row and column headings.

Add row or column headings and gridlines

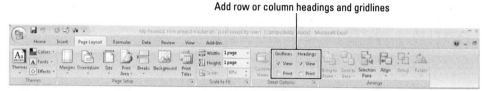

Figure 18-3: Gridlines, row headings, and column headings do not automatically appear in printouts unless certain settings are changed in Excel 2007.

If you want to shrink the height or width of a printed worksheet — or stretch or shrink a printed worksheet to a percentage of its actual size — you need to work in the Scale to Fit group under the Page Layout tab. To shrink a worksheet to fit a maximum number of pages, select the number of pages in the Width or Height lists. To stretch or shrink printed worksheets by percentage, change the percentage in the Scale box.

All done with printing and need to return to the normal view? Go to the View tab and click Normal in the Workbook Views group.

Working with Larger Workbooks

Working with the larger workbooks that Excel 2007 offers isn't really much different from any other version of Excel. Sure, workbooks are limited in size now only by available memory and system resources and your worksheets can hold more than 1 million rows by more than 16000 columns. And you can review more than 65000 pages in print review and 10000 filter drop-down lists can be employed but hey, what's the big deal about a few gazillion rows, columns, pages, and lists among other things? Truthfully, the difference is just that now you can pretty much do what you want in Excel 2007 and you won't be limited by pesky little memory and size issues. But now that you aren't limited in size or imagination, the trick will be to review and analyze quickly the information you are placing into the workbooks.

Here a few things to consider as you work with these larger workbooks. First, because of the new interface, commands are located in different places. To open a new workbook, click the Office

Button and then click New. From there, decide whether you want a blank workbook, one from your templates or Microsoft templates, or to create one from an existing workbook.

Next, due to the larger capacity, you may want to freeze panes more often. You can still freeze panes to lock out specific rows or columns in Excel 2007. This is a particularly useful feature now because of the large size workbooks can become; it lets you keep portions of the sheet visible while the rest of the sheet scrolls. This feature is accessed now via the View tab. After selecting the row or column (or both) where you want the split to appear, click Freeze Panes in the Window group and select the option you want. Notice that when you select Freeze Panes, the drop-down menu automatically offers you the choice of freezing panes, the top row only or the first column only.

A old feature with a new twist in these workbooks is the ability to use a password to prevent others from opening or changing your workbook. It's the same concept as with earlier versions of Excel, but it is accessed differently. To set a password for your workbook:

1. Click the Office Button and select Save As.

2. Click Tools and select General Options.

3. Pick one of these options:

    ▪ Type a password in the Password to Open box. (This will require others to enter a password before they can view the workbook.)

    ▪ Type a password in the Password to Modify box. (This will require others to enter a password before they can save changes to the workbook; they will still be able to view the workbook without a password.)

    ▪ Assign both passwords for double protection; just make sure each password is different.

Caution

If you forget the passwords you assign to a workbook, Microsoft cannot retrieve it. Be sure to write down your passwords in a secure place away from the workbook.

Another trick to working with larger workbooks in Excel 2007 is to filter by using advanced criteria. Often, a simple filter just won't work with large workbooks. Instead of using the AutoFilter, you will use the Advanced command in the Sort & Filter group on the Data tab. This command lets you type in the advanced criteria in a separate criteria range on your worksheet above the range of cells or the table where you want information filtered. Excel then uses this separate criteria range in an Advanced Filter dialog box as its source.

There are dozens of ways to list multiple complex criteria to fine-tune this Advanced Filtering technique; Excel 2007's Help can walk you through the precise steps depending upon your needs (for example, multiple criteria in one column, multiple criteria in multiple columns where all criteria must be true, multiple criteria in multiple columns where any criteria can be true, etc.).

Getting and Using Free Templates from the Web

By now, you have probably noticed that when you use Help in Excel 2007, you are taken to Microsoft Office Online if you are connected to the Internet. While you may usually be seeking instructions, if you take a closer look at Office Online you'll discover a wealth of templates available for your free use. Yep, free. Someone has already gone in, created a template in Excel, and it's just sitting there waiting for you to use it. If you haven't used the templates available from Office Online before, take a few minutes now to check them out. If you are already in an Excel worksheet, just type **templates** in the Help search box and watch how many Excel 2007 templates pop up as in Figure 18-4.

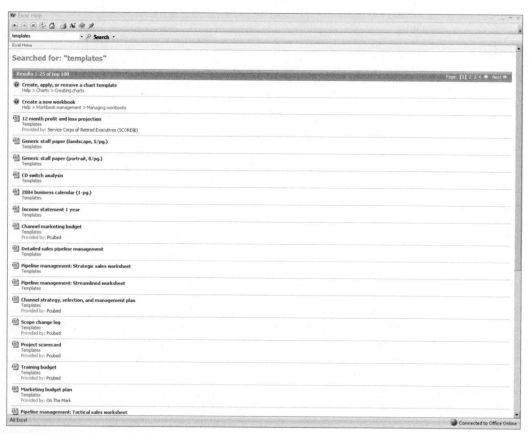

Figure 18-4: Dozens of free Excel templates are available for download from Microsoft Office Online, easily accessed through Excel Help.

You will know the difference between a template and a help topic in two ways: first, the templates display the Excel icon to the left and second, they each say "template" underneath the title. A standard help topic says Help and points to the help topics involved. Not enough templates for you? Scroll down and click All of Microsoft Office Online under Other Places to Look for Templates.

If you are creating a new worksheet and would like to access these templates to help you get started:

1. Go to the Office Button and Click New.

2. Under Templates, choose from Installed Templates, My templates, or New from existing as shown in Figure 18-5.

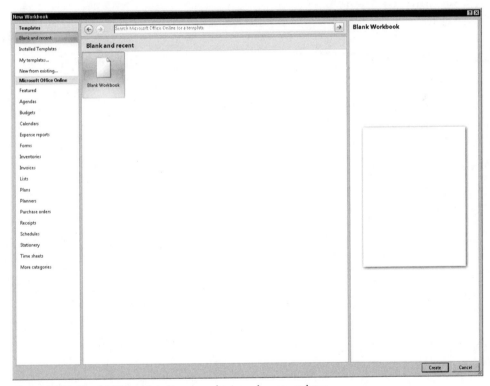

Figure 18-5: Excel 2007 makes it easy to obtain and use templates.

Several templates will show up immediately; others can be accessed by selecting specific templates under Microsoft Office Online.

Summary

This chapter has provided a quick overview of several new features offered in Excel 2007, but we can't cover everything in one chapter. Take the time to explore Excel on your own and don't be afraid to click in a few places that you haven't clicked before. You'll find — like we did — that Excel 2007 offers a variety of small and large features that make working with spreadsheets less intimidating than before. Just click the Undo button on the Quick Access Toolbar if you go somewhere a little too advanced for your skill level and try that command another day.

Part VIII

Keeping in Touch with Outlook

Chapter 19
Performing Common Tasks in Outlook

Chapter 20
Exploring Additional New Features in Outlook

Chapter 19

Performing Common Tasks in Outlook

O utlook is the program in Office that helps you organize your life. Yes, you use Outlook to send and receive e-mail, too, but there's so much more to the program than just e-mail. Organization, contacts, notes, and much more functionality is built into the Outlook program. It just hasn't always been as useful as it is with Outlook 2007.

Microsoft's developers have taken the time to learn what users are looking for when it comes to functionality in Outlook, and much of it has improved. Additional calendaring, task, and even e-mail capabilities have been added, so it takes less time for you to gain control over your inbox and your life.

Exploring the Interface

The first thing you'll notice when you open Outlook 2007 is that it doesn't appear to have changed as drastically as some of the other Office 2007 programs. The changes are simple, clean, and easy to adjust to. But don't let that fool you. There's more functionality hidden behind features that you're accustomed to working with, and those features are easier to access than they have ever been.

New Look

Outlook's new look is similar in appearance to Outlook 2003. The Ribbon that has become part of Word, PowerPoint, and other Office programs is conspicuously missing from Outlook 2003. This is because the designers could find no way to add the Ribbon without cluttering the various views of Outlook.

The toolbars from previous versions of Outlook are still located at the top of the page, and the Office Button has not been included in this version of Outlook, either. The layout, however, is intuitive to use, and with a few mouse-clicks all of the functionality that you're accustomed to having (and then some) is available.

The one place where you will find the Ribbon in Outlook is when you create a new e-mail message. Because creating messages is a Word-based function, you'll find that you have the same controls when creating and replying to e-mail messages that you would have in Word.

New Features and Tools

If it looks the same, the tools and features must all be the same, right? Not quite. There is a wealth of new functionality in Outlook 2007. You'll learn about a lot of that functionality in the pages of this chapter and the next, but here's a sneak peak at what you can do with Outlook 2007:

- Create appointments or to-do items by dragging a message to the appropriate program.

- Create an out-of-office reply.

- Create profiles for separate e-mail accounts or users.

- Create and customize business cards for your contacts.

- Search the entire Outlook program with the click of a button.

- Share calendars, appointments, and journal entries by e-mail.

- Publish a calendar to the Internet.

- Customize Outlook 2007 to meet your specific needs and tastes.

And that's just a sample of the ways in which Outlook works for you to help you get organized and work more efficiently. There's more. A lot more. And you'll learn about all of that in the pages ahead. But for now, let's get started by customizing the Outlook interface to make it feel a little more like your own program.

Customizing the Interface

The default view for Outlook 2007 is the Personal Folders view, which you probably also know as Outlook Today. This view is a quick look at your calendar, task, and messages for the day. And this is the first place you'll begin customizing your interface.

1. Begin by clicking the Customize Outlook Today link in the right corner of the screen. This takes you to Personal Folders - Outlook Today Options.

2. From this screen, you can change your Startup, Messages, Calendar, Tasks, and Styles options.

    - The Startup option allows you to decide if you want Outlook to open in the Outlook Today view each time you open it. If the box next to When starting, go directly to Outlook Today option is not checked, then Outlook will start in the Mail folder each time you open it.

    - The Messages option allows you to select which folders are shown to you in your navigation pane, as shown in Figure 19-1. Select or deselect the check boxes next to each folder to dictate which folders are shown and which are hidden.

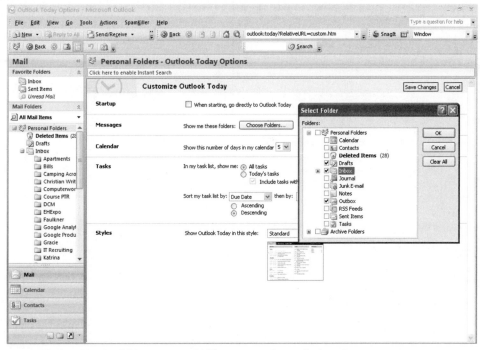

Figure 19-1: Select the folders you would like to see in the Outlook Today view.

- The Calendar option lets you choose how many days will be shown in the Calendar column of Outlook Today. You can choose from one to seven days by clicking the drop-down menu and selecting the desired number of days.

- The options for Tasks are slightly more involved than the other options. You can choose which tasks you want to display (all tasks or just today's tasks), and you can choose the way your tasks are displayed.

- Finally, you'll find the option to change your styles in this menu. Using this option you can set your display style to Standard, Standard (two column), Standard (one column), Summer, or Winter display. If you choose the Summer (orange) or Winter (blue) display, the number of columns shown on the page automatically defaults to three.

3. When you've finished making your selections, click Save Changes in the top right corner so your specifications will take effect.

Each additional program in Outlook also has customization options to allow you to set that program up to meet your personal tastes. For example, if you navigate to your Inbox and select Tools → Options, the Options dialog box appears, as shown in Figure 19-2. From this dialog box you can customize your preferences, mail setup, and other options.

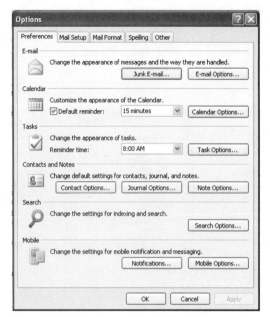

Figure 19-2: Use the Options dialog box to set your
Outlook program options.

The same command string (Tools → Options) opens the Options dialog box from any screen
within Outlook.

Customizing Outlook to your tastes makes it much easier to work in Outlook. Perhaps you like to
start the day in Outlook Today to get a quick overview of what you're doing. Many people prefer to
jump right in with both feet and have Outlook open automatically to their inbox. Your personal preferences determine what works for you and what doesn't, and Outlook gives you some freedom in
using what works to your advantage.

Working with E-mail

For most people, the first thing that comes to mind when they think of Outlook is e-mail. Sure, there
are several other very useful tools included in Outlook, like the calendar and the to-do list, but ultimately, Outlook is about e-mail. So having the e-mail functionality that you would expect to have is
important.

Outlook 2007 has all of that functionality and some extra, too. Creating e-mail profiles, sending
and receiving mail, and adding special touches, like signatures or stationery, to your e-mails is easy
to accomplish with Outlook.

Creating a Profile

The first thing you'll want to do when you access Outlook is probably to create an e-mail profile, or
account. With Outlook, you can create multiple e-mail accounts. If you're prompted to set up an

e-mail account when you open Outlook, follow the prompts and you'll soon have your first e-mail account set up. But what if your e-mail address changes? It happens all the time. You change Internet service providers and get a new e-mail address, or maybe you've found an e-mail service provider online that you like. Changing or updating your profile, or creating a new profile for a separate e-mail box is simple.

1. Go to Tools → Account Settings. The Account Settings dialog box appears.

2. Click the E-mail tab and then select New to create a new e-mail profile. You're prompted to select the type of account you'd like to create.

3. To create a new account select Microsoft Exchange Server, POP3, IMAP, or HTTP and then click Next.

4. Another dialog box appears, as shown in Figure 19-3. Fill in the requested information and click Next.

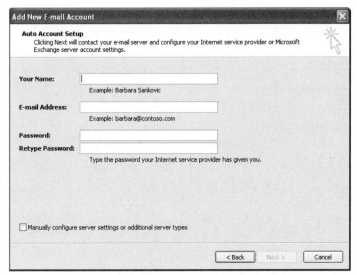

Figure 19-3: Enter your information so that Outlook can automatically detect and configure your profile.

5. Now, Outlook will automatically configure your e-mail account. It could take several minutes for your account configuration to complete, so be patient.

6. When Outlook has finished configuring your e-mail profile, you'll receive a notice that the process was successful. However, if the connection is unsuccessful, you'll be prompted to verify your settings and retry the connection process.

7. Some e-mail programs won't allow Outlook to automatically configure your settings, but you have the option to configure your profile manually. Place a check mark in the box next to Manually configure server settings and click Next. You'll then be taken to the manual

configuration steps. Follow each prompt, and click Finish when you've entered all of your information. Outlook will then configure your account. You should experience more success when setting up a profile manually, however, you'll have to know the address of your incoming and outgoing mail servers. Your e-mail program administrators should be able to give you that information.

8. When you receive a success message, click Finish and then click Close on the Account Settings dialog box, and your new e-mail account is ready to use. All you have to do now is use Outlook to send and receive messages.

Editing and Deleting Profiles

Because change happens, you may on occasion need to change or delete an e-mail profile. Here are the steps for that:

1. Go to Tools → Account Settings.

2. Then, highlight the account that you want to change or delete by clicking the account name one time and select Change or Remove from the toolbar above the account list.

3. If you choose to change an account, the Change E-mail Account dialog box appears. Make the changes that you need to make, click the Test Account Settings box to ensure that your changes have properly taken effect, and then click the Next button. You'll be taken to a screen that confirms your changes were successful.

4. Click Finish to complete the change.

Removing an account is even easier:

1. Highlight the account that you want to remove and then click the Remove button on the toolbar above the account list.

2. You will be prompted to confirm that you want to remove the account. Click Yes and the account will be removed.

Caution

Use caution when removing an e-mail account. Once you confirm the removal of the account, it can't be undone. If you delete an account accidentally, you'll have to reconfigure the account from the beginning.

One other option that you'll notice in the Account Settings dialog box is the Repair option. This is an option that you'll use if your e-mail box begins to behave strangely. It's possible for an e-mail account to become corrupted for no apparent reason. The Repair option allows you to repair any damage to your e-mail profile without deleting and then recreating the account. This is especially helpful if there are items in your inbox that you don't want to lose.

Sending E-mail

Now you have a working e-mail profile. So how do you send e-mail? It's as easy as starting a new message, addressing it, adding a subject line and your text, and then clicking the send icon. Figure 19-4 shows a labeled e-mail message.

Add an e-mail address

Click Send   Add a subject title

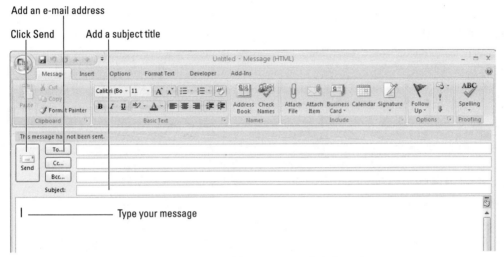

Figure 19-4: Fill in the relevant information, add some text, and click send.

There are some keyboard shortcuts that you can use to make the process easier, too. For example, press the CTRL key and the N key at the same time (CTRL+N) to start a new e-mail message. Or press CTRL+ENTER to send a message. More keyboard shortcuts are available, too. The standard shortcuts for bold formatting, italics formatting, copying, and pasting are available but in addition to these you may find other keyboard shortcuts by pressing the ALT key. This shows the available ALT Commands.

Finally, when you're sending a message, you may want to check your spelling or set the message for follow-up at a later time. These options are available on the Message tab, which should be the default view for creating messages.

You can also set automatic options for spell checking and other functions by going to Tools → Options in the main Outlook window. This action takes you to the Options dialog box you found earlier in this chapter.

Working with Attachments

There will be times when you want to send an attachment with your message or even to embed a document or picture into the message. Outlook 2007 gives you several options for attachments:

- **Attach a file:** Use the Attach File button to attach a file to your e-mail.

▪ **Attach an item:** This command allows you to attach another Outlook item (like a message or an appointment) to your e-mail message.

▪ **Drag a file:** For a quick attachment, you can drag a file from its location on your hard drive to the body of your message. This automatically attaches the file to the message unless it is in a rich text format. When you attach a rich text format file, the file appears to be embedded in the email message although it's actually an attachment.

ATTACHING A FILE

When you choose to attach a file to your e-mail message, it works just like it always has in previous versions of Outlook.

1. Create the e-mail message to which you want the file attached.

2. Select Attach File from the Message tab and choose File or Item.

   A file could be a music file, a document, a picture, or any other self-contained file that you have stored on your hard drive. An item comes from Outlook and it may be an appointment, a calendar, a to-do list, or a folder contained in Outlook.

3. In the dialog box that opens, navigate to the file or item that you want to attach to the message. Select it and click Open.

4. The file or item is attached to the message. Click Send to send the attachment to the message recipient.

Alternately, you can simply drag the item or file that you want to attach into the body of the e-mail message. This automatically attaches the file or item to the message.

INSERTING A FILE

In some cases, you may prefer to insert your file into the body of a message. This is a handy feature if you have a file or item that you want the recipient to see without the frustration of downloading an attachment.

1. Create the message into which you want to embed the file.

2. Go to the Insert tab and select the type of item that you want to embed into the body of the message. You can choose Table, Picture, Clip Art, SmartArt, WordArt, Charts, Shapes, Hyperlinks, Book Marks, Text Boxes, Quick Parts, Date & Time, Objects, Equations, Symbols, or Lines.

3. If necessary, in the dialog box that appears, select the location of the item you want to embed into the body of the message and click Insert. In some cases you won't need to select a location, but you will need to select properties or other defining elements for the item you're inserting.

4. The image or file is inserted and then (and this is the really neat part of this) you're automatically taken to a hidden Picture Tools tab: Format (or whatever tab is appropriate for

the type of object you've inserted). Use the controls on this tab to adjust or reformat the object you've inserted into the message.

5. When you're finished, complete your message and click Send.

The hidden Picture Tools tab is just one of the contextual tabs that you don't see until you need it. These tabs turn up (inline with the other tabs) only when you need them most. For example, if you're inserting a text box, there's a hidden Format tab that appears after you create the text box. When you're finished, these tabs disappear again. So they don't clutter up your work area.

Creating E-mail Signatures

E-mail signatures are like little biographies that you can use to tell your message recipient about you or your company. Most people include titles, contact information, a company name, and maybe even a relevant quote in their e-mail signature.

E-mail signatures are also automatic. You create them one time, and then they appear in your outgoing messages, according to guidelines that you set. For example, you can choose to have them included only in new mails that you create, or you can have them included in new messages and replies, but not forwards, or however else you might choose to set them up.

1. To create an e-mail signature, from your Inbox, go to Tools → Options and click the Mail Format tab.

2. Select Signatures and the Signatures and Stationery dialog box opens, as shown in Figure 19-5.

3. To create a new signature, click New. You're prompted to enter a name for the signature. Type a name for your new signature and then click OK.

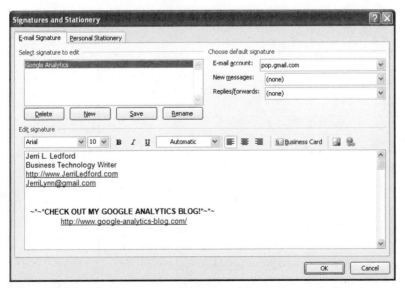

Figure 19-5: Use the Signatures and Stationery dialog box to create signatures to include in your e-mail messages.

4. The name you just typed appears in your signature list, and you're taken to a text editor in which you can create your signature. The text editor contains formatting controls like colors, bold, and italics so you can jazz your signature up. Add the information you want included in the signature, format it in the way you want it to appear, and click OK. Your new signature will be created in the signature list and the signature creator will disappear. If this is the only signature in your list, it will be included in your messages.

5. If you have other signatures, or if you want to change how a signature appears in your messages, you need to go back to the Signatures and Stationery dialog box. In that dialog box, you can use the drop-down menus on the right to set which signature appears on what e-mail account, new messages, replies, and forwards. When you've made your selections, click the OK button and your preferences will be applied to your e-mails.

Using Stationery and Templates

While you were in the Signatures and Stationery dialog box, you may have noticed the Personal Stationery tab. Remember, you got there by going to Tools → Options → Mail Format and then selecting Signatures. You can also get there by going to Tools → Options → Mail Format then selecting the Stationery and Fonts option. This takes you directly to the Personal Stationery tab in the Signatures and Stationery dialog box.

The Personal Stationery tab, shown in Figure 19-6, gives you options for the theme and font that you want to use with incoming, outgoing, reply, and forwarded messages. You can change these settings by clicking the button next to each option. A larger menu appears, from which you can make your selections.

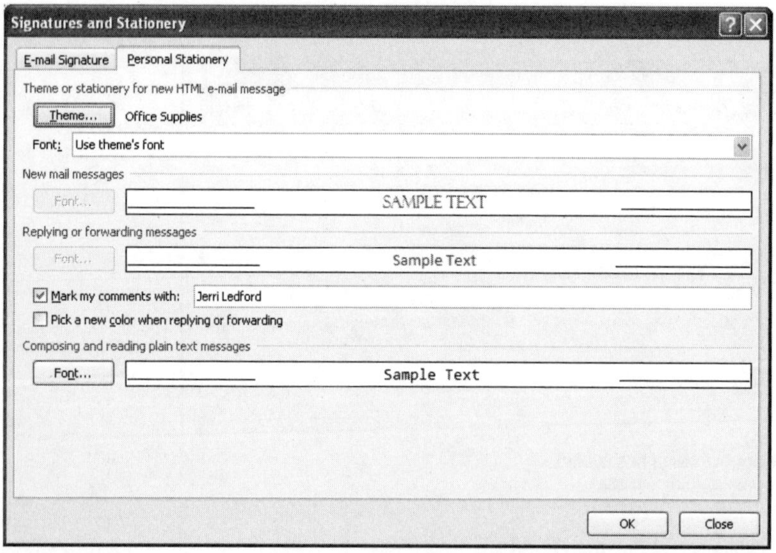

Signatures and Stationery

E-mail Signature | Personal Stationery

Theme or stationery for new HTML e-mail message

Theme... | Office Supplies

Font: Use theme's font

New mail messages

Font... | SAMPLE TEXT

Replying or forwarding messages

Font... | Sample Text

☑ Mark my comments with: Jerri Ledford
☐ Pick a new color when replying or forwarding

Composing and reading plain text messages

Font... | Sample Text

OK | Close

Figure 19-6: Select the stationery options that suit you for incoming, outgoing, and forwarded messages.

When you've finished making your selection, click OK to apply the options and then OK to close the Options dialog box. Then, the next time you create a new message your chosen stationery style will appear in the message.

Creating an Out-of-Office Reply

If you're using Microsoft Exchange Server with your Outlook, then you probably have an option for creating an out-of-office reply. However, computers that are not connected to an Exchange server won't have this option.

The fastest and easiest way to tell if you have this option is to go to the Tools menu. If you're connected to an Exchange Server, you'll find an option there for the Out of Office Assistant. If the option isn't there, then you're not connected to an Exchange Server and you can't use this option.

The autoresponder is designed to let people now when you're away from e-mail. If you do have access to the Out of Office Assistant, you can create an autoresponder by clicking the Out of Office Assistant link. You're taken to the Out of Office Assistant dialog box, as shown in Figure 19-7.

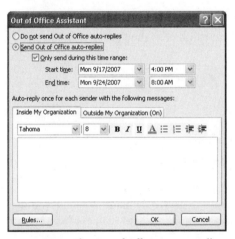

Figure 19-7: The Out of Office Assistant allows you to create an autoresponder to use when you're away from your e-mail box.

Use the options in this dialog box to set up your autoresponder. When you're finished, click OK to create the autoresponder.

When you return from your travels, you can access the Out of Office Assistant again to turn the autoresponder off.

If you don't happen to be connected to an Exchange Server, you're not completely out in the cold for an autoresponder, it's just much more involved to create.

1. Begin by creating a message template to use. Create a new e-mail message by clicking the New option.

2. In the message, go to Options → Format and then click Plain Text. This ensures that you're creating a template based on a plain text format.

3. Type the message that you would like to use as an autoresponder into the body of the message and then click the Office Button and select Save File As and save the file as an Outlook Template.

4. Now, you have to create a rule to automatically send the message. Do this by going to Tools and clicking on Rules and Alerts.

5. The Rules and Alerts dialog box appears. Click New to create a new rule.

6. In the dialog box that appears, select Start from a Blank Rule and then select Check messages when they arrive, and then click Next.

7. Under Which conditions do you want to check? select Sent Only to Me and any other criteria that you want applied to the autoresponder. Then click Next.

8. The next screen asks: What do you want to do with the message? Select Reply using a specific template.

9. Then click the link at the bottom of the Rules Wizard and select the template you created to use an autoresponder and click Open.

10. Now click Next and you're taken to options for setting exceptions to the rule. Select your options and then click Next again.

11. Review your rule setting and click Finish.

12. The rule is created, and now you have an autoresponder, even if you're not using an Exchange Server.

Autoresponders are handy if you're going to be out of the office with limited access to e-mail. It would be great if you could simply click the Out of Office Assistant command, whether you use Exchange Server or another type of e-mail access, but at least using the rules workaround you can create an autoresponder in a pinch.

Managing E-mail

E-mail has become a communication lifeline in most business (and even home) settings. But if you aren't careful, e-mail can take over your life. Fortunately, Outlook 2007 offers many different options for managing your e-mail.

For example, did you know that you can automatically send certain messages to specific folders so that you can deal with them when you're ready? You can also create folders to file your messages in, and you can zap spam before it ever hits your inbox. Keep reading. We'll show you how.

Sorting Options

As overwhelming as e-mail can get, there are ways to make it easier to manage. Sorting options are one of those ways. Consider this: You're away from the office for a week and when you get back there are over 1000 e-mail messages sitting in your inbox. How in the world are you going to wade through all of those messages?

If you use the default sorting option in Outlook, you can go through them by date. But that can be tedious. A better way might be to sort the messages by sender or topic. Outlook gives you 13 options plus the ability to create a custom sorting filter.

To access these options, right-click the Arrange By bar, as shown in Figure 19-8. Then to sort, click on the desired option. All of the messages in the current folder will be sorted according to your choice. If you change folders, however, the sorting will default back to the last sorting arrangement chosen for that folder.

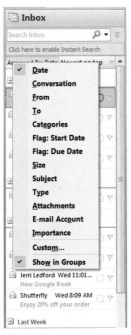

Figure 19-8: Right-click the Arrange By bar to change the sorting method used.

You can also use the View menu to change your sorting options. On the Arrange By menu, select Arrange and then choose the sorting option desired.

Search Folders

Another option for quickly finding the information you need in Outlook is to use Search Folders. Search Folders are useful to find messages when you receive a large quantity of e-mail. You can even use a search folder to find messages if you use rules and filters to automatically separate and file messages so you don't have to.

   1. From the Mail view of Outlook, select File → New and select Search Folder.

2. The New Search Folder dialog box appears, as shown in Figure 19-9.

Figure 19-9: Use the New Search Folder dialog box
to create search parameters for your Search Folder.

3. Select the criteria by which you want to search, and then click OK.

4. The search results are displayed in the navigation pane, just as e-mail within a folder would be.

Search Folders are a quick, and easy, way to find messages of a specific type or from a specific sender. And the search is performed on all of your Outlook folders. And if you find that you perform a search regularly, you can add the search folder to your Favorite Folders view for even faster access.

Once you've created and executed your search, right-click the Search Folder and then click Add to Favorite Folders. The folder is then added to your Favorite Folders navigation pane. The next time you need to run that particular search, all you have to do is click the Search Folder in the Favorites navigation pane.

Search Folders are a useful way of finding and grouping messages according to specific criteria. They can be sent or received messages, and once you find them, it's easy to add the search to your Favorite Folders.

Dealing with Spam

Everyone hates spam. And there's more of it today than there ever has been in the past. Worse, a lot of the spam that's cluttering your inbox could be infected with malware. So, you want to get a handle on spam as quickly and easily as possible.

Previous versions of Outlook included spam controls that were as simple to use as right-clicking on a message. Today, those spam controls are much like they were in the past. If you receive a message that is spam but it manages to get past the spam filter, right-click the message title in your list of messages, and then select Junk Mail and click Add to Blocked Senders List. The message is then sent to the Junk Mail folder and future messages from that sender automatically get tagged as Junk Mail.

You can also manage your Junk Mail Options by going to Actions → Junk Mail → Junk Mail Options. Then you can change the automatic delete selections, add users to the safe or blocked senders lists, or increase or decrease your spam filter's sensitivity, as shown in Figure 19-10.

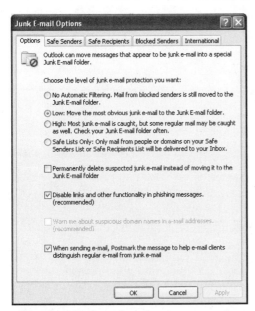

Figure 19-10: Use Junk Mail Options to set the desired options on your spam filter.

Creating Rules

One of the easiest ways to separate and categorize your e-mail is to create a rule that handles the message without any additional thought from you. Rules are guidelines that help Outlook to determine where a message should be delivered to. For example, if you're working on a project, and all of the messages for that project come through with the same subject line or from the same people, you can create a folder specifically for those messages so they're easy to locate.

1. To begin, from the Mail navigation pane, go to Tools → Rule and Alerts.

2. In the Rules and Alerts dialog box that appears, select New Rule.

3. The New Rules Wizard appears, as shown in Figure 19-11. From Step 1 in the wizard box, select the guidelines you would like to put in place with the rule.

4. Then in Step 2 (on the same screen), click the blue link to edit the rule description, and click Next.

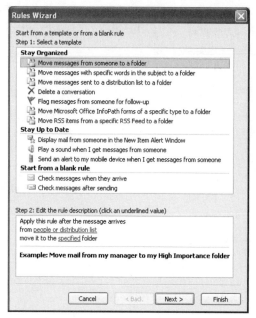

Figure 19-11: Use the New Rules Wizard to create new e-mail rules.

5. Select the conditions and edit the rule descriptions again to further specify rule guidelines and then click Next.

6. Now define what you want done with the messages, and then click Next.

7. Set the exceptions to the rule if there are any, and click Next.

8. Give the rule a name, set up rule options, and review the rule definitions. When you're satisfied that the rule meets your expectations, click Finish and the rule will be created.

After you have created a rule, changing or deleting it is as easy as navigating back to the Rules and Alerts dialog box, highlighting the rule, and selecting Change Rule or Delete. If you choose to change a rule, the Rules Wizard box appears and you can walk through each of the steps again to make the desired changes.

Using the Calendar

E-mail may be the main reason that people use Outlook, but it's not the only reason. Outlook also contains an excellent calendaring application, and with Outlook 2007 that calendar has been made even more useful. New scheduling features, additional organizational tools, and the ability to easily create appointments and tasks make using the calendar even easier than it has been in the past.

Customizing Your Calendar

Just as no two people work the same, no two people use the calendar the same. Your work week might be from 8 to 5, Monday through Friday, while someone else's is 7 to 4, Tuesday through Saturday. Or maybe you prefer to break your days up into 30 minute increments instead of one-hour increments.

All of these features and more are customizable in the Outlook calendar. To makes changes to the appearance and design of the calendar, from the Calendar window, go to Tools → Options and then click the Calendar Options button. The Calendar Options dialog box appears. Use this dialog box to set the days that are displayed in your work week, calendar options including coloring, and advanced options including allowing alternate calendars.

When you've set the options to meet your needs and preferences, click OK and then click OK again to activate your changes. Now, your calendar is customized to work the way you work.

Adding Calendar Items

Now that you've got your calendar set up the way you prefer to work, it's time to put it to use. And that means adding items to your calendar. There are several ways you can add an appointment to your calendar, too, making it easier for you to add to your calendar, no matter what you happen to be doing.

The method of creating an appointment that you're probably already aware of is to use the New option in the calendar page menu. Click New and select Appointment and then fill in the appropriate information. When you're finished, click Save & Close and the appointment is added to your calendar.

Alternatively, you can drag an e-mail onto the calendar and use it to make an appointment. For example, there's a big meeting coming up, and you have to make a presentation during the meeting. So, when the meeting time is set, your assistant sends you an e-mail detailing the date, time, and your responsibilities for the meeting. To create an appointment for that meeting, all you have to do is drag the e-mail to the calendar and drop it. The appointment dialog box appears. Fill in the appropriate information and click Save & Close.

The appointment is created, and the e-mail that you dropped into the appointment will be included in the notes section of the appointment file so that you can easily keep up with all of the information that you need. No more searching for the e-mail containing all the information you need, it's right there with the appointment.

Exploring Scheduling Options

Once you add an appointment to the calendar, it's easy to manipulate it. You can drag the appointment to another day, or click and drag the upper or lower boundary of the appointment to increase the length of time included in the appointment.

And since it's human nature to overschedule yourself, you'll also find that in the Day or Week view, you can see your Tasks in addition to your appointments. If you have a task that will take more than a few minutes to complete, you can drag it onto the calendar and create an appointment for it. This helps you to schedule your time wisely so you're not stressed out when you can't accomplish something that needs to be done.

If it turns out that you have tasks or appointments that you can't complete on the assigned day, deferring them is easy. Simply drag the task or appointment to another date and time. The appointment is moved and automatically adjusted. No stress.

In addition to moving your appointments and tasks around with ease, you can further simplify your life by assigning categories to your appointments, tasks, and e-mail messages. A category is a color code that lets you see at a glance what type of appointment you have set. For example, say you assign a blue category to client meetings. Then, each time you schedule a client meeting, you assign the meeting the blue category. Now, when you look at your calendar, you can tell at a glance how many client meetings you have scheduled in a given time frame. There's more about assigning categories to appointments in the next chapter.

Sharing Your Calendar

Busy people have a hard time scheduling anything. Sometimes it requires back-and-forth communication that can take days to find a date when you're available for a meeting or appointment. Wouldn't it be easier if you could just share your calendar? Guess what, you can.

Outlook 2007 has a function that allows you to publish your calendar to the Web and invite others to use it. Here's how to use it:

1. From the Calendar, click Publish My Calendar in the My Calendars navigation pane. If this is the first time that you've tried to publish your calendar online, you'll be prompted to register to use the service. It's a simple registration that consists of only two steps.

2. When the registration is complete, you'll be taken to the Publish Calendar to Microsoft Online dialog box, shown in Figure 19-12. Select the parameters by which you would like the calendar published, and then click OK.

3. An uploading message appears, and when the upload is complete you'll be prompted to send a sharing invitation for your calendar. Click Yes and an e-mail is opened. Finish addressing the message, add your own note, and click Send. The invitation is then sent to the users you selected.

Figure 19-12: Use the Publish Calendar to Microsoft Online dialog box to set the options for publishing your calendar.

Printing Your Calendar

Sharing a calendar with others is all well and good. Having it available at the click of a mouse is even better. But once in a while you need to have a paper copy of your calendar. You can either copy everything into your Day Planner, or you can print your calendar pages and have everything already included on the print pages.

Printing your calendar is a breeze. From the File menu, select Print. The Print dialog box appears. In the dialog box, select the calendar you want to print, the number of copies, the print style, and the date range that you want to print. When you're finished with your selections, you can preview the print or just select Print.

Alternatively, you can access a Quick Print that prints only the day or week that you select by right-clicking within the time frame. The Quick Print goes directly to the printer, without going through the various options.

Managing Contacts

One more common task that you'll probably use regularly in Outlook 2007 is Contacts. Contacts are your names, address, e-mail addresses, and telephone numbers. In many cases, they're contacts that are added automatically when you respond to an e-mail or download a V-Card. But you can also add new contacts or import them from other Outlook address books.

Flipping back and forth between your e-mail and your contacts gets old fast. Not to mention that it takes valuable time. But there is an easier way. When you're addressing your messages, or if you need to find a contact, you can use the address book from your main e-mail navigation pane.

The address book is indicated by the small address book in the e-mail toolbar. To find a contact, place your cursor in the text box next to the address book and type the name you're searching for and then press enter. If there's only one contact in your address book with that name, that person's contact information is displayed on the screen.

If there is more than one person with the same name, then you'll be shown a list of people whose names match what you typed. Select the name of the person you are searching for and click OK. The person's contact information is displayed.

Now, there are times when all you need is to find a person's e-mail address. If that's the case, Outlook can automatically fill in the e-mail address for you. All you have to do is open a new e-mail message and begin typing the person's name. A list of matching e-mail addresses will be shown, and you can select the e-mail address that you need from the list.

Using the address book in Outlook is pretty intuitive, but there are some interesting things that you can do in Outlook's Contacts. For example, did you know that you can create and customize business cards for everyone in your address book? That feature and others are covered in the next chapter.

Summary

Outlook has always been full of useful features, but Outlook 2007 is by far the easiest Outlook version yet. The new functions that have been added to e-mail, the calendar, and the contacts make it easy to schedule, track, and manage all of the tasks that you need to complete in Outlook. Common features, such as dragging, combined with new functionality such as categories and a consolidated view of your calendar and your tasks will give you the power you need to be more efficient and to accomplish more. These features also add more interest and are easier to use than they have ever been in the past.

Chapter 20

Exploring Additional New Features of Outlook

Bet you thought we were finished with Outlook? Not quite. There are some additional new features that bear mentioning. These features are designed to make your life easier. Some of them you may have seen in the past in some form, but in Outlook 2007 these features get new life and usability. For example, in this new version of Outlook the way you preview files has new life. It's much easier now than it's ever been to see what's included in a file before you download it.

The Integrated Search feature of Outlook is also covered here. This is a wonderful new feature that you'll find you use again and again. Outlook has more, so let's get started.

New Search Features

Outlook has always had search features, but they were slow and cumbersome. The new search features in Outlook 2007 are faster, easier to use, and with the right configuration, they're far more useful than in the past.

Using Integrated Search Features

Take the new integrated search feature. There are two ways that you can search in Outlook. The first is to use the search tool that's included with the program. It's indicated by the text box with a small looking glass next to it, as shown in Figure 20-1, and you'll find this search box in each of the different programs that you open in Outlook.

Search box

Figure 20-1: The search bar is located in each program in Outlook.

The search feature lets you quickly search through Outlook for a specific item. For example, if you need to find all of the messages that Joe sent you, type Joe's e-mail address or name into the search box, and within a few seconds all of them will appear in the preview pane.

The first time you use the search box, it may not return the results that you were hoping for. The search function may be set to search only in the currently selected folder. To change this, click the small black triangle to the right of the search box. This opens a list of options from which you should select Search Options. This opens a dialog box, as shown in Figure 20-2.

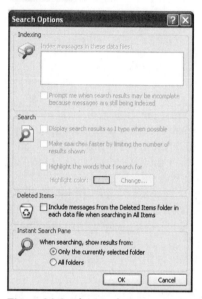

Figure 20-2: The Search Options dialog box allows you to change your search options to include different folders.

Change the Instant Search Pane option to All folders and click OK. Then try your search again. Now the search program is looking at all of your folders in Outlook, and not just in the current folder. When you run the search a second time, you should find that your results are more comprehensive and more accurate.

Using Instant Search

In the Search Options dialog box, you may also notice additional options:

■ **Indexing:** This option allows you to index messages in Personal Folders and Archive Folders

■ **Search:** This option allows you to display search results when you type your search term or highlight the search term in the messages returned in your results. This allows you to see why a particular message was included in the results.

- **Deleted Items:** This option allows you to include messages that you have deleted that contain the search term that you used.

- **Instant Search Pane:** This option allows you to set where search results will be pulled from. You can choose to search only the current folder or all Outlook folders.

Here's the problem with these options; most of them work only if you have Instant Search installed. Instant Search is a function that works only if you are using Microsoft Windows Vista. You are prompted when you open Microsoft Outlook 2007 to install Instant Search, but if you don't have Windows Vista you'll encounter an error with this installation. If you do have Windows Vista, then the search will install and you'll have several new searching capabilities:

- Search across all of the programs in Outlook.

- Search PST files (your personal files in Outlook).

- Search all messages that you have archived or stored.

- Search your Microsoft Exchange Server, if there's one installed.

Once you have installed Instant Search you'll be able to search specific fields within messages, as well. Clicking the double arrow beside the search box opens additional search options. This also appears in your Calendar, Notes, Journal, Favorites, and Tasks views.

The new search capabilities are much more powerful than they have been in the past, and with Microsoft Vista installed you have even more searching capabilities than ever before. Even without Vista, however, you'll find that search is much more functional than it has been in the past.

Previewing Attachments with a Single Click

Announcer voice: Can open attachments in a single click. Makes you feel like Superman, doesn't it?

Well, you can't open them, but you can preview them. When a message arrives in your inbox that contains an attachment, you no longer have to download it or open in a temporary file to find out what's in the attachment.

When the message arrives, you'll see a small paperclip in the right corner of the message title bar. This indicates there is an attachment connected to that message. In the body of the message, there's a line for attachments, which shows you the title, format, and size of the message.

To preview an attachment, click it one time. A warning message appears on the screen. You can choose to preview the file, or if you prefer not to, simply click the message again to be returned to the message view. In this dialog box, you also have the option not to be prompted every time you try to open an attachment. Be very careful about changing this option, because once you do, you no longer receive the prompt and you could accidentally open an attachment that contains malicious software.

Select Preview from the warning message and the file is previewed in the message pane. Now it's not necessary to download that file that Jane sent over to you. You can preview it first to make sure that it's a document that you need before you download it. If, after you preview it, you decide you want to download the document, simply double-click the attachment and select Save from the dialog box that appears.

When you're finished previewing the message, click the e-mail it's attached to and you'll be returned to the message view.

Note

In order for the message preview to work on all message types (.doc, .xls, .pdf, etc.) you need to have that extension installed on your computer. So for example, if you want to preview a .pdf file, then you need to have Adobe Acrobat Reader installed on your computer. If you do not, the document will not be viewable.

Previewing attachments in Outlook has never been easier. You no longer have to download the file completely to preview it. Now it's all available to you at a single mouse-click.

Using the To-Do Bar

One area that's seen the most useful improvements in Outlook is the To-Do bar. Functionality of the past — like the ability to drag a message to your calendar to create an appointment — is still there. But new functionality has been added, too.

Accessing Flagged Messages, Outlook Tasks, and Meetings

There is always something to do: complete tasks, watch over messages that need follow-up, and attend meetings with colleagues or bosses. In the past, Outlook had some capabilities that made this process easier, but they weren't as useful as they could be. Outlook 2007 is much more integrated so accessing flagged messages, tasks, and meetings is much easier now. It's all right there in the To-Do bar on the right side of the screen.

The To-Do Bar is an amalgamation of the various activities that take up your day. And those activities are all right there for you to see at a glance, as Figure 20-3 shows.

Your To-Do bar may be collapsed when you first open Outlook. To expand the bar, simply click the double arrow. When you're finished, you can collapse the To-Do bar again, to allow more space for reading e-mail. Even in the collapsed position, a truncated version of your tasks and appointments is available.

Configuring Automatic Reminders for Procrastinators

If you're like us, you tend to put everything off until the last possible minute. Most people are like that, and the developers over at Microsoft have found a way to help us all stay on task. There's now a reminder function built into Outlook to help you set reminders for the items that you flag for follow up.

If you want to add an audible reminder, right-click on the transparent flag to the right of the e-mail message or task title and select Add Reminder. This takes you to a dialog box, like the one shown in Figure 20-4, that lets you set the particulars for your reminder, including the flag to use, the start date and due date, the date of the reminder, the time of the reminder, and the sound that you would like to hear.

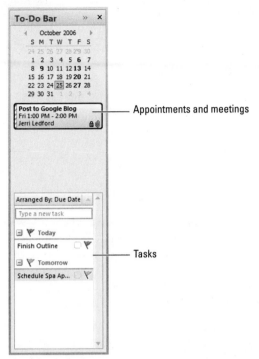

Figure 20-3: The To-Do Bar shows all of your activities in a single, easy-to-use view.

Figure 20-4: The reminder dialog box lets you set the particulars of your reminders.

If you click the Clear Flag button in the dialog box, it will completely remove the flag and any reminder that you have set in the past.

You can also set Outlook up to automatically add reminders to every task or e-mail that you flag. To do this:

1. Select Tools → Options and then click Task Options. The Task Options dialog box appears.

2. Put a check mark in the box next to Set reminders on tasks with due dates and then whenever you drag an e-mail to your task list, or create a new task and set a due date on it, the reminder will automatically be set.

Keeping up with your tasks has never been easier. Even for procrastinators.

Sending a Calendar Page with Calendar Snapshots

As you saw in the last chapter, there are many great new features with Outlook's calendar that make sharing the calendar much easier. Aside from publishing your calendar, though, you can also send a quick snapshot of your calendar to anyone that you can send e-mail to.

When you open your calendar, you'll notice there is a calendar task pane on the left. If you don't see your task pane, click the double arrow on the left above the navigation pane; this expands the calendar navigation pane.

1. In the navigation pane, you'll see there are options for My Calendar. If you click the Send a Calendar via E-mail option, a new e-mail message appears and the Send a Calendar via E-mail dialog box also appears.

2. Select the calendar you want to send, the date range, and the detail you want to send. There are also options to show time within working hours only, and an advanced option that lets you select the layout of the e-mail that you intend to send. These options are all shown in Figure 20-5.

3. When you've set the options, click OK and the calendar will be inserted into your e-mail as an embedded image, as shown in Figure 20-6.

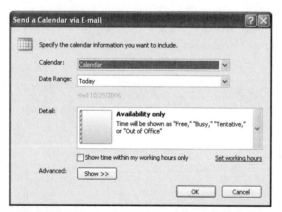

Figure 20-5: The Send a Calendar via E-mail dialog box lets you set the options for e-mailing a calendar snapshot.

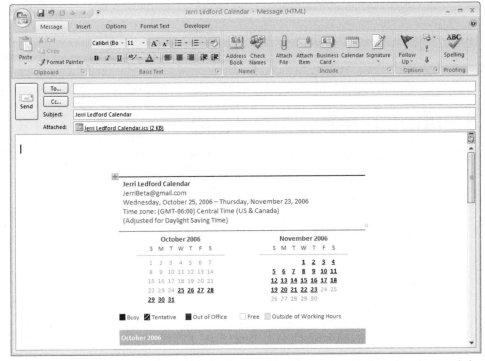

Figure 20-6: Once you've set the options for the calendar you want to include in the message, click OK and it is embedded into your e-mail.

4. Set who you want to send the message to, add any text you would like to include, and then select Send. Your calendar will then be sent to the recipients.

Now it's easy to share your calendar with colleagues, friends, or family. And you control the level of detail that you share.

Customizing Electronic Business Cards

One very interesting new feature of Outlook 2007 is the business card view of your Contacts. This view makes it possible for you to see contacts in business card form, and you can customize those business cards to show specific information and even photographs.

1. To customize those business cards, first go to your contacts. When you open the program, before you begin customization, you should see your contacts displayed as business cards.

2. To customize a business card, double-click on the card or card image. Alternatively, you can right-click the card and then select Open from the list that appears. Then click Business Card on the Contact menu. The Edit Business Card dialog box appears, as shown in Figure 20-7.

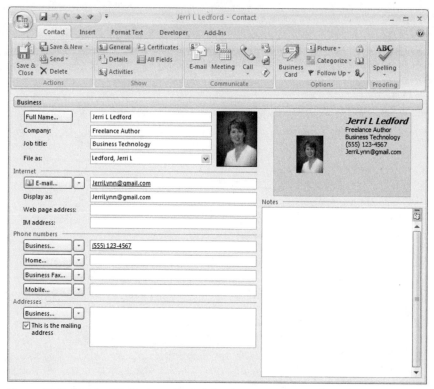

Figure 20-7: Use the Edit Business Card dialog box to customize a business card.

3. Now you can add an image to the card, change the background color, change the size of the image, and add or remove fields from the business card. When you've completed all of these actions click Save and Close. The result might look something like the business card shown in Figure 20-8.

Figure 20-8: A complete business card.

You can add pictures, backgrounds, and additional information to any business card in your contacts list. Pictures are a great way to find people quickly, and if there happens to be more than one person in your contact list with the same name, this helps to stop the confusion.

Configuring the New RSS Reader

Another new feature in Outlook 2007 is the RSS reader. RSS, which stands for Really Simple Syndication, is a phenomenon that's taken off. It seems like every news site has an RSS feed these days, and many of your favorite blogs do, too.

1. When you first click the RSS Feeds link in your navigation pane, you're taken to the Outlook Syndicated Content (RSS) Directory. In this directory, you'll find a few RSS feeds that the developers at Microsoft thought you might find useful. To add one of those feeds to your RSS feed reader, which is located in your Folders list, click the link next to the feed.

2. You may be prompted by a Security Notice. Since these are mostly Microsoft-related feeds, they're safe, so click Yes to continue.

3. Next a small dialog box appears that confirms you want to add the RSS feed to your list. Click Yes to add it or No if you change your mind.

There's also an Advanced button in this dialog box. Click this button to go to your advanced feed options, as shown in Figure 20-9. The RSS Feed Options dialog box lets you select or change the name of your feed, change the folder to which it is delivered, choose download options, and set an update limit on the feed.

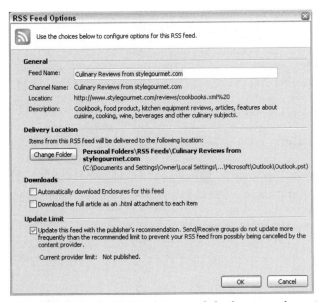

Figure 20-9: Use the RSS Feed Options dialog box to set the options for your RSS feed.

Of course, you probably subscribe to feeds that aren't included in this list, and if you do, you'll want to include those in your RSS feed reader. There are a couple of ways to do this.

First you may want to import a list of feeds that you're already subscribed to and using an RSS aggregator to retrieve and read. Outlook supports the file used to export RSS feeds from an RSS aggregator. This is an OPML file with a .opml suffix. To move your feeds from your aggregator to Outlook, create the OPML file according to the directions provided by the aggregator. Then attach the OPML file to an e-mail message, copy it to a network shared folder, or copy it to a removable storage media. Once you have the file available to you:

1. Import it in the RSS reader by going to File → Import and Export.

2. Then select Import RSS Feeds from an OPML file and click Next.

3. Click Browse to specify where you want the file to be located and then click Open.

4. Finally, click Next and select the subscription check box for each RSS feed that you want to import.

Your other option is to add new RSS feeds as you find them. To do this:

1. Right-click the RSS Feed folder in the Outlook navigation pane, select Add a New RSS Feed from the menu that appears, and then enter the URL of the feed that you want to include.

2. Click Add, and you will be walked through the same security notice as before. You can set the advanced options for the feed now, too.

   Once you click Add to add the RSS feed to your feeds, a new folder is created specifically for that feed. This folder is where all of the new posts for that feed are stored, as Figure 20-10 shows. The entries for the feed act just like new e-mails act. They show up in bold until you read them, then the print appears normal. And just as with e-mail, when you finish reading a post, you can either leave it in the folder, move it to another folder, or you can delete it using the same steps you would use to delete unwanted e-mail.

You can also delete a feed, change its name, or move it by right-clicking on the folder that contains the feed.

If you find a feed that you think another person might be interested in, sharing feeds is easy, too. All you have to do to share the feed is click on the feed folder and then go to the Actions menu and select Share this Feed. A new e-mail appears with the feed attached to it. Add the e-mail address of the person you're sending the feed to and any text that you want to include and then send it.

RSS feeds have become a way of life. Now Outlook makes it easier to integrate those feeds directly into your workflow.

Each feed has a folder   Individual posts appear as an e-mail

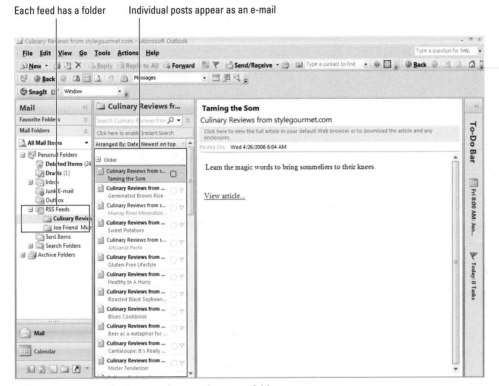

Figure 20-10: New feeds are each given their own folder.

Setting a Task List

Tasks can be a very useful tool in helping you to complete a project or complete certain activities. Outlook has always had useful task-oriented capabilities, but the new task capabilities of Outlook 2007 are even more useful.

The first thing you'll notice about tasks is that they are now viewable in the To-Do Bar. You can also see your tasks by clicking on the Tasks icon in the navigation pane. But the most useful way to view your tasks is in your calendar. When you display your calendar by the Day or Week view, the tasks appear at the bottom of the screen, as Figure 20-11 shows. The tasks are aligned with the day in which the task is scheduled, making it easier for you to keep up with what you need to do in any given day.

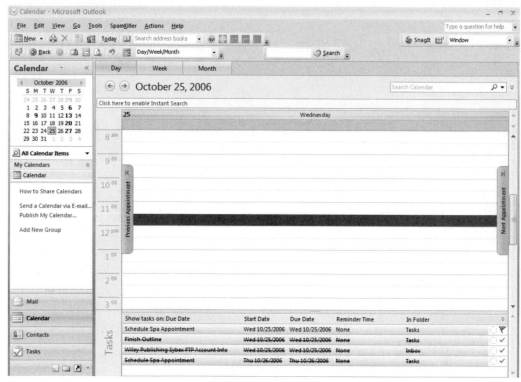

Figure 20-11: Tasks now appear on both the day and week calendar views.

Working with tasks is also more effective than it has been in the past. For example, you have new flagging capabilities for tasks. Say you have a task that you planned to complete today, but due to other requirements, you'll need to finish it tomorrow. You can right-click the flag on the task to change the date that it's due, add a reminder, or to delete the task if it's no longer something you need to complete.

You can also categorize your tasks with the same colors that you use to categorize your mail messages and appointments. Right-click the category box to select the category that you want to apply to the task.

Sometimes, however, a task takes more than a few minutes to complete. If that's the case, you may want to create an appointment in your calendar to allow yourself the time to deal with it. Creating an appointment from a task is easy.

1. Just drag the task to the appropriate time on your calendar and the appointment is automatically created. The task, however, stays in your task list, so when you've completed it you can check off the task as complete.

2. When you drag the task to your calendar, it automatically creates a 30 minute window in which you can complete the task. If you need longer than that, drag the bottom edge of the appointment down to cover the time frame you think will be required.

One last capability of tasks that is useful is the ability to move tasks from one day to the next quickly and easily. To do this, simply drag your task from the original date to the date on which you want to complete it. The task is moved from one place to another without any more input from you at all. It's really that simple.

Of course, completing a task isn't always the end of it. It's nice to have a record of what you have accomplished. When you use the Task view in Outlook, you can sort your tasks by list type, active tasks, date ranges, overdue tasks, category, and even completed tasks.

When you click on a task in the list, the details of that task are displayed in the reading pane, as Figure 20-12 shows. This makes it easy for you to see an e-mail or appointment attached to the task and any related information that might help you complete the task or see what you have completed and what still needs to be done.

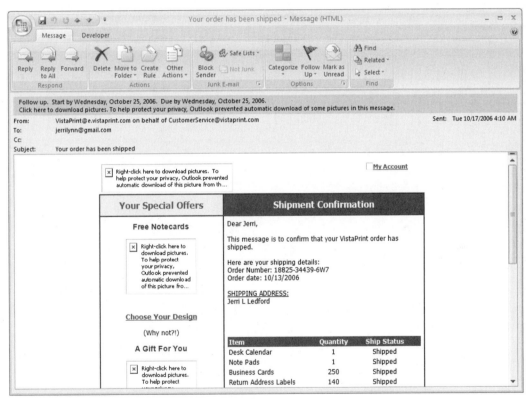

Figure 20-12: Double-click on a task to view any related information attached to the task.

Tasks in Outlook are more powerful than they have ever been. With new flagging and categorizing capabilities you can quickly see what needs to be done and when. The ability to move tasks around and turn a task into an appointment is also a great way to ensure that you're not overscheduling yourself and that you accomplish everything you need to.

But what if you have a task that you think someone else should complete? There's good news. You can send a task to someone through e-mail by right-clicking on the task and selecting Forward from the menu that appears. The task is inserted into an e-mail. Address the message and add any text you want to include, then press send, and the task is e-mailed to someone else.

Using tasks has never been easier, or more useful. The new options make it possible for you to plan better and accomplish more. All you need is a few minutes to create and organize your tasks.

Summary

There's more to Outlook than sending, e-mailing, and managing your appointments. With new search options, you can now find stored e-mails without having to scroll through pages of them. You can preview attachments with a single click, and you can gain control of your chaotic life with the new Tasks features and To-Do Bar.

Then there's the new RSS reader. Now you can have your e-mail and your favorite blogs all in one place. And as if all that weren't enough, you can even add visual cues to your address book with the new business card formats.

Ultimately, it all comes back to one thing: usefulness. All of these new features combine to make Outlook far more useful — and more user-friendly — than it's ever been in the past.

Part IX

Managing Data with Access

Chapter 21
Performing Common Tasks in Access

Chapter 22
Exploring Additional New Features in Access

Chapter 21

Performing Common Tasks in Access

Microsoft Office Access 2007 helps you manage, track, and share information by integrating data from a variety of sources. You don't need a strong knowledge of databases to use Office Access 2007, although it helps to at least have a basic understanding of databases and how they work. This version is much more interactive than previous versions, which means you'll be able to use it more effectively whether beginner or expert, design reports to better suit your needs, and take advantage of stronger integration with Microsoft Windows SharePoint Services.

We don't have the room in this book to give you every detail of Office Access 2007, but this chapter will give you a good understanding of the new interface, how to work with data, databases, and queries, plus tips for creating good tables and reports. Specifically, you will learn how to use the Ribbon, the Report Wizard, run queries, import and export data, create tables and use the new navigation pane.

Exploring the Interface

The first thing you will notice in Office Access 2007 is that it seems more logical than before. In earlier versions of Access, nothing was intuitive, which meant you had to be. And if you hadn't taken a few lessons in Access or sat with someone who could show you the ropes, there was a lot of frustration as you got up to speed.

This interface is designed — finally! — with the user in mind. No matter what your level of experience with Office Access, you'll find this interface makes sense, is easy to follow, and puts you in charge.

Introducing the Navigation Pane

To begin, the Database window is gone. That's cause for cheering for most people. It's been replaced by the navigation pane shown in Figure 21-1, located to the left of your screen and visible at all times, although it is collapsible. Now, when you open a new or existing database in Access 2007, all the objects in that database will appear in the navigation pane. You can also use the navigation pane to import or export data between Excel 2007 and Microsoft Windows SharePoint Services (version 3) and to collect data from Office Outlook 2007.

Figure 21-1: The new navigation pane is located to the left of your screen. The menu and shutter bar Open/Close button are located at the top-right of the pane.

Another thing that the navigation pane has replaced in many cases is the switchboard, the screen that grouped sets of tasks in earlier versions of Access. This change means that you can now manage objects in a database from the navigation pane, as well as create custom categories and groups of objects in the database and display that customized list in the pane.

The Access 2007 navigation pane default is to display all the objects in a database, place those objects into categories, and divide them into groups. Tables and Related Views is the new default category for new databases and its default group is All Tables. Don't forget: Some objects can appear more than once in the Tables and Related Views category. If an object is based on more than one table, it will appear in the groups for each table. To group your objects in a different way, just select another category by using the menu.

Caution

If you delete an object, even one that seems to be a duplicate, remember that you are deleting the object itself. You can break some or all of the database functionality related to the object. A better idea is to hide duplicate objects by right-clicking the object and clicking Hide in This Group.

The navigation pane consists of up to six areas at any given time (some appear only as needed) and you are essentially working with two basic types of items when you are in it: database objects and shortcuts to those objects. Here are the six areas with quick explanations:

- **Menu:** Establishes categories according to the way the pane has grouped database objects. You can right-click the menu to perform other tasks and choose other groupings. The upper section contains categories while the lower section holds groups.

- **Shutter Bar Open/Close Button:** Expands or collapses the navigation pane.

- **Groups:** Displays visible groups as sets of bars. You can use the up or down arrows to expand or collapse a group.

- **Database Objects:** Shows all the objects in a database such as tables, forms, reports, and queries.

- **Blank space:** A right-click here opens a menu that allows you to perform a variety of tasks for the objects in each group.

As we move through this chapter and the next, you'll see how the navigation pane is used to perform a variety of tasks in Access 2007.

Caution

Office Access 2007 does not support some commands often used in switchboards. Therefore, even though switchboards created in earlier versions of Access will work in Access 2007, you may discover some limitations to them. For example, the command to display the Database window does not work in Access 2007.

Exploring the Ribbon

As with other applications in the Office 2007 system, Office Access 2007 uses an area called the Ribbon that takes the place of menus and toolbars found in earlier versions of Access. The Ribbon, shown in Figure 21-2, is a vertical bar across the top of your window that uses a tab system to hold the commands used in Access. Each tab across the top of the Ribbon is called a command tab. The command tab that appears depending upon the context of the task or object you are working on is called a contextual command tab; this tab will be the one containing the commands that typically apply to what you are currently doing.

Figure 21-2: The new Ribbon design helps you find the commands you need faster than before through the use of tabs and logically grouped commands.

These commands are organized into logical groupings. Click the Home tab, for example, and you'll see seven groups: Views, Clipboard, Font, Rich Text, Records, Sort & Filter, and Find. Within each of those groups are command buttons, boxes, and menus. If you want to bold the font in a table, for instance, you would select the cell and text you wish to change, select the Home tab, go to the Fonts group and select the bold button. Some commands have a down arrow; these arrows represent more menu items to choose from.

The Ribbon responds to the actions you take. The idea is that you don't need to see every possible command within Access 2007; you need to see only those commands needed for the work you are performing. Create a PivotChart based on a table, for example, and watch how the Datasheet command tab disappears to make room for the Design command tab. Switch back to your original table, however, and the Datasheet command tab reappears.

Caution

The content of most lists that appear on the Ribbon cannot be added to the Quick Access Toolbar. It is designed to hold commands only.

The dialog box launcher as shown in Figure 21-3 is another new item to watch for in Access 2007. Go back to the Font group (it's not in all groups, by the way) and click the arrow on the bottom-right. You will see a task pane appear that provides more formatting options for your datasheet.

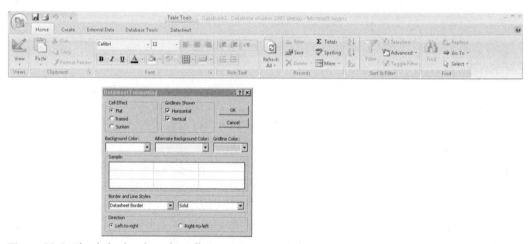

Figure 21-3: The dialog box launcher offers more commands for a group with the click of an arrow. Here, the Datasheet Formatting dialog box is launched from the Font group dialog box launcher.

New Tools and Features

Access 2007 has new features to make it easy to focus on the data you need. For example, AutoFilter lets you sort by using plain-language context menu options (for example, Sort Oldest to Newest) or by choosing from unique values in a column. (Can't recall the name you need? The unique values option can help with that.) Some new features are discussed in detail in this chapter. Other new features include:

- A Layout view that allows you to make design changes while viewing a live form or report.

- Stacked and tabular layouts that can be manipulated as one unit, including the label, and saved with your design for reuse.

- The TextFormat property, which offers rich text support so you can format text in many ways.

- A Totals row that offers many functions: add, count, average, maximum, minimum, standard deviation, or variance.

- The Field Templates pane, which cuts time on field design.

- The Field List pane, which now includes fields from other tables and offers help with automatic creation when it senses relationships between tables.

- A Split Form that allows you to combine Datasheet and Form views.

- Creation of multivalued fields so that, in most cases, you no longer have to model a many-to-many relationship.

- The addition of an Attachment data type for automatic compression of attachments.

- New alternate color background option.

- Embedded macros, which means you can avoid writing code in many cases.

- Easy access to both end-user and developer help from the same Help viewer window.

- A Data Collection option, which automatically creates an Office InfoPath 2007 or HTML form and embeds it in the body of an e-mail.

- The QuickCreate option, which automatically improves the look of your reports.

- The ability to set a property so Access automatically retains a history of all changes to a Memo field.

- The Move Data and Link to SharePoint Site Wizard, which even lets you subscribe to e-mail alerts.

Customizing the Interface

Above the Ribbon is the Quick Access Toolbar. This toolbar holds commands that are independent of the command tab and contextual command tab you are working in. The default commands on this toolbar are Save, Print, and Undo/Redo, but it is easily customized as shown in Figure 21-4; you can add commands that you frequently use to this toolbar so you don't have to flip through tabs and commands.

Figure 21-4: The Quick Access Toolbar can be placed above or below the Ribbon and is easily customized, as the menu options show here.

There are two ways to add command shortcuts to this toolbar: directly from the Ribbon or by using the Program Name Options dialog box. To add a command shortcut directly from the Ribbon, click to the command tab or group that holds the command you want to add. Right-click the command, then click Add to Quick Access Toolbar.

To use the Program Name Options dialog box instead, choose one of these options to get started:

- Click the Microsoft Office Button, click Access Options, and then click Customization.

- Click the Quick Access Toolbar, then click Customize Quick Access Toolbar from the list.

Now, in the Access Options dialog box, click the command category you want from the Choose Command From list. Once you have located the command you want, click Add. You can continue adding command shortcuts from here. When you are done, click OK.

If you prefer to have the Quick Access Toolbar below the Ribbon, just right-click it and select Place Quick Access Toolbar below the Ribbon.

Working with a Database

Databases are just tools to collect, organize, and review information. The information can be on literally any topic and databases come in handy when there is a lot of information to dig through; computerizing them means that the information can be stored in multiple tables in a single database. Access 2007 databases used the file extensions .accdb; earlier versions used .mdb. If you need to, you can save your Access 2007 file with the earlier formats; just choose that option during the save process.

A typical Access database can consist of one or more of the following: Tables, forms, reports, queries, macros, and modules.

Using Access 2007 for the First Time

There are different ways to get started with Access 2007; which way you start will depend on whether you are a first-time user, upgrading from a previous version of Access, or moving data from another database or spreadsheet into Access 2007.

The first screen that appears when Access 2007 is opened is the Getting Started with Microsoft Office Access screen, as Figure 21-5 shows. (Note: This screen will not appear if you started Access by double-clicking a specific Access database file.) The Getting Started screen is where you can create a new database, open an existing one, or view Microsoft Office Online featured content. In the left-hand task pane are Template Categories, with more available in the bottom-center of the screen.

Note

Figure 21-5 shows the options available at press time; Microsoft Online content will change periodically to give you the most up-to-date options.

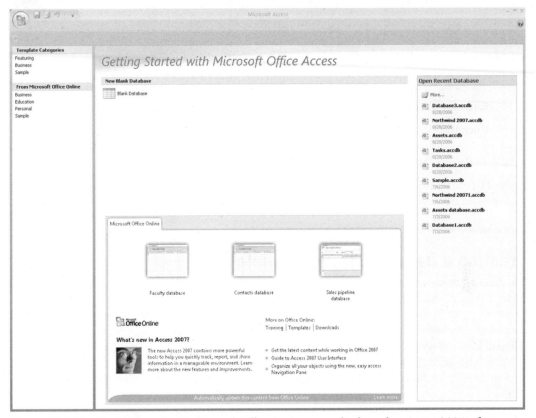

Figure 21-5: The Getting Started with Microsoft Office Access screen displays when Access 2007 is first opened. From here, you can create or open a new database and view Microsoft Office Online content and templates (left- and bottom-center).

Creating a New Database

It's easy to create a new blank database in Access 2007 from the Getting Started screen, as Figure 21-6 shows.

1. On the Getting Started with Microsoft Office Access screen, click Blank Database under New Blank Database.

2. Type in a name in the File Name box (or use the one provided).

3. Click Create.

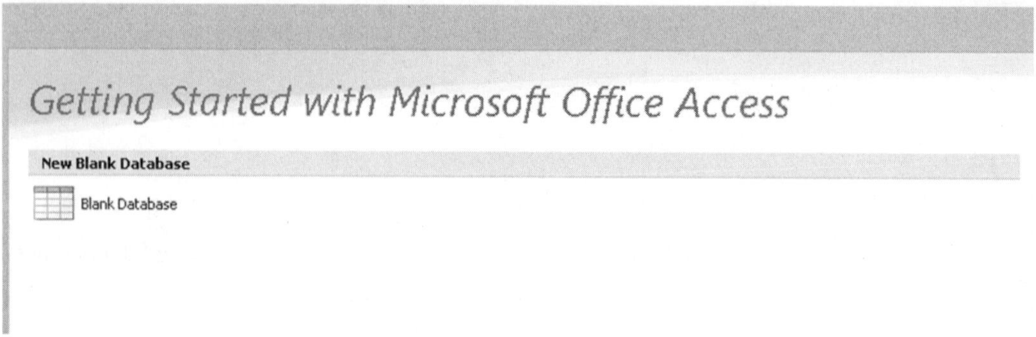

Getting Started with Microsoft Office Access

New Blank Database

Blank Database

Figure 21-6: In the top-center of the Getting Started with Microsoft Office Access screen is the option to create a blank database.

Creating a Database from a Template

Several templates — ready-to-use databases — are included in Access 2007. Access 2007 templates come complete with professionally designed tables, forms, and reports. You can use a template as-is or modify it for your needs; but, if you can't find what you're looking for, you can also download templates from Microsoft Office Online. On the Getting Started with Access screen, notice there are different sections where you can find templates. The left-hand navigation bar features templates in Template Categories and From Microsoft Office Online; the lower-center section of the screen — the Microsoft Office Online tab — offers both featured templates and the option for searching templates online.

To use a template directly from the Getting Started screen:

1. Select one from the screen.

2. In the right-hand task pane, either type a new file name or use the one provided.

3. Click Create. Your new database opens.

To download a template from the left-hand navigation pane:

1. Select the category in the left-hand navigation pane.

2. Select a template.

3. Click the Download button in the right-hand pane.

To download a featured template from the Microsoft Office Online tab:

1. Double-click a template.

2. Click the Download button in the right-hand pane.

To download a template from More on Microsoft Office Online:

1. Click Templates under More on Office Online. The Microsoft Office Online Web site opens in a browser window.

2. Using the Web site's search tools, find the template you want. Follow the site's instructions to download it.

Once a download is complete, the new database is stored in one of the following folders unless you specified otherwise.

- **Microsoft Windows Vista:** c:\Users*user name*\Documents

- **Microsoft Windows Server 2003 or Windows XP:** c:\Documents and Settings*user name*\My Documents

You will be able to open the database using Access or Windows Explorer.

Opening an Existing Database

There are two ways to open existing Access 2007 databases. To open a recently used database from the Getting Started with Microsoft Office Access page, click the database you want to open under Open Recent Database (shown in Figure 21-7) on the right-hand side of the screen.

Figure 21-7: On the right side of the Getting Started with Microsoft Office Access screen is the task pane to open recent databases.

You can also use the Office Button, as Figure 21-8 shows. If you click the button and the database you want appears in the right pane of the menu, just click it to open. Otherwise, click the button and then click Open. Enter a file name or select a file when the Open dialog box appears and click Open.

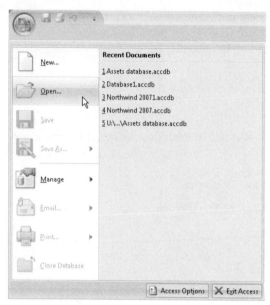

Figure 21-8: You can also open a database using the Office
Button. Here, the cursor is placed on Open to show the
recent databases available to open.

Importing Data into Access

Working in Access 2007 means that you will undoubtedly be importing data from somewhere else
on occasion. You can import all kinds of files into Access 2007: Excel, text, XML, HTML, dBASE,
Paradox, and Lotus. You can even import or link to an Outlook folder. In this section, we take a look
at the two most common import activities used in Access: importing from other Access databases
and from Excel workbooks. To import other kinds of files, use the Import group under the External
Data tab. Some details may differ from the instructions outlined here, but the concept is the same;
you need a source and a destination to get started.

To import data from another Access database, you need to first determine exactly what you want
to do. Do you want to merge two databases and copy everything? Or just copy some tables or table
definitions? Maybe you want to copy a set of related objects from one database to another. Whatever
action you want to take will determine exactly which steps you take during the import process, so be
sure you're clear on it before you begin.

Once you know what you want to do:

1. Find the source database and select the objects for import. Note: Only source file formats
   .mdb or .accdb allow the import of forms, reports, and modules.

2. Close the source database after making sure no user has it open in exclusive mode.

3. Open the destination database. When you do, check that it is not read-only and that you have permission to add objects and data to it. If password protection has been applied, you will be prompted for the password.

4. Go to the External Data tab and click Access in the Import group.

5. Type in the name of the source database in the File Name text box or click Browse to open the File Open dialog box.

6. Be sure Import Tables, Queries, Forms, Reports, Macros, and Modules into the Current Database option is selected and click OK. Figure 21-9 shows you the dialog box where this information is requested. (If you prefer to link to the data, select Link to the Data Source by Creating a Linked Table and follow the prompts.)

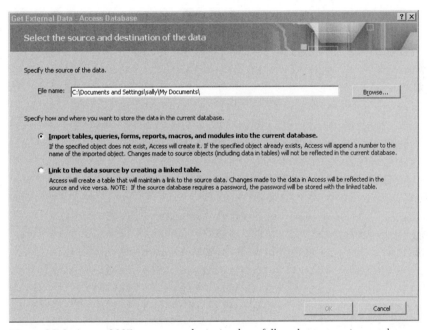

Figure 21-9: Access 2007 prompts make it simple to follow the steps to import data. Here, the prompts ask you to specify how and where you want data stored.

7. Click the tabs as needed and select the objects desired in the Import Objects dialog box. Note: Clicking the object a second time will cancel its selection.

8. Click Options to specify additional settings as shown in Figure 21-10.

9. Click OK. Access displays error messages if it develops any problems during the import. Otherwise, the import wizard box will ask if you want to save the details of the operation for future use. Click Save Import.

10. When the Save as box appears, type in a name for the import specification.

Figure 21-10: Selecting the Options button in the Import
Objects dialog box allows you to further specify the settings you need.

11. If you want the import to run at designated intervals, select Create Outlook Task and follow the Outlook prompts as shown in Figure 21-11. If you are done, click Save Import.

Save import steps check box

Create Outlook Task check box   Save Import button

Figure 21-11: You can save the import steps you just performed and even set them up as an
Outlook Task for recurring imports. This figure shows where you can place check marks to save an
import and create an Outlook Task. Don't forget to click Save!

When you import data from an Excel workbook, it's important to realize that you cannot import all the data from an entire workbook at once — just one worksheet at a time. If you have multiple worksheets to import, you will need perform the following steps for each worksheet. Other considerations to keep in mind:

- Source columns must be limited to 255. Access 2007 cannot support more than 255 fields in one table.

- Rows cannot be filtered or skipped during import.

- Columns cannot be skipped if you are adding the information to an existing table.

- Cells should be in a tabular format.

- Blank rows, columns, and cells should be eliminated.

- Error values should be corrected before import.

- Each source column should have the same type of data in each row. Access will scan the first eight rows to check for data types in the fields and mixed values will cause import problems.

- The first row in the worksheet or named range should contain the names of the columns. (Although this is not a requirement.)

To import data from an Excel workbook:

1. Open the Excel source file and select the worksheet containing the data you want to import to Access 2007.

2. Close the Excel source workbook.

3. Open the Access database where the imported data will be stored. Decide whether you want the data stored in a new or existing table, as shown in Figure 21-12

4. Click Excel on the Import group under the External Data tab.

5. When the Get External Data - Excel Spreadsheet dialog box opens, specify the Excel source file in the File Name box and how and where you want the data stored.

6. The Import Spreadsheet Wizard opens. Place a check mark in the First Row Contains Column Headings box if necessary. Click Next as the wizard prompts you; the button is located in the bottom-right of the dialog box as shown in Figure 21-13.

7. Click Finish.

8. If you want to save the import steps, check the Save Import Steps box.

9. Click Close or Save Import as indicated.

Access creates a table that lists any errors that occurred during the import operation. You can modify the spreadsheet or change import settings if you feel there are too many errors.

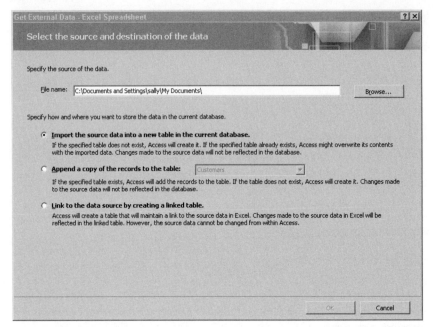

Figure 21-12: Your selections on the Import Spreadsheet Wizard screens will depend upon whether you are storing the data in a new table or appending it to an existing one, and other aspects.

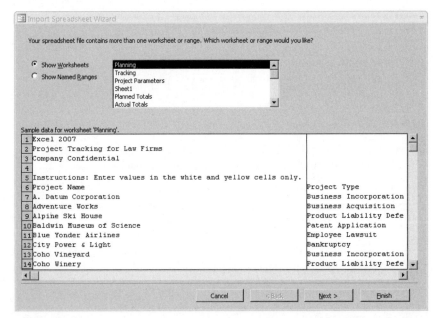

Figure 21-13: Additional selections in the Import Spreadsheet Wizard help you import the exact information needed.

Exporting Data from Access into Excel

Often, you will discover the need to export your Access 2007 data into other applications. Often, that export will need to be made to Excel workbooks although it certainly can be made to other files just like with the importing of information. One notable addition: You can also merge Access 2007 data with Microsoft Office Word using the Word Mail Merge Wizard. In this section, we'll show you how to export Access 2007 data into an Excel workbook.

To export data into Excel:

1. Close the destination Excel workbook. Open Access 2007.

2. Open the Access 2007 source database and select the object you want to export in the navigation pane. (You can export a table, query, or form.)

3. Resolve any error values or indicators.

4. For table and query exports, determine whether you want to export them with or without formatting.

5. Choose the destination Excel workbook.

6. In the Access 2007 source database, open the object and select the records you want to export.

7. Click Excel in the Export group on the External Data tab.

8. Enter the name of the Excel workbook in the Export - Excel Spreadsheet dialog box or Browse to find the file. Figure 21-14 shows where to enter this, along with information for the following four steps.

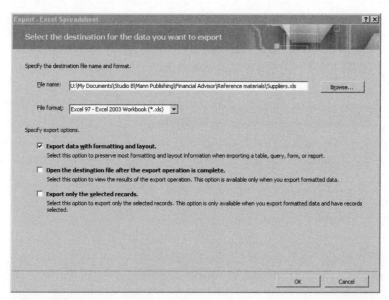

Figure 21-14: Access prompts you to make selections about the Excel destination source, specifically asking for destination file name and format as well as requiring you to make other export choices about formatting, layout, destination files and record selection.

9. Choose a file format in the File format box.

10. Select Export data with formatting and layout (this is automatically selected when exporting a form).

11. Select the check box for Open the destination file after the export operation is complete.

12. Click OK. An error message displays if the operation fails. If the operation is successful, you are prompted to save the details of the export operation for future use.

13. Click Yes, and type a name for the export specification.

14. If you want the import to run at designated intervals, select Create Outlook Task and follow the Outlook prompts. If you are done, click Save Export.

15. The Excel file should now be open on your desktop and showing the exported information.

Caution

If you export a table or query with formatting, only the fields and records displayed in the current view or object are exported. Hidden columns, filtered records, and undisplayed form fields will not be exported.

Creating Good Tables

Database tables aren't really that complicated. The information in a table is simply stored in rows and columns, just like a spreadsheet. Why not just use a spreadsheet, then? Well, because a database table organizes your information much more effectively so that redundancies don't occur (the *normalization* process) and each row in the table is actually a record that can store many fields that correspond to different columns. Spreadsheets simply don't have that capability. Figure 21-15 shows you the row and field concept.

Employees ▾	Last Name ▾	First Name ▾	Address ▾	Department ▾	*Add New Field*
1 Ballew	Joli		123 Anywhere	IT	
2 Ledford	Jerri		234 Anywhere	IT	
3 Slack	Sally		345 Anywhere	IT	
* (New)					

Figure 21-15: In Access 2007, each row is a record. Each column is a field. In this case, each person is a separate record with last name, first name and address fields for each.

Here is an example: Let's say you need to maintain information about every employee in your organization. With a table, you would enter the employee's name once — in a table for employee data. Each row in the table is a record for individual employees; every column for that row holds more specific information about that employee, such as last name, first name, address, department, and so on. The columns with that specific information are referred to as fields.

In this section, we explain how to establish a good table design, how to set field properties, and how to use task buttons and forms.

The Importance of Design

What's in a design? The difference between a database that's frequently accessed and one that is rarely used, that's what. If you're going to go to all the effort of creating a database, then you ought to take the next step and design it with a sharp eye toward layout, color, content, functionality, and maintainability.

Access 2007 organizes information into tables: lists of rows and columns like an Excel spreadsheet. A simple database has just one or two tables; a large database holds many more.

Think about why and how your database will be used — why will people need it? How will they typically access it? Are they skilled in using Access? Do they have a lot of time to play in it or do they need to get in and out quickly? Understanding your audience is critical to good design; if the users don't like using it, they won't. Simplicity in design is essential, but that doesn't have to mean you can't have a lot of information in the database. There are entire books dedicated to the subject of database design, but here are some keys we think will make your design effective:

- Divide your information into major subjects, such as Invoices or Orders. These major subjects will be your tables.

- Break down your fields into the simplest components possible. You might have a lot of fields as a result, but each of those fields houses basic information which makes search, sorting, and filtering functions easier. Each field will become part of a specific table.

- Make the fields useful. For example, you could break down a street address into two fields: street number and name. But why? If your users will not need to extract or sort information by street number or name, it's not useful to separate them.

- Ensure the unique identification of records with key fields. This will avoid problems, for instance, when two employees have the same name.

- Use color only to highlight key information. Don't go overboard with it. Choose a maximum of three colors and use those to draw user attention to important information, not to make things look pretty.

- Develop task buttons that are logical for your audience. What kind of analysis will users typically perform? What kind of reports will they need? Buttons are great but keep them limited to the tasks that are performed most often.

- Test your design. Add a sample table and records, then see if you get the results you were expecting. If not, go back and refine your design.

Setting Field Properties

In Access 2007, you can set default values to a table field or form control. Doing this means Access will enter a value in a new record automatically. For example, you could have Access automatically add the current date to orders. The most common way to add a default value is to add it to table fields. Doing this will apply the value to any controls that are based on that field.

Default values can be set for table fields that are set to Number, Memo, Text, Date/Time, Currency, Yes/No, or Hyperlink data types. To set a default value for a table field, go to the navigation pane and right-click the table you want changed. Click Design View and select the field to change. On the General tab, type a value in the Default Value property box. (See Table 21-1 for examples.) Save the changes and you're all set.

Table 21-1   Field Value Examples — Access 2007

Default Value Examples	Expression
"Yes" is displayed in local language	=Yes
Today's date	Date()
5	5
PST	"PST"
Denver, CO	"Denver, CO"

Understanding and Using Forms

Forms are just an interface you can use to work with your data. They often contain command buttons that perform various functions. You don't need a form to create a database, but many people prefer to use them because they are easy to use and understand. It's also easy to add functional elements, such as command buttons, to forms. These functional elements can be programmed to determine which data appears on the form, and when.

With forms, you can control how other users interact with the data in the database. This helps protect data as well as ensure data is entered properly.

USING COMMAND BUTTONS

In Access 2007, command buttons are added to forms to help users start actions. For example, you might have a form named "Employee Form" in which you work with employee data. The employee form might have a command button that opens a vacation form where you can enter vacation accrual data for that employee.

You can add a command button to a form either with or without the help of a wizard. To do it with the help of the Command Button Wizard, follow these steps:

1. Go to the navigation pane and right-click the form you want to use. If no form has been created, you will need to create one.

2. Click Design View on the shortcut menu. The shortcut won't exist if you create a new form. If this happens, you can access the Design view from the View tab.

3. In the Controls group on the Design tab, make sure Use Control Wizards is selected as shown in Figure 21-16.

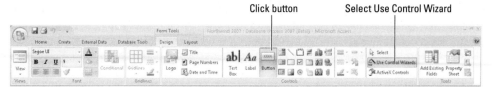

Figure 21-16: You can add a command button to a form with the help of the Control Wizard. This figure shows where the Button and Use Control Wizards options are located on the Ribbon.

4. In the Controls group on the Design tab, click Button as shown in Figure 21-16.

5. Click where you want the command button inserted on the design grid.

6. Follow the directions from the Command Button Wizard (shown in Figure 21-17) and click Finish.

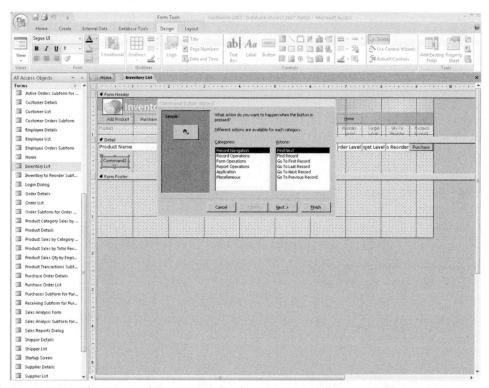

Figure 21-17: The Command Button Wizard makes it easy to install a command button. Here, you can see the options for the command button on the form. The Wizard is asking about the actions that should occur when the button is pressed. Depending upon the choices made in the Categories pane, the Actions pane displays a variety of options.

The wizard automatically embeds a macro in the On Click property of the command button that contains actions your button will perform. If you want to view or edit a macro that's been embedded, go to the navigation pane and right-click the form containing the command button. Click Design View or Layout View on the shortcut menu and then click the command button. Press F4 to display its property sheet. Embedded Macro should appear in the On Click property box that shows in the Event tab. Click anywhere on the property box, then click the ellipses button (…) on the right side of the box. The Macro Builder, shown in Figure 21-18, displays and shows you the action(s) in the embedded macro, as shown in Figure 21-19.

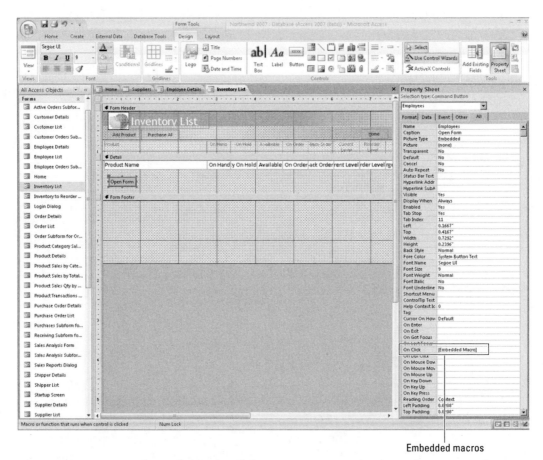

Embedded macros

Figure 21-18: A Property Sheet will show you all the properties associated with your button. Here, the property sheet shows the button has an embedded macro associated with it that becomes active upon a click of the button.

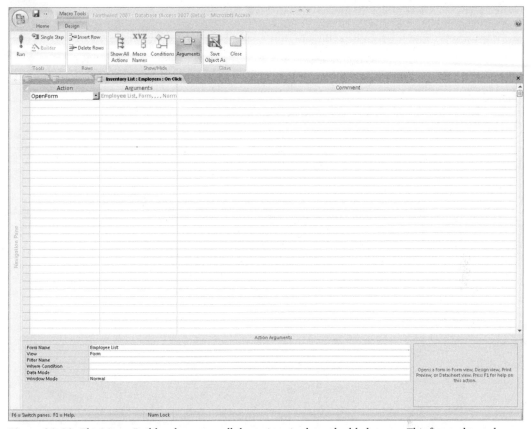

Figure 21-19: The Macro Builder shows you all the actions in the embedded macro. This figure shows the arguments associated with the OpenForm action of an embedded macro.

Caution

The Command Button Wizard creates embedded macros that cannot be run or edited in Access 2003 or earlier versions. If users have not all upgraded to Access 2007, carefully consider the use of this tool.

If you don't want to use the wizard, you can create a command button this way:

1. Go to the navigation pane and right-click the form you want to use or create a new form.

2. Click Design View on the shortcut menu or from the Ribbon.

3. In the Controls group on the Design tab, make sure the Use Control Wizard is not selected.

4. In the Controls group on the Design tab, click Button.

5. Click where you want the command button inserted on the form.

6. The command button should be selected. Press F4 to display its property sheet.

7. Go to the All tab and set the properties to complete the design of the command button.

You can change almost any property on the sheet. Here are the three most common:

- **Name:** Lets you change the name of the button from the default name, Command. The name does not show on the form but can help you refer to the button during a macro or event procedure.

- **Caption:** Lets you type the name you want displayed on the button on the form. Note: This name will not display if a picture is specified under Picture properties.

- **On Click:** Lets you specify what should happen when the command button is selected. If you have an existing saved macro, you can choose it from the drop-down menu. If you want to run an existing built-in function or VBA function, type an equal sign (=) followed by the function name, for example =MsgBox("Hello All").

Note

VBA codes will not run unless granted trusted status.

There are many ways to customize command buttons, from making it transparent to making it appear as a hyperlink instead of a button or even stacking buttons. From the navigation pane, click Design View for your form and take some time to play around with the different ways you can easily change the look and feel of the buttons on your forms.

CREATING A FORM WITH THE FORM WIZARD

The Form Wizard is a great tool if you want to be selective about which fields appear on your form. With it, you can set definitions for sorting and grouping the data and use fields from more than one table or query.

Note

Before you can set definitions for sorting and grouping the data and use fields from more than one table or query, table and query relationships must already be established. See the next section, "Working with Data."

To create a form using the Wizard:

1. Go to the Forms group on the Create tab as shown in Figure 21-20.

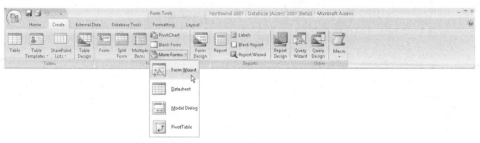

Figure 21-20: The Form Wizard helps you select the right fields for your form. Here, you can see it is accessed via the Create tab.

2. Click More Forms.

3. Click Form Wizard and follow the instructions.

4. Click Finish when you are done.

Tip

Including fields from multiple table and queries on your form? Don't click Next or Finish after selecting the fields from the first table or query when using the Form Wizard. Instead, keep repeating the steps to select the table or query, including the additional fields you want. Once you have chosen all the tables and queries you need, click Next or Finish to continue.

CREATING A FORM WITH THE FORM TOOL

If you just want to create a simple form, use the Form tool. To create a form using this tool, go to the navigation pane. Click the table or query that contains the data you want displayed on your form. Now, go to the Forms group on the Create tab and click Form. It's that simple. Access creates the form and displays it for you in the Layout view. If you want to make changes, you can do that in Layout.

CREATING A SPLIT FORM WITH THE SPLIT-FORM TOOL

Split forms are new with Access 2007. They give you two different views of your data at the same time for easy review and comparison. The two views — a Form view and a Datasheet view — are connected to the same data and synchronized with one another so that selection of a field on one part of the form also brings up the same field on the other part of the form. Editing, adding, or deleting data can be done in either part.

To create a split form, go to the navigation pane. Click the table or query that contains the data you want displayed on your form. Now, go to the Forms group on the Create tab and click Split Form. As with standard forms, Access creates the split form and displays it for you in the Layout view. If you want to make changes, you can do that in Layout.

CREATING A FORM WITH THE BLANK FORM TOOL

Sometimes the various Form tools just don't give you what you need. When that happens, you need to create your form using the Blank Form tool. To create a form using this tool, go to the Forms group on the Create tab and click Blank Form. The Field List pane appears. Click the plus sign (+) next to the table or tables containing the fields you want on the form. Add a field by double-clicking it or dragging it onto the form. (You can add several fields at one time by holding down CTRL and clicking the multiple fields before placing them onto the form.)

If you want to add a logo, page numbers, title, or other items to the form, use the tools in the Formatting tab. More tools can be found by switching to the Design view and using the tools in the Control group on the Design tab.

Using Layout and Design Views

Access 2007 has two really great views to help you work with your reports and forms: Layout and Design. Layout view is an intuitive view. The form is actually running when you are in this view, which means you will see your data pretty much the same way it will appear in the Form view. The nice thing is that you can see the data while you are modifying the form. Layout is a useful view to use when working on the appearance and usability of a form. Some tasks can't be performed in Layout view, however. If you find you can't accomplish something in this view, switch to Design view and you will probably be able to complete the task there. In some cases, Access will display a message advising the switch to Design view.

Design view differs from the Layout view in that the form is not actually running. This means you can't necessarily see all the data while you make design changes. Still, some tasks are easier to perform in this view, so becoming accustomed to the difference between Layout and Design views is something you'll need to do to gain confidence working with Access 2007. Here are some of the key tasks that can be completed in Design view only:

- Adding certain controls (labels, images, lines, rectangles)
- Editing text box control sources within text boxes (without using the property sheet)
- Resizing form sections such as the Detail section
- Changing some form properties, such as Default View or Allow Form View

Working with Data

Data is everywhere. The key to using it effectively in your Access 2007 databases is to ensure the data can be brought back again as needed. The way this is done is by placing common fields in tables that are related, and by defining table relationships between your tables. For example, the order form in Figure 21-21 shows several pieces of information gathered from several tables. Each piece of information on the form is retrieved from interlinked tables, forming relationships that bring information back to the order form as needed.

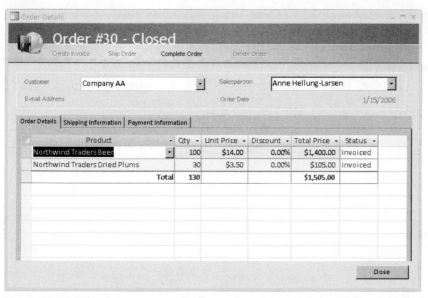

Figure 21-21: The customer information comes from the Customers table, product details from the Products table, invoice details from the Invoices table, and so on. The tables are linked to each other in a variety of ways, forming relationships that bring information from each into the order form as required.

Understanding Relationships

There are so many ways to work with relationships that we will not go into all the details in this book. If you want to create or delete a relationship between tables, it can be done by using the Relationships window in the Database Tools tab. Changing relationships is done via the Tools group on the Design tab. There are three type of table relationships to understand when you are working in an Access 2007 database.

- **One-to-many:** One side of the relationship has many fields. For example, an Employee tracking database might have a Employee table and an Activities table. One employee can participate in many activities — one employee, many activity relationships. Creating a one-to-many relationship can be done by taking the primary key on the "one" side of the relationship and adding it as an additional field on the "many" side of the relationship.

- **Many-to-many:** Both sides of the relationship have many relationships. For example, a single customer might order many products and a single product can appear on many customer orders — many customer relationships and many product relationships can be established. In this type of relationship, a junction table must be created that breaks down the many-to-many relationships into as many one-to-many relationships as needed. This is done by inserting the primary key from each of the tables into the junction table so that the junction table can record each occurrence of the relationship.

One-to-one: Each side of the relationship has just one matching record between them. This type of relationship is not typical. Wherever these relationships exist, fields can be placed into the same table. However, this is not often practical since existing code can often refer to the items as existing in two separate tables; many errors can thus be created.

If you want to view a table relationship, select the table, go to the Database Tools tab and click Relationships. That brings up a relationships table similar to the one shown in Figure 21-22.

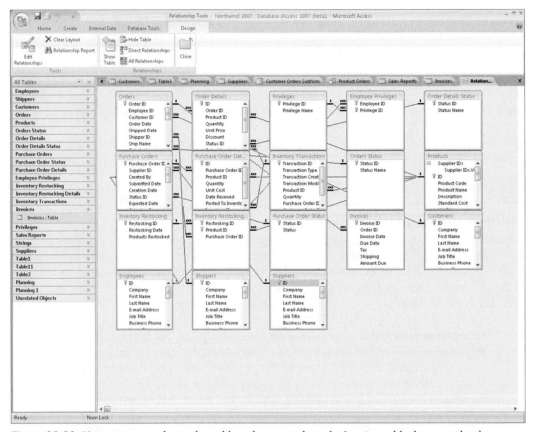

Figure 21-22: Here you can see how other tables relate not only to the Invoices table, but to each other.

Querying the Database with a Simple Select Query

Seeing how tables relate to one another should make it easier to understand how queries work. Queries do most of the work in a database and typically retrieve data from tables, although they can perform other functions, too. Often, the data you need is located in many different tables; a query finds the information and then places it into a single datasheet for easy viewing. You can filter queries as well as update them (in most cases).

Access 2007 offers numerous ways to run queries. The select query is the most common query. A select query gets the data and brings it back; you can view the data, print it, copy it, or use its output as a source for a form or report. You can create simple select queries by using Design view or by working in SQL view; using the Wizard, however, is our favorite method.

To create a simple select query in Access 2007:

1. Click Query Wizard in the Other group on the Create tab.

2. Click Simple Query Wizard in the New Query dialog box.

3. Click OK.

4. Click the table with the data you need under Tables/Queries. (See Figure 21-23.)

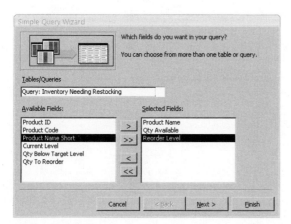

Figure 21-23: The Simple Query Wizard prompts you easily through the steps for creating a simple select query.

5. Select the desired fields under Available Fields and add them to the Selected Fields list.

6. Click Next.

7. Decide whether you want a detailed or summary query if given the option.

8. Title your query and click Finish.

Access will display all of the contact records in the Datasheet view (Figure 21-24); you can restrict the returned records by specifying one or more criteria. When you close the query, it is saved automatically.

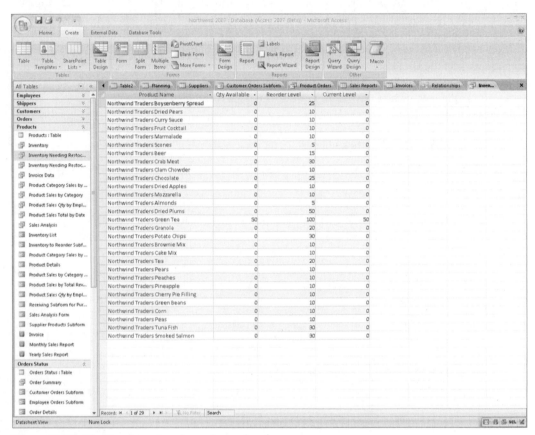

Figure 21-24: The Datasheet view shows the results of your query.

If you find an error in your query, you may or may not be able to edit it. Cross-tab and SQL-specific queries, queries based on three or more tables with a many-to-one-to-many relationship, calculated fields, and queries with a GROUP BY clause cannot be edited. Edits are typically performed in the Datasheet view on the Design tab (shown in Figure 21-25), although they may sometimes be accessed in the Design view instead.

Datasheet is the Default view

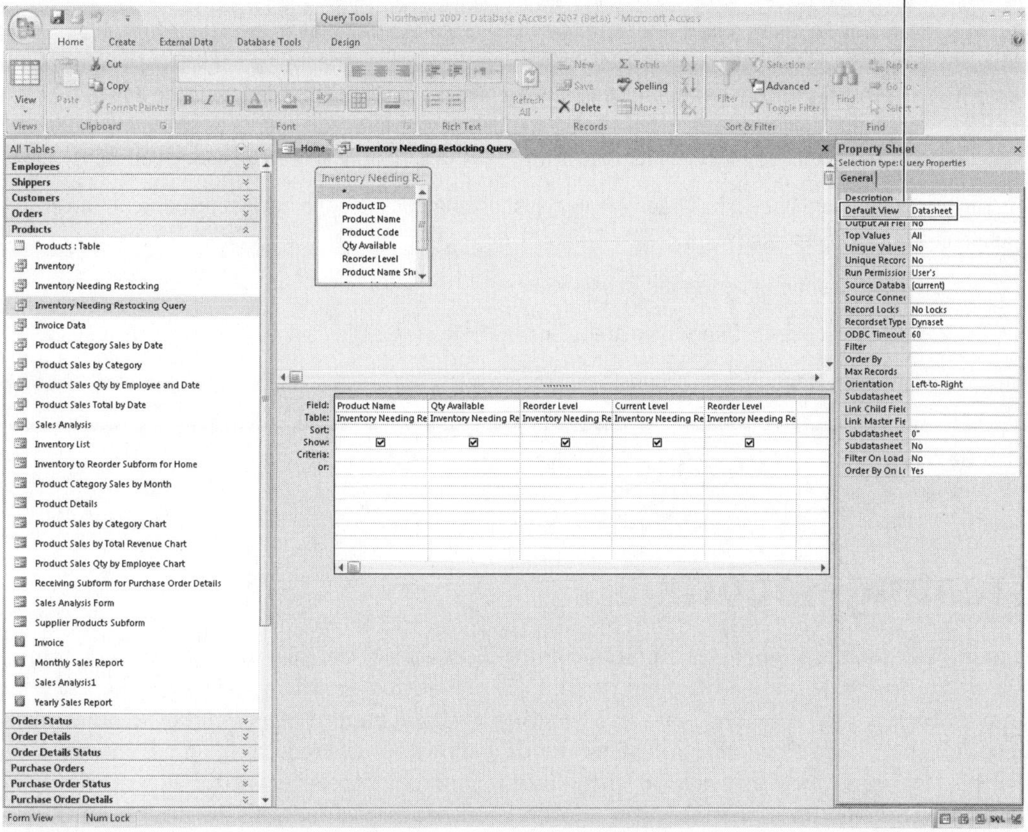

Figure 21-25: Query edits are performed in the Datasheet view of the Design tab.

A Word About Action Queries

Action queries perform tasks with the data they retrieve. For example, you can set up an action query to add or delete data in an existing table or even create a new table.

There are four types of action queries:

- **Append:** Adds records from the query's results to the end of an existing table.
- **Delete:** Removes rows matching specified criteria from one or more tables.
- **Update:** Changes records according to specified criteria.
- **Make-table:** Creates a new table and then places records in it by copying records from an existing table.

Continued

A Word About Action Queries *(Continued)*

Action queries can be dangerous if you're not careful. They make changes to the data in the tables they are based on and typically cannot be undone without restoring data from a backup copy. CTRL+Z usually won't work if you change your mind or make a mistake, so if you're going to run an action query be sure to have a good backup before you start. Each type of action query has specific creation instructions. Check Access 2007 Help for details if you're not sure how to create the one you want.

To run an action query once it has been created, just double-click it in the navigation pane. To run an action query as a select query:

1. Open the action query in the Design view.

2. Click Select in the Query Type group on the Design tab.

3. Click Run in the Results group on the Design tab.

Creating Reports

At some point, everyone has to report on something. Access 2007 can take the pain out of reporting a lot of information by summarizing and presenting your data in a readable, professional format. You can run Access reports whenever you want. You can view them on the screen, print them out, e-mail them, or export them to another program. The data shown always reflects the most current data available. Two new views are available when creating reports in Access 2007: the Report view and the Group, Sort, and Total view. Those are explained below along with details for creating a report.

Using Report View

The Report View is new with Access 2007. With it, you can focus on specific records, find matching text, use a filter feature, perform Clipboard operations, and follow hyperlinks. To use this view, click the table you want to view in report format and select Report under the Create tab.

Using Group, Sort, and Total

Another cool new feature when working with Access 2007 reports is the Group, Sort, and Total feature. It allows you to see the effects of your change requests instantly when you are grouping, adding, or sorting in reports. A new Totals drop-down menu has been added and simple totals can be summed up with a point and click. You can access this tool from two views. In Layout view, click Group & Sort in the Grouping and Totals group on the Formatting tab. In Design view, take the same actions on the Design tab.

Creating a Report with the Report Wizard

Creating reports is pretty easy now with the Access 2007 Report Wizard. To create a report with the wizard:

1. Click Report Wizard in the Reports group on the Create tab.

2. Under Tables/Queries, choose the table or query that contains the fields you want. (You can choose from more than one.)

3. In Available Fields, double-click the fields you want. Access moves them to the Selected Fields list. If you move one accidentally, just click the buttons to move it back.

4. Click Next. Add grouping levels.

5. Click Next. Sort order as desired.

6. Click Next. Choose the layout and page orientation for the report.

7. Click Next. Choose a style.

8. Click Next. Type in a title for the report and select Preview the Report.

9. Click Finish. Your report appears on the screen in Print Preview format.

Summary

In this chapter you learned about the new Access interface, how to work with data, databases, and queries, and tips for creating tables and reports. As you use Access 2007, you will find that the user interface does make it a lot easier to use than earlier versions of Access. There is plenty more to learn about Access, of course, so don't hesitate to play around in it. Try out the templates Microsoft provides on the Getting Started With Access screen and take some risks. You will find a few pleasant surprises on your journey through Access 2007.

Chapter 22

Exploring Additional New Features in Access

In Chapter 21, we discussed Access 2007's new interface, working with databases and data, and creating tables and reports. In this chapter, we'll look at a few more features available with Access 2007, exploring Access templates and macros, data collection, and XPS support. There is so much to know about Access 2007 that we can't possibly share it all in two chapters, but the combination of items included in this book should give you the confidence to dive into the application and begin work.

Using Prebuilt Database Solutions

Templates are a big piece of Access 2007. The folks at Microsoft apparently figured out that it's not that easy to create these databases from scratch all the time and that there are enough similarities between industries and occupations that a lot of people were creating the same type of databases. In Chapter 21, we taught you how to create a database from a template from the Getting Started with Access screen. Besides full database templates, Access 2007 also provides two other templates that might come in handy for you. Here's a look at them.

The first are table templates. You can create a table within an Access database by using a template. The most commonly used types of tables are Contacts, Tasks, Issues, Events, and Assets; by using the drop-down menu as shown in Figure 22-1, you can grab one and get started.

Go to Table Templates in the Tables group on the Create tab and you'll see the menu.

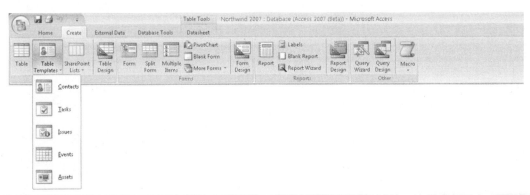

Figure 22-1: Table templates are available on the Create tab.

327

Select the template you want and start typing your data into the first empty cell. You can also paste it from another source just like you would with a table you built yourself.

The second template set that is helpful within a database is Field Templates. Go to the Datasheet tab and click New Field in the Fields and Columns group. (See Figure 22-2.) The Field Templates pane displays, showing a list of standard field types that you probably use quite often. Simply drag the field you want on to the datasheet containing your data and watch for the vertical insertion bar so you can see where the field is being placed. The field template definitions include a setting for the field's format property, a data type and a field name along with other field properties.

New Field command   Field templates

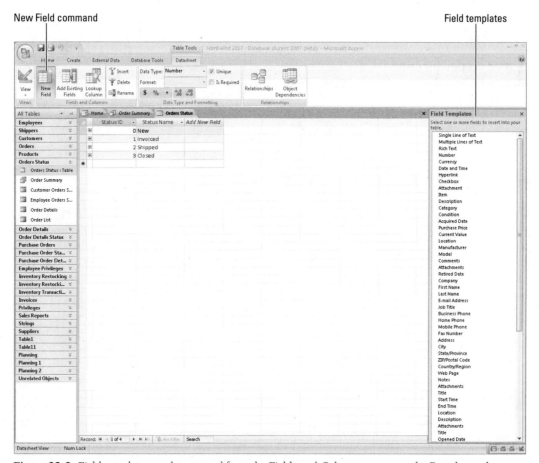

Figure 22-2: Field templates can be accessed from the Fields and Columns group on the Datasheet tab as shown here. This selection brings up a task pane on the right side of your screen. Also shown is the New Field command.

Exploring Macros

New macro features in Access 2007 make it easier to automate tasks, add functionality to your database, and create forms that work right every time. If you didn't know how to write VBA code in previous versions of Access, you were out of luck when it came to using macros. But now, some new features and macro actions included with Access 2007 mean you don't need to know any code to secure your database and add functionality.

Using the Macro Builder

The MacroBuilder will likely become your new best friend. This function helps you create and modify macros to your heart's content, but it works differently than the standard wizard format Microsoft likes to use, so don't think of it as a wizard.

To open and use the Macro Builder:

1. Go to the Create tab.

2. In the Other group, click Macro.

3. The Macro Builder displays as sort of a lined pad of paper with three columns: Action, Arguments, and Comment.

4. Click in a cell in the Action column and you'll see a down arrow; use that arrow to display numerous actions available.

5. In the Arguments column, you can enter or edit arguments for each action if you want.

6. Add more actions by moving to a new row and adding a new action.

Access performs the actions in the order you list them, so pay attention to the order you insert the actions.

Working with Embedded Macros and New Macro Actions

Embedded macros, explained briefly in Chapter 21, give you the ability to add features such as buttons to your forms, reports, and controls. These macros are helpful because they literally become part of the form, report, or control and are retained as copies are made.

To create an embedded macro, open the form or report where you want the macro in either Design or Layout view (right-click to choose the view). If the Property Sheet is not displayed, go to either the Design or Layout tab and click Property Sheet in the Tools group. (Depending on the view you have chosen you will locate the Property Sheet in different areas. Remember, views and tabs are different but are often referred to by the same name, so you need to pay attention to both the view and the tab you are working in.) Then take these steps:

1. Click the control or section containing the event property where you want the macro embedded.

2. Click the Event tab under Property Sheet.

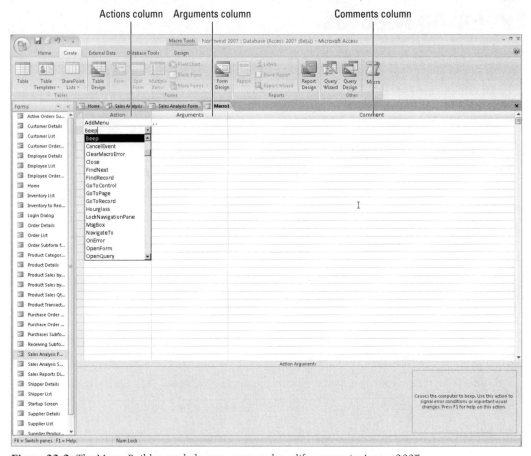

Figure 22-3: The Macro Builder can help you create and modify macros in Access 2007.

3. Click the event property where you want the macro embedded.

4. Click the ellipses box.

5. Click Macro Builder in the Choose Builder dialog box and click OK.

6. Using the Macro Builder, click in the first row of the Action column.

7. Click the action you want from the Action drop-down list and enter any required arguments in Action Arguments.

8. Repeat step 7 to add another action; when your macro is finished click Save.

9. Click Close.

Your macro will run each time the events specified are triggered. Note that even though Access 2007 lets you build a macro group as an embedded macro, only the first macro in the group will run when triggered by the event.

Three new macro actions can be used to create and use temporary variables in your macros. The actions — SetTempVar, RemoveTempVar, and RemoveAllTempVars — refer to temporary storage places for values and can be used to control running macros, pass data to and from reports and forms, and so on. These are accessible in VBA, by the way.

A couple of new macro actions you will want to play with when you have some time:

- **SingleStep:** Lets you enter single-step mode in your macro so you can see exactly how the macro works one action at a time.

- **OnError:** Lets you define how Access 2007 should handle errors that arise.

- **ClearMacroError:** Clears the last error in the MacroError object, which gives you the opportunity to perform specific actions when errors occur as your macro runs.

Access 2007 offers the option of shutting out macro actions that do not have trusted status. When the Show All Actions button is not highlighted in the MacroBuilder, macro actions and RunCommand arguments will run only if they have trusted status.

Tip

Macro objects are visible in the navigation pane; embedded macros are not.

Sharing Tracked Information with Others

As you know by now, Access 2007 is a great tool for helping you track information. As a companion to that tracking ability, new and improved features allow you to share the information with others fairly easily. Several of these involve Windows SharePoint Services or SharePoint sites so we won't discuss them here, but there are three that do not:

- **Data Collection feature:** This new feature allows you to embed information into the body of an e-mail message. Through this feature, Access 2007 automatically creates a form in Office InfoPath 2007 or HTML format. You choose the recipients of the e-mail from Outlook 2007 or Access and tell it the information to include. When the form is completed and returned by recipients, Outlook 2007 recognizes the incoming form and gives you the option of saving the data automatically back into your Access 2007 database.

- **Exporting to PDF and XPS:** PDF (Portable Document Format) and XPS (XML Paper Specification) capture information exactly as it's shown in your database for easy viewing. Details of these formats are explained later in this chapter.

- **Improvements in importing and exporting data:** Explained in more detail in Chapter 21, these improvements even allow you to save import and export operations and reuse them as often as you like.

More about Data Collection

It's easy to create the e-mail that automatically creates a form for recipients. The Data Collection Wizard will help you walk through the process, which does make this a fast and easy process. Don't forget to start Outlook 2007 before you use the Data Collection feature.

To create an e-mail for data collection:

1. Select the database item you want to populate with information from recipients.

2. In the Collect Data group on the External Data tab (shown in Figure 22-4), select Create E-mail.

Create E-mail

Figure 22-4: On the External Data tab in Access 2007, the Data Collection activities are performed in the Collect Data group.

3. Follow the prompts of the Data Collection Wizard. Note that on the Customize the E-Mail Message dialog box, you have the ability to change the e-mail subject line and its content, although Access will automatically fill those items in for you. Figure 22-5 shows a sample e-mail that is generated.

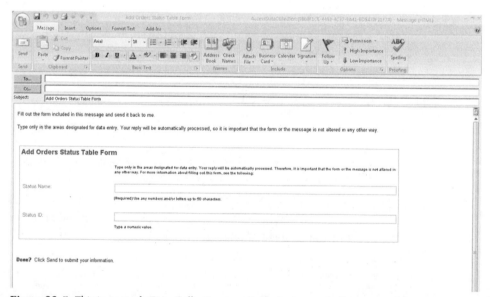

Figure 22-5: This is a sample Data Collection e-mail that is automatically generated for you.

To see the status of your e-mail, select Manage Replies in the Collect Data group on the External Data tab. The Manage Data Collection Messages dialog box opens (Figure 22-6), offering you several options and giving you information about the message (when it was created, for example, or what was included on the form).

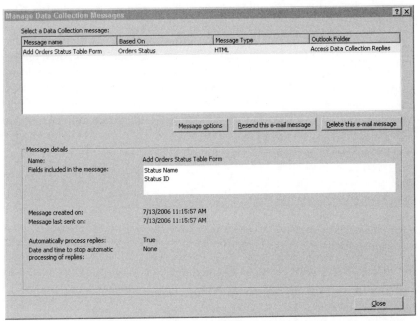

Figure 22-6: The Manage Data Collection Messages dialog box allows you to organize and manage your messages according to your preferences.

If Outlook 2007 is not running when replies are returned, don't worry. Processing will automatically begin the next time you start Outlook. If you prefer manual processing of the replies, be sure to choose that option during the Data Collection setup.

Caution

When using the Data Collection feature, remember these items: (1) the database cannot be password-protected, (2) the database cannot be open in the exclusive mode, and (3) the name or location of the database cannot change after you send the e-mail message.

Incorporating PDF and XPS Support

In the previous chapter, we discussed aspects of importing and exporting data with Access 2007. Another new feature is the ability to export data to a PDF or XPS (XML Paper Specification) format. This ability allows you to distribute your Access files — even to those who don't have Access installed — with all the formatting characteristics of the original file. The installation of a free XPS viewer from Microsoft allows others to see the file without the application.

XML Paper Specification or XPS is new, so if you choose this option you should include the viewer link for your recipients the first time you send them a file in this format. XPS is based on the Extensible Markup Language (XML), sort of a universal computer language explained in more detail in Chapter 10. This format preserves the formatting you establish and allows file sharing, but does not allow data in the file to be copied or changed. Here's a handy tip: Check your document in Print Preview before saving in either PDF or XPS format. You will probably want to switch to Landscape format for your page layout.

To save a file in XPS format:

1. Click the Office Button.

2. Place your cursor over the arrow in the Save As selection and click Save the current database object as PDF or XPS.

3. Type or choose a file name in the File name list.

4. Choose XPS Document (*.xps) under Save as type (Figure 22-7).

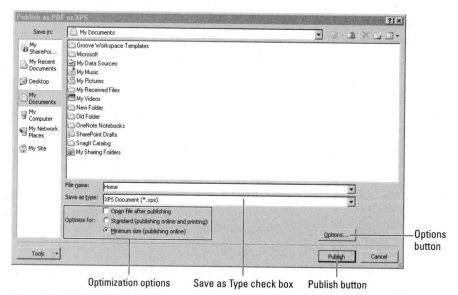

Optimization options   Save as Type check box   Publish button

Figure 22-7: The Publish as PDF or XPS dialog box offers choices for print quality, compressed file size, and other options.

5. Next to Optimize for, decide whether file size or print quality is more important to you and click either Standard (publishing online and printing) for highest print quality or Minimum size (publishing online) for compressed file size.

6. Click Options and select any options you want. Click OK.

7. Click Publish in the Publish as PDF or XPS dialog box.

Caution

If you have not used the Publish as XPS feature previously, you will probably be required to download and install a viewer the first time you use this publishing option to see the file after it has been saved. It's a free download; just allow yourself a few extra minutes to update your system. Also, if you do not see the XPS Save As options in your Save as type list, then the feature may not be available because of your organization's policy.

Understanding the New Report Functions

Two new report functions in Access 2007 can help you create reports that are concise, understandable, and easy to analyze. Take some time to play around with Mode Editing and Grouping; both are great ways to fine-tune your reports for your readers.

Mode Editing

When you create a report, you will often want to edit it. Access 2007 offers two ways to edit reports. In one (Layout view), the report is actually running; in the other (Design view), it is not.

In Layout view, your data appears about the same way it will show up on the report. That makes this view very useful for setting column widths, adding group levels, and making other changes. However, some things do appear differently than on the printed version, so be sure to check the report in Print Preview before the final print. Also, some specific actions cannot be performed in Layout view and must be performed in Design view (adding line numbers, for example).

Design view lets you see things like headers and footers, plus it gives you a broader ability to add visual pieces such as lines, rectangles, labels, and images. Also, you can edit text box control sources in the text boxes without the use of the property sheet and make other property changes.

Grouping Information

In the previous chapter, we talked briefly about the new Group, Sort, and Total feature. When you create a report, it's often helpful for your audience to have the records organized by groups. Doing this lets readers understand your report from a visual perspective, which is a key way in which readers learn. In Access 2007, groups are a collection of records displayed with introductory and summary details. Here is how to build a grouped report using the Report Wizard shown in Figure 22-8:

1. Click Report Wizard in the Reports group on the Create tab.

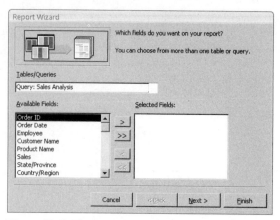

Figure 22-8: The Report Wizard can help you create grouped reports.

2. Choose a table or query that contains the fields you want on your report from the drop-down menu. (You can choose from multiple tables or queries by moving between steps 2 and 3 as needed.)

3. Click the buttons between Available Fields and Selected Fields to move fields from one place to the other. (Double-clicking fields also performs this action.)

4. Once you have completed your selection of all tables, queries, and fields, click Next.

5. The Report Wizard asks you to determine grouping levels. (See Figure 22-9.) Click the buttons between the field names list and the report layout diagram to determine groups and priority.

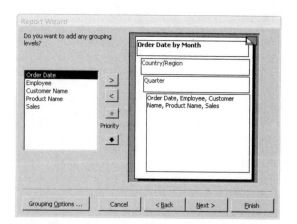

Figure 22-9: In the Report Wizard, you can choose your grouping levels.

6. Click the Grouping Options button to see grouping intervals available for group-level fields. Make your selection and click OK.

7. Click Next.

8. Now the Report Wizard asks you to determine the sort order and summary information you want included (Figure 22-10). Make your selections — don't forget to look at numeric summary choices that may be available via the Summary Option button — and click Next.

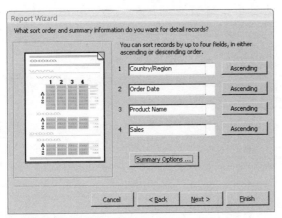

Figure 22-10: The Report Wizard can help you sort your summary information.

9. Determine your layout by answering the layout questions. Click Next.

10. Choose a style. Click Next.

11. Title your report. Be sure Preview the Report is selected. Click Finish.

That's it! Your report should appear on the screen for print preview as shown in Figure 22-11. If you want to make changes, you can do that through Layout or Design view. Just right-click the report and choose the view you desire from the menu.

Using New Field Types

In Access 2007, columns are also called fields. These columns — or fields — are where you store the information and items you want to track. Access 2007 has a couple of new fields that you should know about, so we've given you a brief overview here.

Sales Analysis1

Order Date by Month	Quarter	Country	Order Date	Product Name	Sales	Employee
January 2006						
	1					
		USA	1/15/2006	Northwind Traders Beer	$1,400.00	Anne Hellung-Larsen
		USA	1/15/2006	Northwind Traders Dried Plums	$105.00	Anne Hellung-Larsen
		USA	1/20/2006	Northwind Traders Dried Apples	$530.00	Jan Kotas
		USA	1/20/2006	Northwind Traders Dried Pears	$300.00	Jan Kotas
		USA	1/20/2006	Northwind Traders Dried Plums	$35.00	Jan Kotas
		USA	1/22/2006	Northwind Traders Chai	$270.00	Mariya Sergienko
		USA	1/22/2006	Northwind Traders Coffee	$920.00	Mariya Sergienko
		USA	1/30/2006	Northwind Traders Chocolate Biscuits Mix	$276.00	Michael Neipper
February 2006						
	1					
		USA	2/6/2006	Northwind Traders Chocolate Biscuits Mix	$184.00	Anne Hellung-Larsen
		USA	2/10/2006	Northwind Traders Chocolate	$127.50	Jan Kotas
		USA	2/23/2006	Northwind Traders Clam Chowder	$1,930.00	Mariya Sergienko
March 2006						
	1					
		USA	3/6/2006	Northwind Traders Curry Sauce	$680.00	Laura Giussani
		USA	3/10/2006	Northwind Traders Coffee	$13,800.00	Anne Hellung-Larsen
		USA	3/22/2006	Northwind Traders Chocolate	$1,275.00	Jan Kotas
		USA	3/24/2006	Northwind Traders Boysenberry Spread	$250.00	Nancy Freehafer
		USA	3/24/2006	Northwind Traders Cajun Seasoning	$220.00	Nancy Freehafer
		USA	3/24/2006	Northwind Traders Chocolate Biscuits Mix	$92.00	Nancy Freehafer
		USA	3/24/2006	Northwind Traders Green Tea	$598.00	Mariya Sergienko
April 2006						
	2					
		USA	4/3/2006	Northwind Traders Chocolate	$127.50	Andrew Cencini
		USA	4/5/2006	Northwind Traders Beer	$1,218.00	Nancy Freehafer
		USA	4/5/2006	Northwind Traders Chocolate Biscuits Mix	$230.00	Mariya Sergienko
		USA	4/5/2006	Northwind Traders Clam Chowder	$289.50	Anne Hellung-Larsen
		USA	4/5/2006	Northwind Traders Crab Meat	$552.00	Anne Hellung-Larsen
		USA	4/5/2006	Northwind Traders Curry Sauce	$1,000.00	Mariya Sergienko
		USA	4/5/2006	Northwind Traders Mozzarella	$1,740.00	Robert Zare
		USA	4/5/2006	Northwind Traders Olive Oil	$533.75	Anne Hellung-Larsen
		USA	4/5/2006	Northwind Traders Ravioli	$1,950.00	Robert Zare

Thursday, July 13, 2006   Page 1 of 2

Figure 22-11: Your report should appear on the screen for print preview. Here, you can see how the information has been grouped for easy analysis.

Using Attachments

The Attachment data type means your attachments are automatically compressed now. You can add multiple attachments to a single record, too, and even attach different types of files, such as image or document files, to the same record. You need to add an attachment field to at least one of the tables in your database to add attachments, and that can be done in the Datasheet and Design views.

To add an attachment in the Datasheet view:

1. Be sure your table is open in the Datasheet view, then click the first available blank column. Add New Field will be in the column header.

2. Click the down arrow next to Data Type in the Data Type and Formatting group on the Datasheet tab.

3. Click Attachment. A paperclip icon appears in the header row of the attachment field.

4. Save your changes.

After you add the attachment field, you can attach and open files by double-clicking the attachment field and choosing the appropriate buttons for your attachment in the Attachments dialog box that opens.

Creating Multivalued Fields

With Access 2007, you can create a single field that holds multiple values. This will come in handy in a variety of situations. For example, suppose you need to store a list of products to which you have assigned a sales representative. In previous versions of Access, this wasn't easy to do and involved the modeling of a many-to-many relationship. Now, simply create a multivalued field and your days of frustration are over. A Lookup Wizard helps you create a lookup column, which is how you create your multivalued field.

To create a multivalued field in Access 2007:

1. Open a table in Datasheet view.

2. Go to the navigation pane and double-click the table where you want the lookup column.

3. Click Lookup Column in the Fields and Columns group of the Datasheet tab.

4. The Lookup Wizard (Figure 22-12) appears. Typically, a user would choose the first option, "I want the lookup column to look up the values in a table or query," but you must decide which option you want. Select it and click Next.

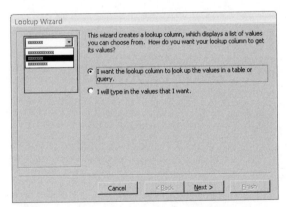

Figure 22-12: The new Lookup Wizard helps you create a multivalued field in Access 2007.

5. Select a table or query from the list. Click Next.

6. Choose the fields you want in Available Fields, using the buttons in the middle to move items back and forth. Click Next.

7. Determine the Sort Order. Click Next.

8. Adjust the columns. Click Next.

9. Type in a label for the lookup column. Don't forget to check Allow Multiple Values if you need that option. Click Finish.

A lookup column is created for you. There are other things you can do with the multivalued field, such as modify its design or use multivalued fields in a query. Take a few minutes to explore your options.

Summary

This chapter was designed to hit the highlights of the new features we found most innovative and helpful. You will undoubtedly uncover some new features in Access 2007 that we haven't covered in this book. That's great; it means you are confident enough to play around in Access 2007 and click on some buttons that you might not have tried otherwise. This program can be intimidating, but, if you get stuck somewhere, use the Help provided by Microsoft. It's fairly comprehensive and will likely have exactly the answer you need. Happy database-building!

Part X

Publishing with Publisher

Chapter 23

Performing Common Tasks in Publisher

Desktop publishing hit the world by storm in the early nineties. At the time, it was a specialized industry that offered small and medium-sized businesses an alternative to professional printing houses that could often be very expensive. Then Microsoft released the Publisher program, and slowly but surely, desktop publishing has become a way of doing business.

It's no longer necessary to send every print job out to be done by someone else. With a laser printer and Publisher, you can create nearly every piece of collateral you'll need, right from your own computer. Publisher is, above all else, a desktop publishing program, but it does provide some Web page creation capability, as well.

In this chapter, you'll learn how to add pictures, objects, and other graphic elements to documents, as well as how to create a business information set. And you'll even find out how to prepare your publication to take to a commercial printer using the new Pack and Go feature in Publisher. There's more, too, so keep reading.

Exploring the New Interface

One of the first things you'll notice when you open Publisher 2007 is that the Ribbon that's so useful in Word and Excel is missing in Publisher. All of the functionality still exists (and a little more, too), but because of the space the Ribbon takes, the designers opted to leave it out of Publisher.

New Look

Not only is the Ribbon missing, but also the interface for the Publisher program has changed. As Figure 23-1 illustrates, the new interface is divided into three sections: Publication Types (a master list), Popular Publication Types, and Recent Publications.

The new interface layout makes it easier for you to find publications on which you may be working or to quickly see your options for creating new documents. Additionally, the standard toolbar is right there at the top of the page, so you can perform some of the more traditional functions in Publisher just like you always have.

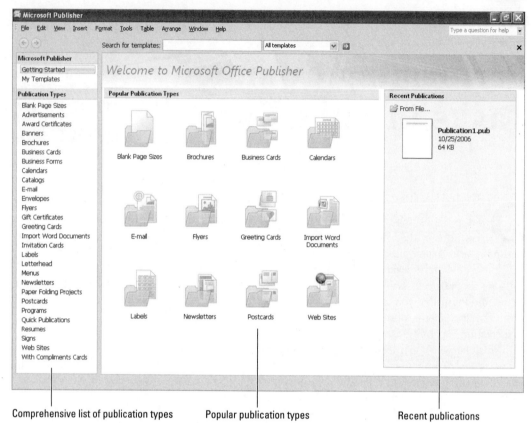

Comprehensive list of publication types   Popular publication types   Recent publications

Figure 23-1: Publisher features a new interface layout that makes it faster to navigate to the publication you'd like to create.

For example, if you've been creating a new set of stationery for a company function and you want to work on it more, you have two options for accessing that document. You can either select it from the Recent Publications menu on the right side of the page or you can click the File menu, select Open, and navigate to the location of the publication to open it. This is especially helpful if you've worked on numerous publications since the last time you opened the stationery.

Additionally, there's a new search box located near the top in the middle of the page. This search box lets you search for templates on your computer or online. Simply enter keywords that describe the template you're searching for and click the green arrow button to the right of the search box. Your search results will be returned into the user interface.

Finally, in the upper-left corner of the interface you'll find back and forward arrows. These arrows allow you to navigate back or forward when you're working in Publisher. For example, suppose you search for an invoice template and a template that suits your needs is not returned. You don't have to close out of the program to get back to the main navigation page. Instead, click the back arrow and you're returned to the previous page. It works just like the back and forward navigational buttons on a Web browser.

New Features and Tools

In addition to the changes in the user interface, you'll also find some new features and tools in Publisher 2007. If you own your own business, for example, then you have probably already established a brand identity for your business. This brand identity includes your business logo, any standard color scheme that you use, fonts that are specific to your logo, and taglines or addresses — anything that's unique to the way you present your business. With Publisher 2007, you can use those elements of your brand identity across a variety of publications. Create, customize, and reuse publications that include your brand identity quickly and easily using the design templates and other features of Publisher.

For example, it's easy to quickly create and save a document color scheme or business information set and then apply those settings to the publications you create.

CREATING YOUR OWN BUSINESS INFORMATION SET

To create your own business information set, follow these steps:

1. First, create a new publication. The first time you create a publication in Publisher, all of the color schemes and business information will be set to a default setting. When you find a template that resembles the publication you'd like to create, left-click the template.

2. On the right side of the interface, you'll see a customization pane, like the one shown in Figure 23-2.

Figure 23-2: Use the customization pane to select or create a business information set.

3. In the customization pane, select Create New from the Business information drop-down menu.

Note

If you've never created a business information set for Publisher, then the only option you have may be Create new. If you've already created a business information set, then you can use this drop-down box to select the business information set that you would like to use with your publication. You can create and save multiple business information sets.

4. The Create New Business Information Set dialog box appears. Replace the default company information and logo (if desired) in the dialog box, create a name for the business information set that makes it easy to identify, and then click Save.

   Now you have the option to add that business information set to any publication that you create in Publisher. All you have to do is select the business information set by name in the Customize pane when you create a new publication.

CREATING A CUSTOM COLOR SCHEME

You have the same option when creating a custom color scheme for your documents.

1. Start by selecting a new publication template.

2. When you left-click on the desired template, the Customize pane appears on the right side of the page.

3. Click the Color Scheme drop-down menu and select the Create New option from the bottom.

4. The Create New Color Scheme dialog box appears, as shown in Figure 23-3. Select the colors that you would like to use, name the color scheme, and then click Save.

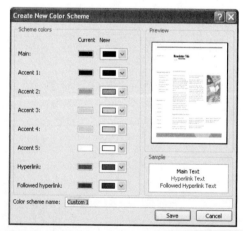

Figure 23-3: Choose the colors desired for your custom color scheme.

Once you've created your color scheme, you can always select it from the list of available schemes to apply it to a publication. And like the business information sets, you can create multiple, unique color sets to use as needed.

In addition to these features of Publisher, there are many others that make creating professional, high-quality publications easier than ever before. Here's a short list of some of the great new tools and features that you'll find in Publisher 2007:

- **Improved template functionality:** Now you can select from a library of hundreds of templates. You can even locate, preview, and open templates from the Microsoft Office Online Template Gallery while you're working in Publisher.

- **Get Help with tasks:** The new Publisher Tasks helps you to complete common Publisher activities, such as creating, publishing, and distributing your publications. Tasks also helps when it comes time to add text and images, change publication designs, send your publications as e-mail messages, or compile a mailing list. Tasks even provides tips for writing effective communications.

- **Build custom publications faster:** The Catalog Merge Wizard is improved in Publisher 2007, so it's easier than ever to build custom publications such as data sheets, directories, and catalogs. The Wizard makes it easy to merge text and photos from a database so you can create publications on the fly.

- **New publishing options:** Now you can publish your Publisher documents as Portable Document Format (PDF) or XML Paper Specification formats for easy sharing and printing. You'll even have control over options for online viewing, high-quality printing, or preparing for a commercial press.

Using Publisher is easier and more efficient than it's ever been. With just a few keystrokes, the program lets you create documents and publications that look like they were professionally designed and created.

Working with Text

Did you know that the way words appear on paper and in digital form is a highly refined craft? It's called typography, and scores of people spend all of their time making sure that the text you read is more than just words on a page. In effect, the fonts themselves can amplify and shade the meaning of your texts. Because of the time that's been put into developing the various fonts in all of the Office programs, including Publisher, you can use these fonts to enhance any document or publication.

Publisher gives you easy options for enhancing your text through effective design elements, such as fonts and layout. And because of the Live Preview option in Publisher, you don't have to commit to any change until you're satisfied that your text makes exactly the statement you want it to make.

Working Inside a Text Box

In Publisher, your main textual element is a text box. If you create a publication from a template, text boxes will already be placed in the document. All you have to do is highlight the existing text and replace it with your own.

You can remove or replace those text boxes if you wish, or if you're creating a new publication from scratch, then you'll need to add your own text box or boxes. It's easy to do. Just click the Text Box Tool on the Objects toolbar.

Then when you place your pointer over the publication, it changes to a cross. Place the cross at the corner of where you want your textbox to appear, and then click and drag the cursor to the end of the section in which you want to place the text box. The text box is inserted into the document.

Now you can type text into the text box and format it using the text controls that you're familiar with. You'll find these tools in the Formatting toolbar. You can also change the formatting options for the text box, too:

1. Right-click inside the text box.

2. In the menu that appears, select Format Text Box, as shown in Figure 23-4.

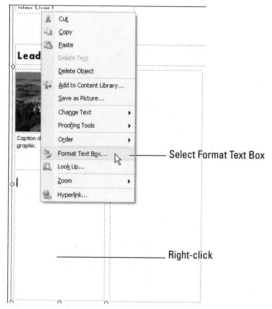

Figure 23-4: Select the Format Text Box option to change the appearance of your text box.

3. The Format Text Box dialog box appears, as Figure 23-5 shows. Change the format settings — including borders, colors, layout, size, and alternative text.

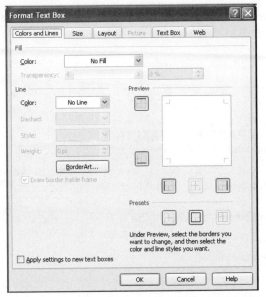

Figure 23-5: Select the text box attributes to change in the Format Text Box dialog box.

4. When you're satisfied with your selections, click OK and your preferences are applied to the text box.

Tip

If you want to apply the same text box formatting to all of the text boxes you create within a publication, you can set Publisher to automatically format new text boxes. Right-click on the text box that has the formatting you'd like to duplicate and then select Format Text Box. When the Format Text Box dialog box appears, select the Colors and Lines tab, and then select the Apply Settings to New Text Boxes option. Now any new text boxes you create in the document will automatically be formatted in the same manner.

Exploring Formatting Options

In addition to the formatting options on the formatting toolbar, you also have some other formatting options when you're using Publisher 2007. Here are some of the formatting options you have when using the text box tool:

- Change font colors
- Change fonts

- Change font sizes

- Apply bold, underlining, or italics to text

- Change the direction of text

In addition to those basic formatting options, you also can use some special formatting on your text to give it more personality.

INSERTING A SYMBOL, SPECIAL CHARACTER, OR FRACTION

Occasionally you'll want or need to insert a symbol, special character, or fraction inside a text box. Some of these elements aren't included on your keyboard, so you have to take some additional steps to insert them. Even so, it's not too difficult a task. To insert symbols or special characters:

1. Place your cursor in the publication where you would like the symbol or special character to appear.

2. Then, click the Insert menu and select Symbol.

3. The Symbol dialog box shown in Figure 23-6 appears. For symbols, select the Symbols tab or for special characters select the Special Characters tab.

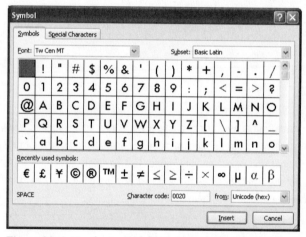

Figure 23-6: Use the Symbol dialog box to select symbols or special characters to insert into your document.

4. Select the symbol or special character you would like to insert in your document and click Insert.

The fastest way to insert a fraction into your document is to use the AutoCorrect function. By default, AutoCorrect is set to turn specific numerical entries into fractions. For example, if you type the combination 1/2, when you press the space key the text is replaced by the fraction for one-half (½).

USING AUTOCORRECT

Alternatively, you could create an AutoCorrect entry to insert the fraction. Here's how:

1. To find the correct keyboard shortcut, got to Insert → Symbol and click on the Symbols tab.

2. Scroll through the symbols until you find the fraction that you would like AutoCorrect to create. When you find it, copy the symbol by highlighting it and pressing CTRL+C. After you copy the symbol, close the Symbol dialog box by clicking Cancel.

3. Now you need to create the AutoCorrect option, so click on Tools → AutoCorrect Options.

4. When the AutoCorrect dialog box shown in Figure 23-7 appears, type the entry you would like to replace in the Replace text box.

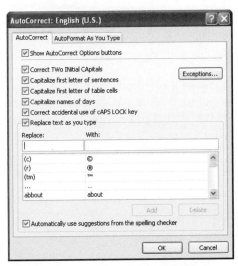

Figure 23-7: Use the AutoCorrect dialog box to create AutoCorrect entries.

5. Then paste the symbol you would like to replace the text within the With text box.

6. Click Add and the new AutoCorrect entry is added.

You can use the AutoCorrect function to replace various entries with symbols or special characters. Use care when creating the entries to replace, however. Be sure it's not an entry that could create difficulties in the future. For example, if you choose to replace the letter *a* with the at-symbol (@) using an AutoCorrect entry, every time you type *a* as a standalone word, the letter will be replaced. This could become frustrating if the entry that you choose to trigger a replacement is a common entry.

ADDING SHADOW TO TEXT

One text feature that can really make text stand out is to add a shadow to it. The shadow can appear below, to the side, or even above text, and when used properly it makes the text very eye-catching. Don't overuse it, though, because too much shadow can make your text unclear and difficult to read.

Adding shadows to all or part of your text is a simple process.

1. Highlight the text to which you would like to add shadowing.

2. From the Standard menu, select Format → Font.

3. In the Font dialog box that appears, place a check mark next to the Effects entry Shadow.

4. Click Apply and then OK. The shadow will be applied to the selected text.

You can use shadow with single words or entire blocks of text. And you can change the color of the text to add even more visual power. But again, use the shadow feature sparingly, as it can make text difficult to read.

ADDING SUPERSCRIPT OR SUBSCRIPT TEXT

Another way to really bring attention to text is to raise or lower the text within a line. For example, if you've ever seen a newsletter with words or even whole lines of text that are higher or lower than the rest of the text in any given section, you know that your eyes are immediately drawn to these entries.

Text that is lower than the other words or lines around it is call subscript text. Text that is above the other words or lines around it is called superscript text. You can add subscript or superscript text to your publication using the same Font dialog box you used to add shadow to your lettering.

1. Highlight the text that you would like to designate as subscript or superscript.

2. On the Standard toolbar, select Format → Font.

3. In the Font dialog box that appears, place a check mark next to the Effects entry Subscript or Superscript.

4. Click Apply and then click OK. The subscript or superscript formatting will be applied to the selected text, as shown in Figure 23-8.

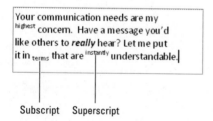

Subscript   Superscript

Figure 23-8: Add emphasis to words or lines of text by using subscript or superscript alignment.

Subscript or superscript text will add emphasis to your document. Most frequently, subscript and superscript notations are used to show there is additional information on a particular word or topic, however. So, again, use these elements sparingly. Overdoing the emphasized text will serve only to underplay any emphasis you intended.

ADDING STYLE WITH DROP CAPS

Drop caps, or dropped capital letters, are another element that can really add style to your publication. A drop cap is usually used to indicate the start of a new paragraph in a document, and many times they're only used for the first letter in the first paragraph of a section. Drop caps are another of these elements that you can overdo if you use them too frequently. To add a drop cap to your publication:

1. Click anywhere in the paragraph that you want to change, or highlight the letter that you would like to apply the formatting to.

2. Click Format → Drop Cap.

3. The Drop Cap dialog box appears. Select the type of drop cap you would like to apply to the paragraph and then click Apply and OK.

4. The drop cap formatting you selected will be applied to your publication.

You can also create a custom drop cap that meets your specific needs by selecting the Custom Drop Cap tab in the Drop Cap dialog box. Once you've selected the tab, set your specifications, and then click Apply and OK and your custom formatting will be applied.

Checking with Spell Check

All of the fancy formatting in the world will do you absolutely no good if the publication that you create goes out with spelling errors in it. Fortunately, Publisher has a Spell Check option to allow you to proof your spelling before you send any errors out into the world.

To access Spell Check all you have to do is place your cursor within a text box and then select Tools → Spelling → Spelling.

Publisher automatically checks the current text box for spelling errors. If errors are found, you'll be prompted to replace them with correct words. When the Spell Check for that text box is complete, you'll be prompted to check any additional text boxes within the publication. You can choose to check them or not, depending on your needs.

Creating Live Links

One element you might want to add to your document is a way to move from one section to another or from the document to a related Web page, with ease. In Office, this ability to move about freely is created using live links. A live link can connect you to another section of the document or publication you're in or it can take you directly to a Web site where you might find additional information, the opportunity to sign up for an ongoing newsletter, or many other capabilities that you couldn't have in the past.

Creating a live link that takes you to a Web site isn't as automatic as it is in Word. Instead of typing the Web site URL and pressing the space bar or return key to activate the link, you actually have to apply a hyperlink to the address. It's easy though.

1. Type the URL or text you would like to use as a live link, and then highlight the text.

2. Right-click in the highlighted area and select Hyperlink from the menu that appears.

3. The Insert Hyperlink dialog box appears. Type the URL you would like to link to into the Address text box and then click OK.

4. The hyperlink will be applied to the text or URL that you highlighted, and the color of the text will change to indicate there is a hyperlink included.

If you prefer to link to another area in your document the process is a little different. You still need to highlight the text you would like to use as a hyperlink. And you still right-click and select Hyperlink. But when the Insert Hyperlink dialog box appears, select Place in this document from the Link to options on the left side of the dialog box. As Figure 23-9 illustrates, a list of the places within the document to which you can link will be displayed. Select the area you would like to link to, and then click OK.

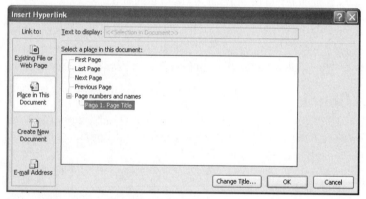

Figure 23-9: Select the segment of the document or publication to which you would like to create a link.

The live link is created; when a user clicks on the link, they're taken to the place in the document that you specified. This is especially useful if you're working with large documents that span dozens or hundreds of pages. It allows users to quickly find and access the information they need without having to scroll through page after page of information that's of no value to them.

You can also use this same dialog box to create links to new documents or to create e-mail links or links to other documents on your computer or your network. Live links are literally the freedom to move from one document to the next or within a document without the frustration of opening and closing files and windows or searching for exactly what you need.

Working with Multiple Pages

One last element of working with text that you should understand is the way in which Publisher handles multiple pages. It can be a little confusing, because Publisher displays only one page at a time, even when there are dozens of pages in a publication.

Note

By default, Publisher displays one page at a time, even in multiple page documents. You can change the way publications are viewed to see two pages at a time if you prefer to work that way, of if you'd like to see how a two-page spread might appear. To change this, click on the View menu and select Two Page Spread. Your publication view changes to show you two pages at a time except in the areas where there is no facing page.

If you're new to Publisher, switching between pages could prove to be challenging the first time you use it. It's not nearly as difficult as the designers make it appear, however. If you're working on a multiple page document, you'll notice there are several small boxes with numbers in them under the publication pane. Figure 23-10 illustrates. These boxes indicate the pages in your publication. To switch between the pages of the publication, click one of the numbered boxes, and you'll be taken to that page.

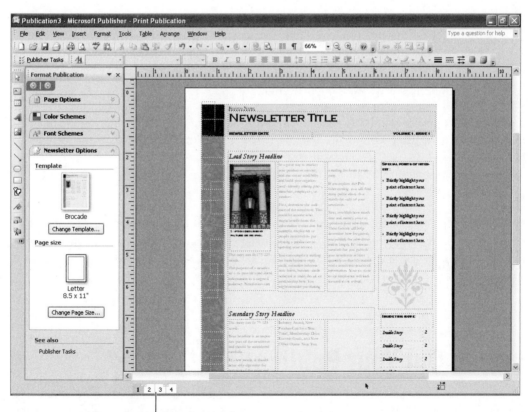

Click a numbered box to switch pages

Figure 23-10: Switch between pages in a publication by clicking the numbered boxes at the bottom of a page.

Of course, being able to switch from one page to the next doesn't ensure that your text will flow properly between pages. If you have a text box that extends beyond a single page, you'll want to be able to extend it without having to create a new text box on the next page and recreating all of your formatting options in the new text box. Publisher gives you the ability to easily flow text from one page to the next.

When adding text to a text box, if there's more text than will fit in the designated area, the text goes into what Publisher defines as Overflow. The text overflow can't be seen, but it's there, and is indicated by a small box that contains the notation A at the bottom of the text box. To move this text to a new text box without having to reformat it:

1. Create a new text box. If you're working with a publication template, there may already be a text box into which you'd like to flow the additional text.

2. To connect the two, click the text box that contains the overflow text. This causes all of the controls for the text box to appear.

3. On the Connect Text Boxes toolbar, click the Create Text Box Link icon.

4. Your pointer changes to a pitcher indicating that there is text to be poured into a new text box. Click the text box you would like to flow the text to, and it will be inserted into the box, formatting intact.

5. If you have more text than will fit in the second text box, you can perform the same steps again until all of your text is out of overflow.

Now you not only have a way to access multiple pages in your publication, but you can flow text from one page to the next, or from one text box to the next, without having to reformat a new text box each time your text overflows the current text box.

Note

Publisher also offers an automatic way to flow overflow text from one textbox to the next if you're pasting text into a publication. When you paste the text, if it will not fit in the designated text box, you will be prompted to automatically flow the text to a new text box. Select Yes and Publisher handles all of the flowing requirements automatically.

Laying Out Your Publication

Now you know how to handle the text in your publication, so it's time to get to the dirty work of laying out a publication from scratch. Publisher makes it easy to create professional-looking documents with a few clicks of a button. In no time at all, you can have an eye-catching, professional publication ready for distribution.

Creating a Layout

It all begins with creating a layout. And you have two options for the layout of your publication. You can use a template, something we've already covered in this chapter, or you can create your own layout from scratch. That's what we'll address now.

Creating a layout from scratch starts with a blank page, and it's something you might feel the need to do if there are no templates available that suit your needs. One example is if you want to create a document with specific content for a client, like a success story or an informational article. There are many different templates in Publisher, but none that really suit your needs. Now, assume you have the content already written, and all you need to do is plug it into a professional, eye-catching format.

1. Start by selecting New from the File menu.

2. You should be taken to the front page in Publisher, where you can select Blank Page Sizes from the Publication Types pane.

3. When you select this option, the different sizes of publications are shown. Select the size you want to use, and then you can apply customized formatting such as themes, font schemes, and business information sets in the Customize pane.

4. When you've selected the options you want applied to your new publication, click the Create button, and the page is opened for you. Now you can begin adding elements, such as pictures and text boxes, or adding and arranging the pages to suit your needs.

Arranging Pages

As you're creating your publication, you may want to add or rearrange pages. Adding pages is as simple as right-clicking on the numbered icon that represents a page and then selecting one of the page adding options. Unless you're creating pages that have duplicate options, you'll be prompted to decide where you want to add the page — before or after the page you right-clicked on. But what happens if you decide to change the location of a page?

Don't worry. You don't have to recreate the page. Even once you've completed the design and layout of your publication, you can rearrange the order of the pages. Simply click and drag the page to the location that you would prefer. The page, and everything on it, is moved.

This makes rearranging your pages fast and easy, so that newsletter you're creating can be rearranged quickly if the story on the third page becomes first-page news.

Adding Objects

You'll probably also want to add a variety of objects, like lines, clip art, and maybe even drawings to your publication. These objects add visual appeal and help to illustrate the points that you're trying to make with your publication. They should be easy to add, right? They are. Every element that adds to a publication is available to you through the Objects menu in Publisher.

ADDING LINES

Lines are one way that you can set sections of text apart. Use them like dividers or as decoration on a page. They're easy to add, and with the options that you have available for formatting lines, you can create a variety of different line styles that offer enhancement and functionality.

1. To add a line to your publication, click the Line button on the Objects toolbar (remember, this is a vertical toolbar on the left side of the page). When you place your pointer inside the document, it changes to a cross.

2. Next, drag in your publication from the spot where you want the line to begin to the spot where you want the line to end. If you decide later that you don't like the line where it is, you can change the location or delete it.

3. When you release the mouse button, the line is created in your publication. To change the appearance of the line, right-click on it and select Format AutoShape from the menu that appears.

4. The Format Auto Shape dialog box shown in Figure 23-11 appears. Use the options in this dialog box to change the color, style, height, and type of line that is shown.

Figure 23-11: Use the Format AutoShape dialog box to add style and visual appeal to your lines.

5. When you've made your selections, click OK and the changes are applied to your line.

To add a quick graphic element to your publication, lines are an easy choice. Create one, add your own style, and with a few clicks, you have an eye-catching element that serves to enhance the appearance of the publication or to set elements of the publication apart from the rest.

ADDING CLIP ART

Clip art is another element you'll likely add to many of the publications that you create. And adding a clip is no more difficult than adding any other element. The value of clip art, however, is tremendous. The right picture can speak volumes without any words having to be written, so be sure you choose pictures that do more than just look pretty on the page.

To insert clip art into your publication, you can begin in one of two ways. One way is to begin with the frame.

1. To insert the frame first, click the Picture Frame button on the Objects toolbar. A submenu appears from which you can choose Clip Art, Picture from File, Empty Picture Frame, or From Scanner or Camera.

2. Select one of the options, navigate to and select the clip art or picture that you want to use, and double-click it. The picture will be inserted into your publication.

If you want to start with an empty frame, then select the Empty Picture Frame option. You can then drag within your publication to draw the frame to the size that you would like your clip art or picture to fit into. When you've drawn the frame, right-click on it and select Change Picture from the menu that appears to locate the clip art or picture that you would like to add.

An alternate way to add clip art or a picture to your document is to select Insert → Picture and then choose the type of picture that you would like to insert. If you select clip art, you are taken to the Clip Art pane in which you can search for and select the clip art you'd like to use. If you select picture, you are taken to the Picture dialog box from which you can navigate to where the picture you want to use is stored.

Once you've inserted a picture into your publication, you can change the appearance of the picture by right-clicking on it and selecting Format Object from the menu that appears. The Format Objects dialog box appears. On the Colors and Lines tab of the dialog box, you can select what type of lines you would like to frame the picture. If you don't want any lines at all, select the No Lines option in the Color drop-down menu.

When you've created the lines you want around your picture, you can change the coloring of the picture by going to the Picture tab. Use the drop-down menu to control the color of your picture (including grayscale, black and white, or washout) and use the sliders to control the brightness and contrast of the picture.

In addition to these ways in which you can manipulate pictures, you can also use the Format Object dialog box to change the way your picture affects text — how text wraps around the picture — or you can change the size of the picture. Additionally, if you plan to insert clip art or pictures into a publication that may be used on the Web, you can add alternative text which will appear in the event that the picture doesn't display.

CHANGING COLOR SCHEMES

You've already learned about color schemes and how to select them. But did you know that you can change the color scheme in a document with a few mouse clicks? You can. With the document that you would like to change open, select Color Scheme from the Format Publication pane. (If you don't see the Format Publication pane, you can make it appear by selecting Format → Format Publication.) The color scheme options for your publication are displayed, as shown in Figure 23-12.

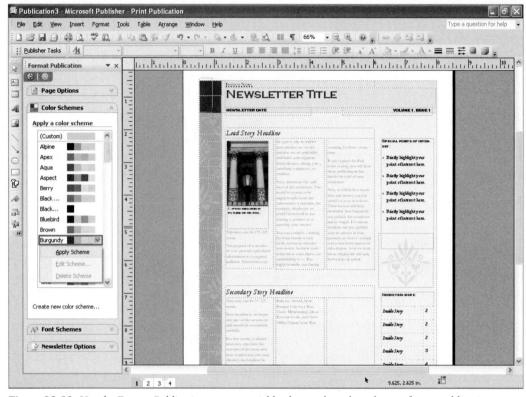

Figure 23-12: Use the Format Publication pane to quickly change the color scheme of your publication.

To change the color scheme of your publication, select the color scheme that appeals to you. Don't worry. If it doesn't appear the way you expect, changing it back or to another scheme can be accomplished by clicking a different color scheme.

Remember from earlier in this chapter that you can also save custom color schemes; these you can apply to any publication in the future.

Finalizing Your Publication

When you've finished the design of your masterpiece and you're certain that it's exactly as you want it to look, then all that's left is to finalize your publication. Unlike some of the other new Office programs, there is no specific finalization command set for Publisher. But that doesn't mean that you're without finalization options.

Many of the publications that are designed in Publisher are designed for printing. But meeting all of the specifications needed for printing can be a difficult and time-consuming process. To help alleviate some of the difficulties, Publisher 2007 includes a set of commercial publishing tools, including a Pack and Go Wizard, that make preparing your files for a commercial printer a snap.

To use the Print and Go Wizard, you must first complete the design of your publication. Then follow these steps to prepare your publication for the printer.

1. From the File menu select Pack and Go → Take to a Commercial Printing Service.

2. As Figure 23-13 shows, the Pack and Go Wizard appears.

Figure 23-13: Use the Take to a Commercial Printer pane to set the options needed for professional printing.

3. Follow the Wizard prompts to select how you want to pack the file. Click Next between each option and then click Finish on the last screen.

4. The file processes and then a message appears to let you know if the packing process was successful or not, as seen in Figure 23-14.

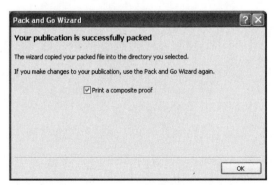

Figure 23-14: The Wizard shows a message to let you know if the packing process was successful.

Summary

Publisher 2007 gives you so many new options for creating publications that convey your message in a stylish, eye-catching manner. Graphics and objects are just two ways that you can add visual appeal to your publication. You can also create your own design sets that make putting together consistent publications a snap. In other words, you have more capabilities and they'll take far less time to use. You can go from nothing to a complete publication in minutes. And when you're done, use the Pack and Go option to pack it all up to take to the printer.

Your creations are limited only by your imagination. And even then, you still have many options left, some of which are included in the next chapter. And those options will have you creating and reusing content in ways that you never dreamed possible, so keep reading.

Chapter 24

Exploring Additional New Features of Publisher

There are so many new or improved features in Publisher 2007, it's hard to cover them all in the space provided in this book. We've done a pretty good job of hitting some of the most frequently used features, but there's more that you might like to know about. For example, did you know that you can use Publisher to create Web documents and convert other formats to Web documents? You can also create and use a content library to speed the creation process, and use some of Publisher's tools to ensure that your magnum opus is well designed.

In this chapter, you'll find information about those features and others that will make life so much easier, and good designs so much faster, when you're using Publisher 2007.

Accessing New Design Templates

One of the features that make using Publisher a fast and easy exercise in desktop publishing is the availability of templates, which are professionally designed publication layouts to which you may add graphics and text. And Publisher comes loaded with an impressive number of templates. Still, those templates may not be what you're looking for, so what are your options for finding additional templates?

In the past you had to navigate to the Microsoft Web site to find the templates that you needed if they weren't already loaded with the program. Finding those templates in Office Online is much easier now, and you can do it right from the front page of the Publisher program.

The first thing you'll need is an active Internet connection. If you have broadband Internet, you're probably already active, but if you're using dial-up service, be sure to create an active Internet connection before you try this.

1. Open Microsoft Publisher 2007.

2. At the top of the front page, you'll see a search box. Type a search term that describes the template you would like to find, and then use the drop-down menu to select the location you would like to search. To search online, click On Microsoft Office Online, as shown in Figure 24-1.

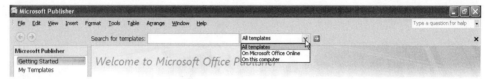

Figure 24-1: Use the drop-down menu to choose a search location.

3. Click the green arrow button to the right side of the drop-down menu (or press the Enter key on the keyboard) and the program searches for the templates online. You'll notice that you also have the option to search All templates or On this computer. The All templates search searches both online and on your computer, while the On this computer option searches for only those templates that are stored on your computer.

4. Search results are shown in the center of the main page in Publisher, as shown in Figure 24-2, without the need to download a file before you can preview it.

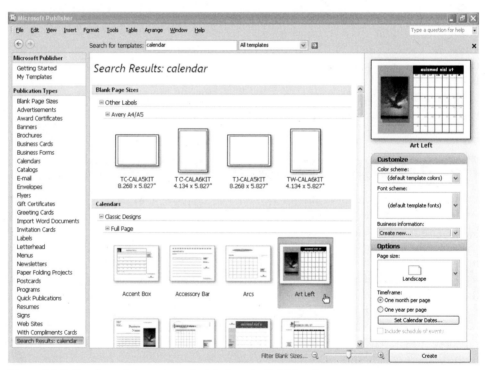

Figure 24-2: Search results are returned, right into the Publisher front page.

5. When you find a design you like, click the design name and then click the Create button, and the file begins downloading.

6. The downloaded file opens in Publisher. Then you can work with the file in the same way you would work with any other Publisher file.

With Publisher, your capabilities are endless. And if there's not a template to support your needs, you can always search online for the right one. Templates make life so much easier, but they leave you plenty of room to add your own personal or corporate style to your publications.

Importing Word Documents into Publisher

Another very useful feature of Publisher 2007 is the ability to import Word documents into Publisher templates to create new marketing materials. This allows you to quickly apply a professional look and feel to a document that's been created in Word.

1. Open Publisher and select Import Word Documents from the Publication Types task pane.

2. A variety of templates into which you can import the document are shown.

3. Select the template you would like to use.

4. Then, using the Customize task pane, select the color scheme, font scheme, business information set, page size, and number of columns that you would like your document to have. When finished making your selections, click Create.

5. As shown in Figure 24-3, you will be prompted to select the Word document that you would like to import. Navigate to the document, highlight it, and then click OK.

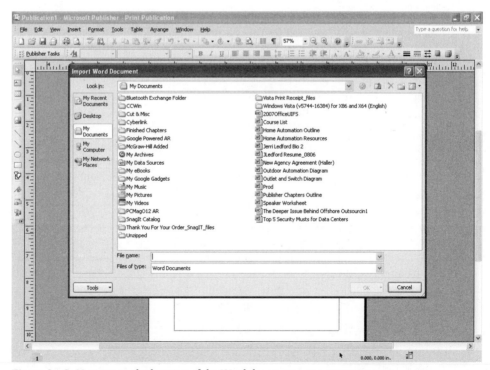

Figure 24-3: Navigate to the location of the Word document you want to import.

6. The Word file is imported into the template, and a new publication is created. There will be areas in the template that will still require your input, but the hard part of formatting the document is done for you.

Using the Import Word Document feature is an easy way to apply the look and feel of your corporate collateral to any document you've created. The ability to pick and choose color schemes, font schemes, business information sets, and the layout lets you control how the document will appear when your publication is complete.

Customizing the Content Library

The content library is another feature in Publisher that decreases the time it takes to create a publication. The content library is a collection of frequently used content that you can plug into any publication with a few clicks of the mouse, rather than retyping that text each time you want to use it. For example, a paragraph (like the company information paragraph) that you use frequently in documents can be added as a content library entry, and then each time you need to have that information, all you have to do is add it from the content library.

To add content to the library:

1. Highlight and right-click on the content within your document and select Add to Content Library. The Add Item to Content Library dialog box appears.

2. Add a title for the content, select a category, and click OK. The content is then added to your content library.

To add content from the library to a document:

1. Place your cursor in the place within your publication where you want a content item added.

2. From the menu bar, select Insert → Item from Content Library.

3. The Content Library task pane opens to the left of your document. From this task pane, shown in Figure 24-4, select the content that you want to add to your document, and then using the drop-down menu, select Insert. Alternatively, you can double-click on the content that you want inserted into the document.

Using the content library, you can quickly add repetitive content to your documents. This is especially helpful if there are marketing or legal elements that need to be included in all of the corporate documents that are created within your organization. And even if you just have a phrase, address, or tagline that you like to include in your publications, you'll find that the content library decreases the time it takes for you to populate your publications with all the right words.

Figure 24-4: Select the content that you want to add
to your publication from the Content Library task pane.

Using Publisher Tasks

An additional new feature of Publisher 2007 that you might find useful is the Publisher Tasks pane.
Publisher Tasks is a collection of task-oriented help files and information that helps you to quickly
get up to speed with the various tasks you can complete in Publisher.

By default, the Publisher Tasks pane is hidden in the Publisher Tasks toolbar, shown in Figure 24-5.
When you click the toolbar, the task pane opens, and a variety of content is available to help you
understand the features of Publisher.

Each of the entries on the task pane links to a Help topic or Web site that explains how to use that
feature more fully. If you're just getting started with Publisher, the Publisher Tasks options is a quick
way for you to get up to speed on the various features, capabilities, and concepts of the program.

Publisher Tasks toolbar

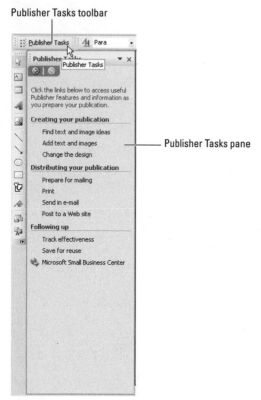

Publisher Tasks pane

Figure 24-5: The Publisher Tasks toolbar and pane help you quickly get started using the features of Publisher.

Double-Checking with Design Checker

One of the most frustrating problems you'll come up against in Publisher is having a page that doesn't print or appear digitally as you would expect it to. To help alleviate this problem, Publisher has a feature called Design Checker that can check the design elements of your page and help you to correct them.

You can access the Design Checker, shown in Figure 24-6, from within any Publisher publication by selecting Tools → Design Checker from the menu bar.

When you click on a design error in the Design Checker, you're given access to a drop-down menu, as shown in Figure 24-7. From that menu, you can move to the error in the publication, change it automatically if there's an automatic option available, or choose to never check for that design element again.

If there are no design errors in your document, the message "There are no problems in this publication" is displayed in the Design Checker task pane.

Figure 24-6: The Design Checker checks your publication for design elements that might create unwanted print or digital results.

Figure 24-7: Use the drop-down menu next to each error to correct or ignore a design problem.

Converting Your Publication for the Web

Finally, having the ability to turn your print publications into Web publications will reduce the amount of time it takes for you to move your message from one format to another. And Publisher gives you several options for creating electronic versions of your documents, from Web sites to e-mails.

Converting to a Web Publication

One of the neatest features of Publisher is the ability to convert your print publications to Web publications. And Publisher 2007 provides wizard-style capabilities that make the conversion easy.

1. Open the publication that you want to convert to a Web publication, and then select File → Convert to Web Publication.

2. If you have not saved your document, or if you have made changes to it without saving, Publisher prompts you to save the publication before converting. If you intend to use the publication for print, as well as for the Web, or if you will be making changes to the publication in the future, select "Yes, save my print publication and then convert it to a web publication." Then click Next.

3. Next, you're asked if you would like to add a navigation bar to the publication. The navigation bar helps users to move through your publication easily. Click "Yes, add a navigation bar" or "No, do not add a navigation bar," and then click Finish.

4. A Web publication will be created. Then you can manipulate it in the same ways that you would manipulate any other Web publication, including publishing it to a Web site or sending it via e-mail.

Publishing to the Web

Once you've created a Web-ready publication, then you'll either want to send it via e-mail or publish it to a Web site. You can accomplish that by selecting File → Publish to the Web. The Publish to the Web dialog box appears,. The first time you use this feature, you may see an option to find a Web hosting provider on the Microsoft Office Online site. If you don't already have a Web hosting provider, you can use this option to find one.

In the dialog box, enter the Web site to which you want to publish the file in the File Name box. Then click Save. Publisher attempts to access the Web site. You may be prompted for a user name and password, as shown in Figure 24-8. Enter your username and password and click OK.

If you have an existing Web site, you will be prompted to replace the existing index file with the new file that you're trying to publish to the Web. Otherwise, the file will publish to the Web without the prompt to replace the existing file.

Select Yes to replace the existing file or No to change the location to which you want to the file published. When you've made your selection, click Save and the file is published to the Web.

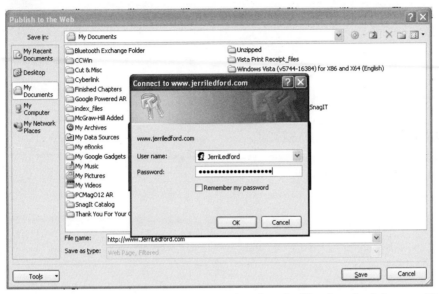

Figure 24-8: Enter your username and password to allow the file to be uploaded to your Web site.

Caution

When you use Publisher to create files, including Web sites, that you plan to publish to the Web, the resulting Web publication may not display properly for all users. Publisher creates files that are optimized for Internet Explorer. Users with different browsers may not see your Web site or publication as you intend.

Summary

The capabilities in Publisher 2007 are designed to help you create documents and Web content quickly and easily. New features like the ability to quickly access templates and import Word documents into Publisher files will have you creating professional, eye-catching documents in no time.

The Design Checker will help you to determine if your publication is designed properly so there are no surprises when you print, and of course, you can pack your publications up to take them to a commercial printer if you find that you need binding, thousands of copies, or other services that aren't available in your office.

Finally, you can tie your online identity seamlessly to your print identity using the Publish to Web feature. In just a few mouse clicks, you can create documents that look great in any format.

Publisher has finally become a truly useful desktop publishing program, that really works, right from your desktop. So go. Create professional, eye-catching documents.

Part XI

Doing Even More with Office

Chapter 25

Web Design with Office

You've learned quite a bit about Office 2007 in this book, but we've barely scratched the surface regarding Microsoft Office 2007 and creating Web pages. Yes, we know Microsoft took out FrontPage, but that's okay. There are plenty of other ways to create and publish a Web page in the new Office applications.

In this chapter we'll cover the basics of incorporating Web design with the Microsoft Office suite. You'll learn what programs support the option to save your work as a Web page, how to incorporate existing documents and data, how to add hyperlinks, and finally how to spice up, save, and then publish your work.

Introducing Web Design

Support for creating Web pages and Web content is included in every Office 2007 program. You can turn any Word document, any Excel spreadsheet, any PowerPoint slide, and any Publisher creation into a Web page (or part of one). Excel tables, Access databases, whatever, can all be integrated too. Even Outlook's calendars can be added. But what exactly is a Web page, does it have to be posted on the Web, and how does Office fit in?

Understanding Web Pages

Web pages are documents that usually include text, and that frequently contain content in additional media such as pictures, animations, videos, and sound. Web pages also contain links (hyperlinks) to other pages. Web pages can be stored on a Web server for the world to access via the Internet, or, on an intranet server that only specific people, such as those in a designated company or school, can access. You can also keep Web pages on your own hard disk for personal use.

Web pages can be published for a small, home-office network, a large, corporate network, or the largest of networks, the Internet. On any of these, a group of Web pages that contain a similar theme, purpose, or topic are combined together to form a Web site.

You can take Web page design beyond the normal Internet/intranet usage though. You can use Office and the applications in it to create documents, spreadsheets, tables, and charts, and link those to each other for easier access. For instance, if you've created a PowerPoint presentation for the monthly sales meeting, and you don't want to have to update the sales figures inside the presentation each month, you can simply link to the most up-to-date chart or table and have the presentation basically update itself each time you open it. You can then publish these pages to an intranet for colleagues to access anytime they need to.

You can also use Office to create a Web site on your own computer, preview it on your own computer, and edit it on your own computer, to make sure it's completely perfect before sending it off to the Internet or the company intranet.

Understanding HTML

HTML stands for Hypertext Markup Language and is the coding system of the Internet. HTML is what is used to format Web pages so browsers can display them and people can access and read them. The code <b>, for example, denotes a specific text should be bold. More complex coding offers more complex formatting including font color and size, and even how the page layout should look. HTML also tells Web sites what part of a text is a hyperlink and what part is not.

Office is compatible with HTML. Word, Excel, Access, and the other applications can all save and read HTML documents. You can thus create a document in Word, save it as an HTML document, and then use and view it as a Web page in just about any Web browser. (Internet Explorer is one of the most popular browsers and we suggest it for viewing Office Web pages.)

You don't have to create a document from scratch though. You can open any document, table, chart, slide, or database, save it as HTML and go from there. In the olden days you'd have to code that by hand. Now, it's as simple as choosing the appropriate extension from the Save As dialog box.

You can view the HTML code that's in the background if you'd like to see what it looks like. Once saved with the proper extension (.htm or .html) and published, you can open the published data in your Web browser and look at the HTML code that powers the page. (Don't worry; you'll learn the specifics for doing that later.) Once it's published and opened in your Web browser, just locate the View Source button. In Figure 25-1, using Internet Explorer 7 Beta, View Source is under the Page tab.

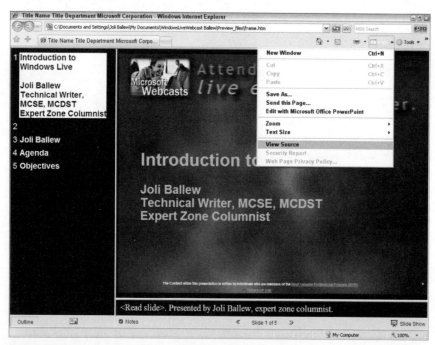

Figure 25-1: To view the HTML code that's behind the scenes, open the Web page in any Web browser and select View Source.

After locating the View Source option, click it to reveal what's going on behind the scenes. All of the Office applications create this HTML code automatically. It's amazing really, considering all of this had to be done by hand not all too long ago! Figure 25-2 shows some sample HTML code.

```
frame.htm - Notepad
File  Edit  Format  View  Help
<html>

<head>
<meta http-equiv=Content-Type content="text/html; charset=windows-1252">
<meta name=ProgId content=PowerPoint.Slide>
<meta name=Generator content="Microsoft PowerPoint 12">
<link id=Main-File rel=Main-File href="../Preview.htm">
<link rel=Preview href=preview.wmf>
<title>Title      Name Title Department Microsoft Corporation</title>
<![if !ppt]><script src=script.js></script><script>
<!--
var gNavLoaded = gOtlNavLoaded = gOtlLoaded = false;
function Load()
{
        str=unescape(document.location.hash),idx=str.indexOf('#')
        if(idx>=0) str=str.substr(1);
        if(str) PPTSld.location.replace(escape(str));
}
//-->
</script>
<![endif]>
</head>

<frameset rows="*,25" border=0>
 <frameset cols="25%,*" id=PPTHorizAdjust framespacing=2>
  <frameset rows="100%,*">
   <frame src=outline.htm title="Outline" name=PPTOtl>
  </frameset>
  <frameset rows="*,40" id=PPTVertAdjust framespacing=2 frameborder=1
   onload="Load()">
   <frame src=slide0090.htm title="Slide" name=PPTSld>
   <frame src=slide0090.htm title="Notes" name=PPTNts>
  </frameset>
```

Figure 25-2: HTML code tells the Web page how to format the pages you've published.

Again, no worries. You're not supposed to be able to look at this and have any idea as to what all of this code means. However, if you look closely enough, you may see things you recognize. At the top is <html>, which means everything to follow is written in HTML. Following that is <head>, and that's code for a kind of heading. That's really all you need to know about that for now. You're not in the business of writing HTML code and neither are we. What we are in the business of doing is creating Web pages, easily and simply.

Creating Basic Web Pages

As you know by now, you can turn any existing document or any new one into a Web page that can be published to a Web site. In this section we'll look at Word documents and PowerPoint slides.

Microsoft Word Documents

We're going to start with Word 2007 because it seems to be the Office application most familiar to the most people. In real life, if you were planning to create a Web site, you'd likely start with Publisher, as detailed in the previous two chapters. However, in the interest of reaching the most readers possible, and to show that you can use any Word document you've already created to create a Web page, we'll start with Word.

To open an existing Word document and transform it to a Web page that you can view in any Web browser and ultimately publish:

1. Open Word 2007, click the Office Button, and open any document in the Recent Documents list.

2. Click the Office Button and select Save As.

3. In the Save As dialog box, in File name, create a name for the file.

4. In Save as type, select Web Page (*.htm;*.html).

5. In Save in, browse to an appropriate location to save the files. We'll choose the folder Web Sites. You may choose any folder you like, and may prefer the default folder My Webs. The results are shown in Figure 25-3. (Don't click Save yet!)

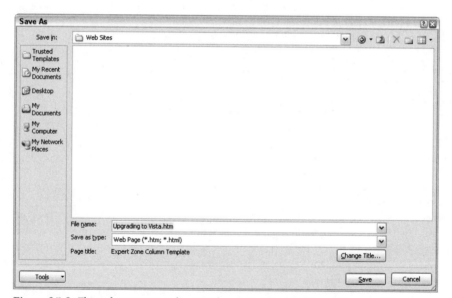

Figure 25-3: This is how to save a basic Web page in Word 2007 on Windows XP.

6. Click the Tools button located in the bottom-left corner of the Save As dialog box, select Web Options, and work through the tabs. Do not change anything here; for now, only know these options are available. Click Cancel.

7. Click Save.

8. If the document is a long one, it may take a few minutes for the process of converting the file to complete. Notice the view changes too. Note that if Word finds anything that can't be converted in the document, a "Word Compatibility Checker" box appears, telling you what has to be changed to create the Web page, and gives you an opportunity to continue or cancel the save. You may want to go back and make changes, or, you can click Continue and let Word fix it for you.

Browse to the location of the saved file. In our example, it's located on the Desktop, in My Documents, in the subfolder Web Sites. Notice there are two items in that folder. One is the document you converted to a Web page, and the other is a folder containing associated Web page files. Figure 25-4 shows the new HTML document and the new file folder.

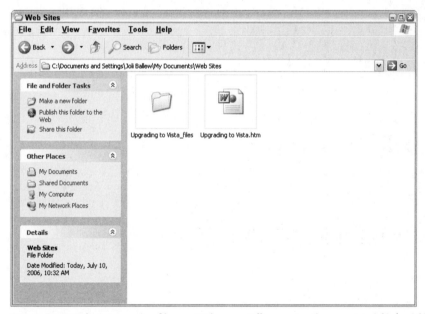

Figure 25-4: When you save a file as a Web page, Office creates the associated file and file folder by default.

Figure 25-5 shows what's in the new folder. Word created this folder for you. These are support files and are needed to successfully publish the page later.

It isn't important at this time to know what's going on behind the scenes or what the items in Figure 25-5 do or mean. That's the beauty in using Office 2007 to create Web pages; you don't have to know.

Figure 25-5: Files associated with your new Web page are created and stored inside the new folder.

PowerPoint Slides

Let's look now at PowerPoint 2007. You probably have an existing presentation. To open an existing PowerPoint presentation and transform it to a Web page that you can view in any Web browser and ultimately publish:

1. Open PowerPoint 2007, click the Office Button, and open any presentation in the Recent Documents list.

2. Click the Office Button and select Save As.

3. In the Save As dialog box, in File name, create a name for the file.

4. In Save as type, select Web Page (*.htm;*.html). Do not select Single Web Page (*mht; *mhtml). Single Web Page is best for sending a presentation via e-mail. Web Page is best for creating Web pages for a Web site.

5. In Save in, browse to an appropriate location to save the files. We'll choose the folder Web Sites. You may choose any folder you like, and may prefer the default folder My Webs.

6. Click the Tools button, Web Options, and work through the tabs. Do not change anything here; for now, only know these options are available. Click Cancel.

7. Click Save.

8. If the presentation is a long one, it may take a few minutes for the process of converting it to complete. Notice the view changes too.

Browse to the location of the saved presentation. In our example, it's located on the Desktop, in My Documents, in the subfolder Web Sites. Notice there are again two new items in that folder. One is the presentation you converted to a Web page, and the other is a folder containing associated Web page files. These are support files and are needed to successfully publish the page later.

Note

You can also publish Outlook calendars to the Web.

Working with Hyperlinks

Hyperlinks are what make the Internet work like it does. Without hyperlinks, you'd have one heck of a time getting from one Web page to another! Hyperlinks let you click and go immediately to somewhere else on the Web, your company's intranet, and even on your own computer. That being said, you'll want and need to add, edit, test, and remove hyperlinks on your Web pages. In this section, we'll show you how to do all of that.

Adding and Removing Hyperlinks

Creating and deleting hyperlinks is pretty much the same no matter what Office application you're using, so let's continue with Word, since it's the most familiar to the most people.

ADDING HYPERLINKS

To add and delete a hyperlink in a document saved as a Web page:

1. Open Word 2007, click the Office Button, and open the Web page you created earlier in this chapter. You'll find it in the Recent Documents list.

2. Highlight a word or short phrase you'd like to configure a hyperlink for, and right-click.

3. From the resulting drop-down list, select Hyperlink. This is shown in Figure 25-6.

4. In the Insert Hyperlink dialog box shown in Figure 25-7, add the hyperlink to the Address window by any of the following means, all of which are available and configurable from the Insert Hyperlink dialog box:

   ▪ By locating a specific file or Web page in the current folder, recently browsed pages, or recent files

   ▪ By locating a place in the document

   ▪ By creating a new document

   ▪ By typing in an e-mail address

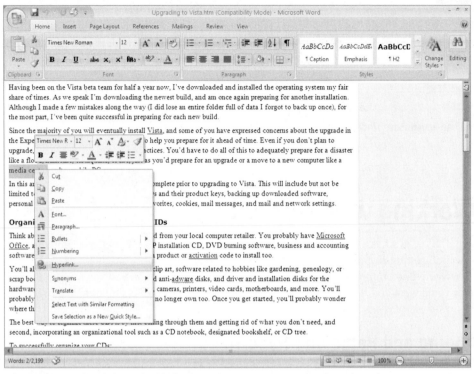

Figure 25-6: Right-click any highlighted word or text to access this drop-down list.

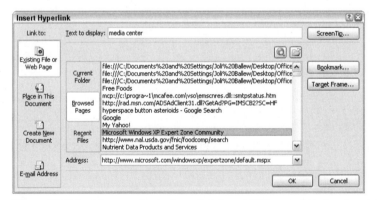

Figure 25-7: In this example, the hyperlink is to a Web page that already exists on the Internet.

5. Click OK.

In the example in Figure 25-7, the address, which starts with `http://`, indicates that the hyperlink is to an existing page on the Internet. Notice also that it was retrieved from the Browsed Pages button, which resulted in us not having to manually type the address. (Manually typing in an address is a good way to make a mistake with the hyperlink via typographical error.)

You don't have to use a hyperlink to the Internet though. If you have an intranet (an internal Internet in your office or company), you can choose to link to a place on your own intranet. You can also choose to link to a document on your own hard drive. Figure 25-8 shows an example of the latter. Here, the link is to a file on an external hard drive, F:\, in a folder called Diabetes, to a document entitled Diabetes May To August.xls, an Excel file. This would be an appropriate hyperlink for a doctor so that he or she could access a patient's daily logs from inside the patient's file. The file could be updated at each appointment, making accessing the file quick and simple.

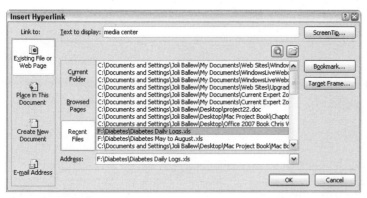

Figure 25-8: In this example, the hyperlink links to a file on the computer's own hard drive.

And although we won't cover every aspect of this dialog box, note that you can create a hyperlink to an e-mail address. Click the E-mail Address button in the Insert Hyperlink dialog box and you'll see the options shown in Figure 25-9.

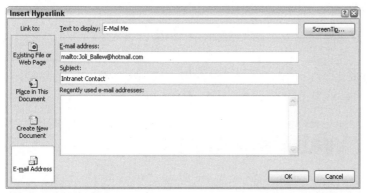

Figure 25-9: A hyperlink to an e-mail address allows those who click to send you an e-mail using their own e-mail client.

EDITING AND DELETING HYPERLINKS

Deleting a hyperlink is as simple as right-clicking and selecting Remove Hyperlink. Editing is not much more difficult.

To edit an existing hyperlink:

1. Right-click the hyperlink and select Edit Hyperlink.

2. In the Edit Hyperlink dialog box, make the appropriate changes. The Edit Hyperlink dialog box is exactly like the Insert Hyperlink dialog box, except for its title.

3. Click OK.

Testing Hyperlinks

There are several ways to test a hyperlink to verify it works, but prior to actually publishing or previewing a page, the best way to test a hyperlink is to CTRL-click it. The results depend on what type of hyperlink you select to test.

You can CTRL-click to test a hyperlink for any of the following:

- **An existing Web site on the Internet:** Your Web browser opens automatically and tries to access it. If the hyperlink works, you'll see the desired Web site; if not, you won't. Close the Web browser to return to the document.

- **An internal Web page on your own hard drive or a network drive:** Your Web browser opens automatically and tries to access it. If the hyperlink works, you'll see the desired Web site; if not, you won't. Close the Web browser to return to the document.

- **A new document:** The new document opens in the appropriate application. Click ALT+TAB to return to the original document containing the hyperlink.

- **A place in the current document:** You are taken to that part of the document. Use the scroll bar to return to the original hyperlink in the document.

- **An e-mail link:** Your default e-mail client opens. Usually, this is Outlook 2007.

If a hyperlink doesn't work, right-click the hyperlink and select Edit Hyperlink and try again. Most of the time, it's a typographical error, although occasionally the Web page, document, or internal link is not longer available on your network or the Internet (as the case may be).

Tweaking Your Web Page Settings

You were encouraged to look through the tools available in the Save As dialog box using the Tools button in previous examples. If you did that, you likely have a good idea as to what's available there. If you're new to creating Web pages and Web sites, it's prudent not to mess with the default settings too much. However, if you know your audience or have specific needs or ideas for how your Web page should look, you can make changes if needed.

To access the Web Tools in any Office application, open a Web page you've previously created, click Save As, and click the Tools button. From the choices in Tools, click Web Options. What you'll see if you are in Word is shown in Figure 25-10. Here you can see that there are tabs for Browsers, Files, Pictures, Encoding, and Fonts. PowerPoint and Excel also offer these tabs. However, what you'll find under these tabs differs in each application.

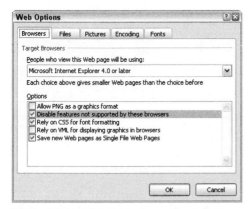

Figure 25-10: Web Options are offered via the Save As → Tools menu. This is Word's.

Figure 25-11 shows an example from Excel. Compare what's under the General tab here to what's shown in Figure 25-10, from Word. There's significantly less to work with. As you work through Excel's other tabs though, you'll find more tools, tools which are necessary only for Excel documents.

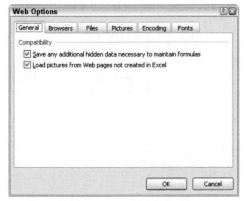

Figure 25-11: Web Options are offered via the Save As → Tools menu. This is Excel's.

Figure 25-12 shows an example in PowerPoint. Under General here, you can decide what colors to use, whether to show slide animation while browsing or to resize graphics as needed. These things are inherent to PowerPoint only.

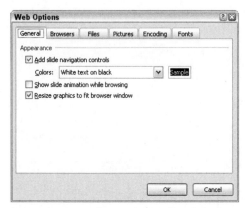

Figure 25-12: Web Options are offered via the Save As → Tools menu. This is PowerPoint's.

As you can see, it would be nearly impossible to go through every tab for every application. However, you can. For the most part, it's self-explanatory, and if you need help with any part of it, click the question mark at the top of the dialog box and look up what you don't understand. For the most part, the defaults are fine.

There are a few defaults that you may want to change though. For instance, on the Browsers tab, there's an option that tells the Office application what Web browser your users will be using to view your Web page. The default is Microsoft Internet Explorer 4.0 or later. If you'd like though, you can add Netscape Navigator, or choose different versions of Internet Explorer as the default.

You can also change the screen size you think your users will be using. By default it's 800 × 600, but if everyone in your intranet has his or her monitors set to 1024 × 768, you should consider changing that setting.

Another default is to let Office organize your files in a folder it creates, as shown earlier. If you have your own way of doing things though, perhaps a Web design program you import your Office files to, you'll want to disable this feature.

We'll leave it up to you to explore the other choices.

Previewing Your Web Pages

Before you publish your Web page to the Internet or an intranet, you'll want to preview it to verify it looks and works the way you want it to. As always, there are many ways to do this; one way is to manually open the Web page in Internet Explorer. To do this:

1. Browse to the location on your hard drive that contains the Web page you created. In our case, it is in My Documents\Web Sites.

2. Right-click the Web page you created, from the drop-down list point to Open With, and click Internet Explorer.

3. Double-check the formatting and hyperlinks, noting that you can use the back and forward controls just as if the Web site were published to the Internet.

4. When finished, close Internet Explorer.

5. Edit any file as needed.

Publishing Your Web Pages

Publishing your Web pages involves publishing them to a Web server. A Web server is a computer on the Internet or on your local intranet that manages and stores Web site files. If you don't have a Web server, you're not going to be able to publicly publish your Web pages. If you do have a Web server, for the most part, publishing to it is as easy as saving a file.

To publish a Web site to the Internet, you'll need to find a Web hosting provider and purchase a domain name if you want to set up a personal Web site all your own. To publish to an intranet Web server, you'll need to obtain the required information from your network administrator.

Note

To publish a Web site on the Internet, you generally have to subscribe to a Web hosting provider and purchase a domain (Web site) name. However, purchasing a domain name is not necessarily required; you can get an account from a provider, such as MySpace.com, that provides you with an area to post Web pages for a small personal Web site using the provider's domain name as the base of your Web address.

To publish to a Web server, open the presentation, document, database, or other item, click the Office Button or File menu and select Publish. You'll be given lots of choices and they'll differ depending on what application you're using. In Publisher 2007 for example, you can choose from Blog, Document Management Server, and Create Document Workspace. You'll see similar options in other Office applications.

Summary

In this chapter you learned how to use Microsoft Office applications to create, save, and edit Web pages. Because Office is compatible with HTML and can save in that format, creating, saving, and publishing Web pages is much easier than it used to be. Office does all the work of providing the HTML code, and creates additional files and folders automatically, which will help speed up the process of previewing and publishing.

Chapter 26

Using Office 2007 with Vista

W indows Vista is to Windows XP as Office 2007 is to Office XP (or Office 2003 or Office 2000). Windows Vista is an operating system. In fact, it's Microsoft's newest operating system and should be available in early 2007. Windows Vista is Windows XP on steroids. As you'd probably guess, there are a lot of versions of Vista, including a stripped down version with just the basics to a version for media enthusiasts that includes just about anything you can think of, including the ability to watch, pause, rewind, and fast forward live TV and subscribe to any kind of online media from movies to music. Just like Office 2007, Windows Vista can be installed as an upgrade. But Vista is more than an upgrade (as is Office 2007); it's a completely new technology, with new features, and awesome new tools for getting things done. You'll probably want to upgrade or install Vista once you find out about its new features and what it brings to the table.

Because Windows Vista is such a technological advance, Office 2007 on Windows Vista is completely different from Office 2007 on any other operating system. That's because Vista has new and improved technologies that other operating systems don't have, not even Windows XP. The technologies that affect Microsoft Office are fairly specific though, and what you'll be most interested in are those technologies and features that revolve around searching for and organizing data. If you haven't seen Office 2007 on Vista yet, this is going to blow your mind. If you have Vista, in this chapter you'll learn how to get the more out of it with regard to Office 2007.

Exploring Office's Open Dialog Box

When you opt to open a file with any application in Office 2007, you see the familiar Open dialog box, shown in Figure 26-1. It's okay; it's functional after all, but that's about it. You click the buttons on the left to jump to a specific area or you use the Look In box to manually browse for the file you want.

The Open dialog box for Office 2007 on Vista is quite a bit more sophisticated. Figure 26-2 shows the difference.

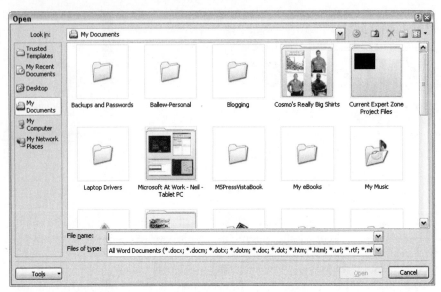

Figure 26-1: The Open dialog box in Office Word 2007 looks like this on Windows XP.

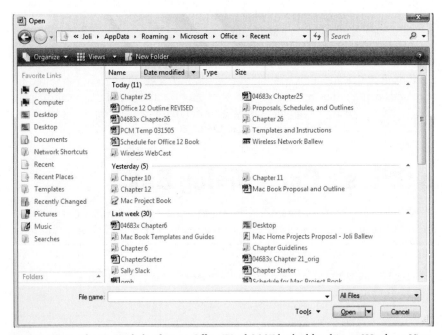

Figure 26-2: The Open dialog box in Office Word 2007 looks like this on Windows Vista.

In this example, we're using the Open dialog box in Word 2007, and we've clicked on Recent. These are all of the Word documents we've recently edited, worked on, or created. Notice how they're sorted too, by date. There are myriad ways to sort the data shown.

Figure 26-3 shows the Open dialog box in PowerPoint 2007 on Vista. In this example, we've selected Searches from the left pane. In the right pane notice the folder names. These Search folders were created by Vista for use in all aspects of the operating system, even Office. As you can see there are many quite useful default folders, each containing virtual links to the named files inside:

- Attachments

- Favorite Music

- Fresh Tracks

- Important E-Mail

- Last 7 Days E-Mail

- Last 30 Days Documents

- Last 30 Days Pictures And Videos

- Recently Changed

- Shared By Me

- Unread E-Mail

- User's Files

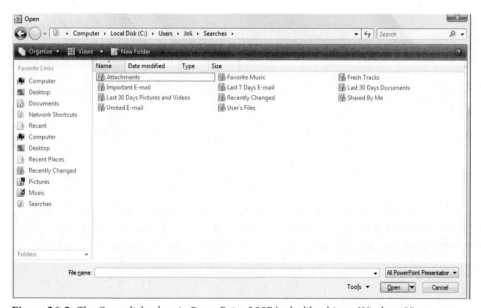

Figure 26-3: The Open dialog box in PowerPoint 2007 looks like this on Windows Vista.

Looking inside any of those folders yields the ultimate search results. Perhaps you're looking for something you created in the last 30 days, say a document. Opening the Search folder Last 30 Days Documents puts all of the files that match these criteria at your fingertips. Figure 26-4 shows what we see when clicking the Recently Changed Search folder. If you wanted, you could sort these results by date as well.

You can also sort data using the following options (this list does not include all available options):

- Name
- Date Modified
- Type
- Size
- Title
- Word Count
- Due Date

And for media of varying types:

- Camera Model
- Duration
- Encoded By
- Beats Per Minute
- Flash Mode
- Lens Maker
- Genre
- Year
- Composer

And this doesn't even skim the surface of how Search Folder data can be sorted and grouped!

Note

This may all seem a bit overwhelming, and if you're an XP user you may be disappointed with Microsoft for not including this technology in your version of Microsoft Office. The thing is though, this isn't a feature of Office, it's a feature of Windows Vista, and applications that can run on Vista are able to use Vista's technologies to offer it up. You can't get this functionality in Windows XP because Windows XP does not include it in the operating system.

Figure 26-4: The default Search folders enable you to find what you need quickly.

Searching from the Start Menu with Vista

Vista lets you search in new and exciting ways, certainly in more ways than simply using an application's Open dialog box. In Figure 26-5, you can see there's a Search box right there in the Start menu itself.

Type anything in the Start Search box and wait to see the results. In Figure 26-5, we've searched for Office. Notice the initial search provides links to Office applications, as well as a few links that have Office in the title. For more results, click Search the computer.

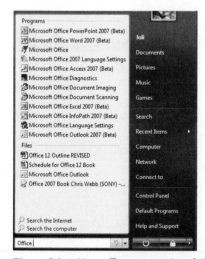

Figure 26-5: Vista offers its own Search features.

When you choose to search the computer, the Search Index window opens, showing the results. Figure 26-6 shows the results for Office. Notice here we've grouped the results alphabetically. Grouping and customizing the Search Index window is done in the same manner as it always has been done; click the title bar and make a choice from resulting drop-down list.

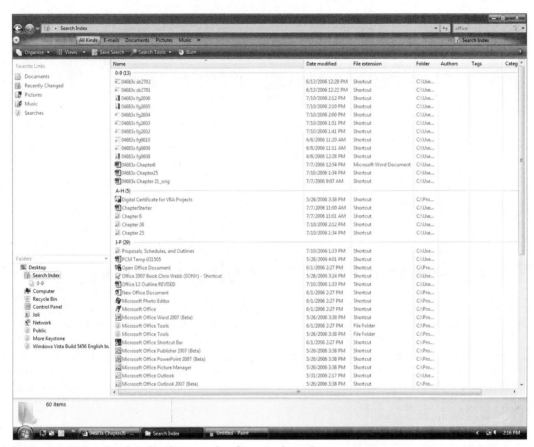

Figure 26-6: Vista Search Index shows results of a manual search.

Beyond searching your own computer and network though, note that you can also search the Internet from the Start menu. To do this, type your query into the Start Search box and click Search the Internet.

Creating Manual Searches

You can create your own searches using the search function in Vista, using the Search choice on the Start menu. This isn't the Start Search box, it's an item called Search located on the Start menu itself. Figure 26-7 shows this option.

Figure 26-7: A more sophisticated search option is available from the Start menu.

When you click this option, a new Search window appears. You can use this window to perform a search for almost anything including e-mails, documents, pictures, music, video, and more. As you can see in Figure 26-8, the Search window allows you to type a word in the Search box in the top right, or, lets you configure advanced options. In this figure, we've chosen to search for anything on the hard drive that contains text. (Notice All Kinds is selected in the title bar.) The text we searched for was Chapter 26, and the results clearly show success. The results are all shortcuts to a network drive, and include figures and a file folder.

Saving Searches with a Search Folder

Once you've performed a search, you can save the results in the form of a folder. The Search Folders you create will be *live*, meaning each time you open a saved Search Folder, the information in it will be updated.

We can use the previous search as an example. In that search, we found everything on the computer that contained the text Chapter 26. If we save that folder and then create other documents or images later that contain that same text, references to them will appear in that folder the next time we open it.

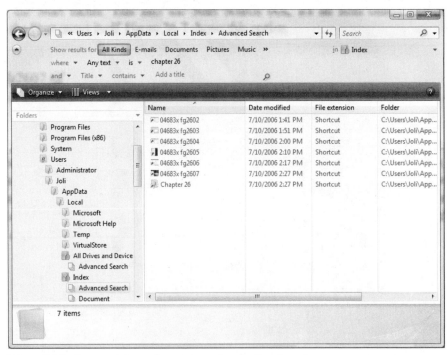

Figure 26-8: You can define your searches using the Search options.

Note

The actual file isn't in the Search Folder; the files and images are stored on a network drive, your hard drive, or somewhere else. If Vista created actual copies of the file to include in a folder, we'd have a mess on our hands. There would be all kinds of versions of each file floating around, or at the very least, a complicated system in place to keep them all on the same page. That's not how Search Folders work; what's inside of the folders are really only virtual data, not real data. In a way, they're shortcuts.

To save a search and create a Search Folder:

1. Right-click anywhere in the Results pane and select Save Search.

2. In the Save As dialog box, name the search so you'll recognize it later.

3. Click Save.

The next time you click Searches in the Open dialog box or any other Search window, you'll see this one. Figure 26-9 shows an example.

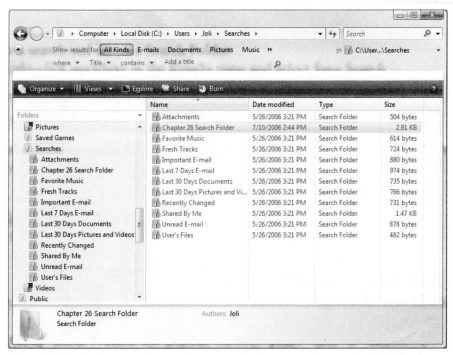

Figure 26-9: Saved Search Folders allow you to virtually group any type of data easily.

Tip

Consider creating Search Folders for projects, picture types or subjects, or anything you can sort by date.

Using Outlook and Vista

This entire chapter revolves around the Search functions in Vista. Outlook has its own special Search functions though. As with other applications there are default Search Folders already created, and you can certainly create your own. (Unlike the other features mentioned in this chapter, these items have been incorporated to work with XP too.) Search Folders already created in Office 2007 when combined with Vista include the following:

- Categorized Mail

- Large Mail

- Unread Mail

These are located under Personal Folders, Search Folders. Once you start getting e-mail using Outlook 2007, virtual copies (not duplicates) of the e-mail will appear there.

You can also use Outlook's new Search box to search any Personal Folder for e-mail that contains a specific word. To look for e-mail from a specific person, for instance, select the Personal Folder to search (Deleted Items, Inbox, Sent Items, etc.), type the name in the Search box, and click the Search icon. Results will appear and you can look through them to find what you need.

Creating Your Own Search Folders

As with other Office 2007 applications, you can create your own personalized Search Folders. To do so, right-click Search Folders, select New Search Folder, and set the criteria. Here are some of the criteria from which you can choose:

- Mail flagged for follow up

- Mail from and to specific people

- Old mail

- Mail with attachments

- Mail with specific words

The last option is one of the most useful. If you need to retrieve an e-mail that contains information about a "distribution widget" for instance, but you have no clue regarding what it refers to; why, where, or when the e-mail came in; or who sent it, this offers your best shot at finding it.

You can also create custom Search Folders in Outlook that contain additional, more-specific criteria you select. This can include just about anything you can imagine too. Criteria can include if the messages have additional subjects in the CC line or if they have been flagged by you or someone else. What's really nice though is the ability to create a Search Folder for your RSS feeds.

Using Outlook for RSS Feeds

With Outlook 2007, you can subscribe to, read, organize, and search RSS feeds from inside Outlook. No more using an online subscription service or going to a particular Web site to get your fix. With Outlook, it's all right there. Outlook has an RSS folder in the Personal Folders list that contains the RSS feeds you've subscribed to. Figure 26-10 shows an example.

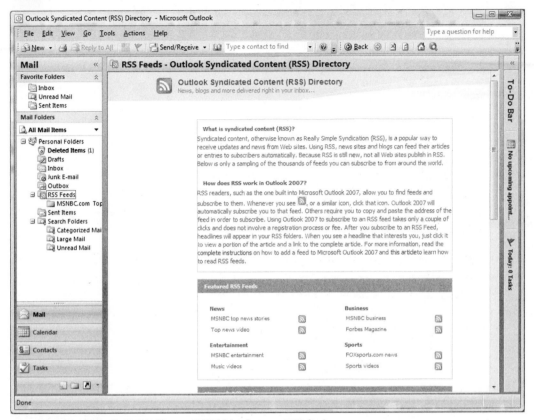

Figure 26-10: Outlook 2007 offers an RSS folder for your RSS feeds.

Here, MSNBC.com is listed as a subscribed-to RSS feed. With an RSS feed configured, you can now search these RSS feeds for the information you need. To do so, simply click the RSS folder, and in the Search window, type your query.

Finally, you can create a Search Folder that looks for certain data in your RSS folder. To do this:

1. Right-click Search Folders and select New Search Folder.

2. In the New Search Folder dialog box, shown in Figure 26-11, select Create a custom Search Folder.

3. Click Choose to set the criteria for the Search Folder.

4. Name the folder and click Browse.

5. Select RSS Feeds, click OK.

Figure 26-11: Create a new Search Folder for RSS feeds.

6. Click Criteria and configure your settings. This will likely include a specific word at first, and then you can configure more advanced settings once you get a feel for it.

7. Click OK, OK, and OK again to exit and create the folder.

Summary

Office 2007 looks a lot different on Vista than it does on Windows XP. It's more than a cosmetic change though; it's a complete technological breakthrough. With Vista, you'll get more than you ever expected from Office 2007, from searching to organizing to saving Search Folders. It's well worth it if you can afford it; Vista is the operating system of the future.

Chapter 27

Exploring Office Enterprise

Microsoft Office 2007 comes in eight flavors. In this book, we focused on one of them, Microsoft Office 2007 Professional. We believe this will be the most popular version for offices, as it contains a vast majority of the applications end users will need in an office setting. However, large enterprises and worldwide corporations will require and have additional applications. You may have access to some of these additional applications in your office. Because you may come across these additional programs where you work, we'll introduce the other versions and the applications that come with them.

We'll also cover the Microsoft Office suites that offer less than Microsoft Office 2007 Professional. If you have a student heading off to college, for instance, you may want to pay for only the necessities, in this case Microsoft Home and Student 2007. If you need only Word, Excel, and Outlook at home, you may decide to opt for Microsoft Office 2007 Basic.

Introducing the Seven Office Suites

Table 27-1 shows the names of each of the eight Microsoft Office suites and what is included with each version.

In this book, we've covered the applications in Microsoft Office Professional. In the following sections, we look at the other applications that were not addressed.

Understanding OneNote

OneNote comes with the Home and Student and the Enterprise versions of Microsoft Office 2007. The high school or college student will benefit the most from this application, when it's used in conjunction with a laptop. Enterprise users will benefit in brainstorming sessions or when traveling to seminars.

Table 27-1   The Eight Office Suites

	Basic	Home and Student	Standard	Small Business	Professional	Ultimate	Professional Plus	Enterprise
Word	✓	✓	✓	✓	✓	✓	✓	✓
Excel	✓	✓	✓	✓	✓	✓	✓	✓
Outlook	✓		✓	✓	✓	✓	✓	✓
PowerPoint		✓	✓	✓	✓	✓	✓	✓
OneNote		✓				✓		✓
Publisher				✓	✓	✓	✓	✓
Outlook with Business Contact Manager				✓	✓			
Access					✓	✓	✓	✓
InfoPath						✓	✓	✓
Communicator							✓	✓
Integrated Enterprise Content Management						✓	✓	✓
Electronic Forms						✓	✓	✓
Advanced Information Rights Management and Policies Capabilities						✓	✓	✓
Groove						✓		✓

Basically, OneNote is a digital notebook, much like the physical notebook your student carries to class or you take to board meetings. You can do everything with this digital notebook that you can with a physical one. Here are some of the tasks you can accomplish:

- Gather and organize notes, including handwritten notes.

- Gather and organize pictures and graphics, including scanned documents from professor's handouts or handwritten notes from the office.

- Record, organize, and listen to recorded audio from lectures, foreign language labs, business seminars, and more.

- Reduce the amount of time you spend searching through class notes, handouts, printouts, lab notes, and research notes.

- Collaborate using OneNote's comprehensive collaboration tools.

- Automatically create backups of your most important data.

- Create notes from brainstorming sessions, cram sessions, and lab sessions.

- Transfer information from mobile devices.

- Avoid duplicate work, especially when collaborating.

- Use the shared digital whiteboard to work digitally with others in real time.

OneNote may be the reason you choose Home and Student version of Microsoft Office over other versions. It's an extremely powerful application, and can be a productive tool to help your student study better and work more efficiently.

Understanding Outlook with Business Contact Manager

This application is Outlook on steroids. Beyond the usual Outlook you'll be able to improve contact and customer management, project management, and marketing using e-mail and calendar functions. You can do all of this and more within the familiar interface of Outlook.

With Outlook combined with Business Contact Manager you can accomplish the following tasks:

- Manage sales leads and share customer data with colleagues.

- Manage marketing activities.

- Track a customer's e-mails, contact information, phone calls, appointments, and related documents.

- Track the time spent on a customer, which can then be sent to a billing application.

- View, forecast, and convert sales opportunities into real sales, in conjunction with other Microsoft Enterprise products.

- Create a custom mailing list from customer contacts and incorporate mail merge capabilities from Word.

- Track project information including messages, meetings, quotes, potential clients, and e-mail, all from one place.

- Assign to-do tasks for others in the company and have them automatically delivered and added to a person's Project Tasks list.

Understanding InfoPath

InfoPath is an application for creating rich, vibrant forms. Teams and organizations can use the personalized forms they create to gather, share, and recycle information. Having all of the information that's been gathered readily available and centrally managed leads to improved teamwork and decision-making for the organization. InfoPath is a must for all form-based businesses, as it helps businesses of this kind manage and efficiently structure their business.

With InfoPath you can accomplish the following tasks:

- Incorporate different form types so end users can fill out the forms using familiar tools, such as Outlook, an Internet browser, or a mobile device.

- Validate information so you know it's right before you use it.

- Build forms with an easy-to-use drag-and-drop interface.

- Convert Word and Excel documents into forms you can use.

- Create PDF records of form data.

- Incorporate SharePoint for greater flexibility and effectiveness.

Understanding Communicator

As you would expect, Communicator is used to enhance communications between coworkers and colleagues. This includes e-mail, instant messaging, voice, and video, as well as technologies for VoIP. All of these methods are integrated. This means if you're in an instant message conversation and you think that a video chat might be more productive, you can switch to that immediately. Because it's all integrated, there's no need to switch to another communication client.

With Communicator you can accomplish the following:

- Communicate with others in real time, using a variety of media.

- Communicate using one easy-to-use and integrated interface.

- Find colleagues and their status, and use the information to figure out the best method of communication with them.

Understanding Integrated Enterprise Content Management

Enterprise Content Management is a key component of Microsoft SharePoint Server 2007. It offers an integrated, dependable, and reliable way to protect documents, records, and Web content. This protection and management starts when data is first created, and follows the content from it's creation to archive.

With Enterprise Content Management you can accomplish the following:

- Access the information you need more quickly than ever.
- Achieve compliance with government regulations.
- Provide a scalable repository for data.
- Streamline review and approval workflows.
- Create custom content and review workflows.
- Repurpose existing content, including PowerPoint slide sets, reducing the need to recreate data.
- Generate and embed barcodes in documents.

Using Electronic Forms

In conjunction with InfoPath, electronic forms can be made available as standalone forms. These forms can be made appear in an InfoPath browser, or in a Word or Excel document. They can even be embedded in Outlook 2007 e-mail messages. By inserting forms into these types of documents and applications, you can more easily acquire the information you need from clients.

Here's some of what you can do with Electronic Forms:

- Create useable, intelligent forms for clients, partners, and suppliers.
- Integrate data received via forms into servers and content management applications.
- Incorporate data validation tools to reduce the amount of errors created in forms.
- Control who can create and publish forms inside your company.
- Create advanced forms and custom forms.

Understanding Information Rights Management and Policy Capabilities

Information Rights Management and policy controls help organizations safeguard their data from unauthorized use. This also enables workers to define precisely how recipients can use the information contained in their Office documents.

With Information Rights Management you can accomplish the following:

- Define who can open, modify, print, forward, or take other actions with your data.

▓ Create templates that can be used to protect accounting reports, merchandise specifications, customer data, and e-mail messages.

▓ Create policy statements and embed them in e-mail messages.

Understanding Groove

Groove is collaboration software. It allows coworkers and colleagues to work together inside digital collaborative *workspaces*. Colleagues do not need to be in the same office, or even the same country to make use of Groove, and all have access to the tools needed to collaborate effectively.

With Groove you can accomplish the following tasks:

▓ Use specialized tools including Files, Discussion, and Calendar.

▓ Use built-in templates.

▓ Invite anyone, even a person who is not a coworker or does not have Groove, to the workspace.

▓ Push changes to colleagues' computers. This makes comparing and converting documents unnecessary.

▓ Use built-in presence awareness tools to know who is working on what, and when.

▓ Synchronize SharePoint documents with Groove.

▓ Work with teams from other countries in their own language. Groove supports 29 languages, with new languages being added regularly.

Learn About the New Office Applications Online

At www.microsoft.com/learning/default.mspx, you can access online tutorials to learn about the Office products we introduced in this book and the ones we briefly detailed in this chapter. You'll need a .NET Passport to log in, you'll have to fill out a short survey, and you'll need to agree to the Terms of Use, but after that, just select the course you want and watch the demonstration.

Summary

Although in this book we focused on the applications in Microsoft Office 2007 Professional, there are other versions and additional applications available. Only the largest companies and corporations employ most of these applications, save OneNote. Most of these applications make collaborating or securing data more efficient and effective, such as creating custom forms with InfoPath or connecting on a project with others using Groove.

Index

A

Access 2007, 295–340
    attachments, adding, 299, 338–39
    database, creating, 301–3
    database, opening existing, 303
    Data Collection, 299, 331–33
    Design view, 318, 335
    dialog launcher, 298
    e-mail, embedding information into, 331
    exporting data from, 309–10, 331
    fields, new types, 337–38
    filtering data, 298
    forms, 312–18
    Getting Started, first time use, 300–304
    grouping information, 335–37
    importing data to, 304–8
    interface, customizing, 299–300
    Layout view, 318, 335
    macros, 299, 329–31
    multivalued fields, 299, 339–40
    navigation pane, 295–97
    new features, 298–99
    PDF files, exporting data to, 334–35
    queries, 321–24
    Quick Access Toolbar, 299–300
    reports, 324–25, 335–37
    ribbon in, 297–300
    switchboards, limitations, 297
    table data relationships, 319–20
    tables, 310–12
    templates, 302–3, 327–28
    tracking, 331
    XPS format, saving file in, 334–35
Action queries
    running, 324
    types of, 323
Activation, 7–10
Active X controls, and manual update, 53
Ad-Aware, 17

Add-Ins
    Excel, 220
    Word, 158
Address book, Outlook, 277
Advanced
    Excel, 220
    PowerPoint, 195
    Word, 158
Adware
    dangers of, 14, 16–17
    protection against, 17
ALT key, shortcut feature, accessing, 180
Animations, PowerPoint, 193, 204–5
Antivirus software
    configuring, 14–16
    McAfee options, 15
Append, action query, 323
Asterisk (*), search with, 68
Attachments
    Access, adding, 299, 338–39
    e-mail messages. *See* E-mail attachments
Audio. *See* Sounds
AutoCorrect, 82–84
    to add math symbols, 83–84, 351
    Publisher, 350–51
    to save keystrokes, 82–83
    Word, 83–84
AutoFilter
    Access, 298
    Excel, 237–38
Automatic updates, 20–22, 51–52
AutoRecover, 72
Axes of charts, 241

B

Backup, 41–49
    CD backup, 42, 45–46
    dragging files method, 44–45
    DVD backup, 42, 45–46

CD, burning presentation to, 215–16
charts, creating, 207–8
clip art, inserting, 92–93, 202–3
collaboration features, 208–9
command tab, insert objects, 92–93
contextual tab, adding/editing shape, 95–98
date and time, 200
diagrams, creating, 207
File menu button, 194
file protection, 117–18
finalization tools, 193
fonts, changing, 199–200, 215
Galleries and Quick Styles, 105–7
headers and footers, 200
interface, customizing, 194–96
intuitive navigation, 192
lists, converting to diagrams, 211–12
Live Preview, 193, 200
multiple monitor presentations, 193
new features, 192–93
objects, inserting in presentation, 200, 202–6
placeholders, 214
presentation template, choosing, 197–98
publishing options, 193
Quick Access Toolbar, 195
ribbon in, 88, 191
sharing between applications, 161, 250–51
slide layouts, custom, 213–15
slide libraries, 198–99
sounds, adding, 203–4
symbols, 200
text boxes, adding, 200–201
text formatting, applying, 215
Trust Center, 195
View Toolbar, 196
Web pages, creating, 380–81
WordArt, 200
Word documents, importing to, 365–66
XML file types/extensions, 127
Presentation template
PowerPoint, choosing, 197–98
viewing online, 198

Preview
e-mail attachments, 281–82
mail documents, 176
styles, Word Live Preview, 11, 155, 160
Web pages, 386–87
Printing
Calendar, 277
from Excel, 251–52
Publisher, packing process, 360–61
Privacy
Microsoft information collection, 9, 58
See also Security
Product key, 5, 7
Profile, e-mail, creating/changing/deleting, 262–64
Program viruses, protection against, 14
Proofing
Excel, 219
PowerPoint, 194
Research feature, 171
Word, 157
Protecting documents. *See* File protection
Public MSN Profile, 9
Publisher 2007, 341–71
AutoCorrect, 350–51
business information set, creating, 345–46
Catalog Merge Wizard, 347
clip art, inserting, 359
color scheme, customizing, 346–47, 359–60
content library, 366–67
Design Checker, 368–69
drop caps, 353
Galleries and Quick Styles, 108–9
help feature, 367–68
hyperlinks, 353–54
interface, new, 343–44
layout, creating, 357
lines, adding, 358
multiple page documents, 354–56
new features, 345–47
pages, rearranging, 357
PDF/XML formats, 347
printing, preparation for, 360–61

GET YOUR
PC MAGAZINE SUBSCRIPTION
@ http://go.pcmag.com/vistaoffer

Your purchase of PC Magazine Office 2007 Solutions includes a one-year subscription to *PC Magazine* ($19.97 value). To start your subscription, go to **http://go.pcmag.com/vistaoffer** and tell us where to mail your issues. Offer valid only in the United States.

PC Magazine is the authoritative source for technology experts. *PC Magazine* is published 22 times a year. Each issue includes trusted, lab-based product reviews, "First Looks" at emerging technologies, award-winning commentary & feature articles and time-saving tips & tricks.